Stealing Dreams

Stealing

A FERTILITY CLINIC
SCANDAL

Dreams

Mary Dodge *and*
Gilbert Geis

NORTHEASTERN
UNIVERSITY PRESS
BOSTON

NORTHEASTERN UNIVERSITY PRESS

Library of Congress Cataloging-in-Publication Data
Dodge, Mary, 1960–
Stealing dreams : a fertility clinic scandal / Mary Dodge and Gilbert Geis.
p.   cm.
Includes index.
ISBN 1-55553-585-2 (cloth)
1. University of California, Irvine. Center for Reproductive Health.
2. Ovum—Transplantation—Moral and ethical aspects. 3. Human reproductive
technology—Moral and ethical aspects. 4. Fertility clinics—California.
5. Physicians—California—Malpractice. I. Geis, Gilbert. II. Title.
RG133.5.D63   2003
362.1'96692'00979496—dc21   2003005450

Designed by Gary Gore

Composed in Photina by Coghill Composition, Richmond, Virginia.
Printed and bound by the Maple Press, York, Pennsylvania.
The paper is Maple Tradebook Antique, an acid-free stock.

MANUFACTURED IN THE UNITED STATES OF AMERICA
07 06 05 04 03   5 4 3 2 1

To Lucie, Phillip, Michael, and Jere

To Dolores and in memory of Robley

IT IS FAIR TO SAY THAT THE DRIVING FORCES BEHIND MODERN SCIENCE ARE MONEY AND POLITICS....FOR A SCIENTIST, NEW FINDINGS REPRESENT NOT ONLY A TRIUMPHANT FURTHER INSIGHT INTO THE ENIGMAS OF THE NATURAL WORLD, BUT ALSO DIRECT FISCAL AND SOCIAL GAINS: MORE GRANT MONEY, GREATER STATUS AMONG ONE'S PEERS, PERHAPS PUBLIC ACCLAIM AND A LUCRATIVE INTERNATIONAL PRIZE. LIKE JOURNALISTS, WHOSE PARAMOUNT AIM IS TO GET A SCOOP OR CATCH THE NEXT BIG TREND RIGHT AS IT BREAKS, SCIENTISTS ADORE THE CUTTING EDGE: IT'S WHAT THEY LIVE FOR; IT'S WHAT REDEEMS ALL THE HOURS IN THE LAB WATCHING EXPERIMENTS FAIL.

GINA MARANTO, *Quest for Perfection* (1996), p. 276.

Contents

Chronology

1978	Sergio Stone joins UCI Medical School
1984	Ricardo Asch and José Balmaceda perfect GIFT procedure
1986 March	Asch and Balmaceda recruited to UCI
1989	Mary Piccione becomes executive director at UCIMC Saddleback clinic opens
1990	CRH closes Garden Grove and opens at Pavilion II Stone joins partnership with Asch and Balmaceda
1991 September December	Debbie and John Challender start infertility treatment Thefts reported at clinic; Bruce Murdy begins first audit; Toula Batshoun mentions egg transfers to Murdy
1992 August October November	Challenders' son J.D. born Marilyn Killane starts working at CRH David Swanberg begins second audit; Norbert Giltner mentions egg transfers
1993 July September	Laurel Wilkening becomes chancellor of UCI Debra Krahel starts work at UCIMC Patricia and Edward Haynes's malpractice suit filed
1994 March	Robert Chatwin begins third audit of the clinic

March 15	Killane reports wrongdoing at CRH and requests whistle-blower protection
April	Wilkening's office informed of egg transfers by internal auditors
May 24	Challenders meet with UCI officials
June 1	Sidney Golub claims patients have not been contacted
July 27	Krahel and Carol Chatham fired
September 10	Three whistle-blowers file complaint against the university
October 10	Outside accounting firm hired to do another audit of the clinic
October 20	Charles Wiggins and Allen Snyder appointed to investigate management practices
November 2	Clinical Panel appointed to investigate medical issues
November 3	Settlement negotiations begin between the university and the whistle-blowers

1995

January 26	NIH site visit
February	UCI halts research at the clinic
March, April	Agreements reached between the university and the whistle-blowers
March 17	Clinical Panel report completed
April 6	Wiggins and Snyder report completed
April 7	KPMG financial report completed
April 14	UCI orders the clinic closed, effective June 2; order to vacate by April 28
May	Wiggins and Snyder supplemental report submitted
May 12	KPMG supplemental report submitted
May 16	Lawsuit filed against the doctors by the university Doctors placed on leave by the university
May 25	UCI amends suit, alleging the doctors took eggs without consent
June 2	University terminates practice management agreement with CRH
June 6	Challenders' press conference Whistle-blowers' stories become public
June	Asch resigns from medical staff

June 14	Tom Hayden convenes Select Committee on Higher Education
June 22	Piccione and Herb Spiwak fired
September	Balmaceda leaves U.S. for Chile
September 19	Raid on homes and offices of doctors
September 22	Wilkening petitions for Stone's dismissal
October	Asch settles in Mexico
November 11	Orange County Superior Court issues order for Asch to return to U.S.

1996

January 19	Deposition of Asch in Tijuana
January	Asch's and Balmaceda's faculty salaries cut off
April 25	Stone indicted
June 27	Balmaceda indicted as co-defendant and declared a fugitive
November 14	Asch indicted

1997

September	Stone's trial begins
	Wilkening resigns
October 30	Stone convicted of mail fraud

1998

| May | Stone sentenced |
| October | Stone CPT hearings begin |

1999

| July | University settles 107 of 113 suits; the university files suit against the partnership; Asch CPT hearings held |

2000

March	Stone is dismissed by the university
July	Asch is dismissed by the university
	Swanberg's notes disclosed

2001

| January 17 | Balmaceda arrested in Buenos Aires; flees Argentina and returns to Chile |

Stealing Dreams

CHAPTER 1

Setting the Stage

■ Three women employed at the medical center operated by the University of California, Irvine, after first seeking whistle-blower protection, informed authorities and the media that wrongdoing was afoot at the Center for Reproductive Health. The center was run by world-renowned fertility specialists. The most serious allegation was that the doctors were taking eggs from some patients and implanting them into others without the consent of the "donors." There also were claims of insurance fraud, research misconduct, and misappropriation of funds by the physicians.

Media coverage sought to pinpoint the villains and flesh out the story. An editor of the *Orange County Register*, the local newspaper, immediately (and accurately) saw the charges as an avenue to a Pulitzer Prize. University officials moved into action, creating a smoke screen to avoid charges of personal responsibility or inadequate oversight. The university's first move was to pay off the whistle-blowers with almost a million dollars as part of a settlement agreement that stipulated that they remain silent.

By the time the scandal had wound down several years later, the

3

scene was strewn with destroyed reputations and careers, much of it the product of a process of scapegoating. Two of the doctors fled the country; the one who remained was convicted on criminal charges in a trial that at best can be called controversial. The fertility clinic story throws light on in vitro fertilization and other recently developed medical procedures for making babies. It also is a story replete with evasions, nastiness, and injustice.

John and Deborah Lynn Challender were the first to go public and in time they became the most outspoken of the slightly more than one hundred couples who believed that they had been duped and despoiled in the worst fertility clinic scandal in the annals of reproductive medicine. The Challenders were interviewed by Tom Brokaw, Oprah Winfrey, Maria Shriver, Maury Povich, Phil Donahue, Gordon Elliott, and others. Their story was translated into a third-rate television drama on *Lifetime* featuring Linda Lavin as a whistle-blower employed in the fertility clinic and Marilu Henner as Debbie Challender. Numerous popular magazines, including *Redbook*, *Vogue*, and *People*, provided sympathetic accounts of the Challenders' experience.

The Challenders had been patients at a medical facility run by the University of California, Irvine (UCI). The university chancellor, Laurel Lynn Wilkening, was a forty-eight-year-old planetary science scholar and rather new to the job, though she had been second in command at the University of Arizona and the University of Washington. Later she would say of the fertility clinic situation, "I have never encountered such depraved behavior on the part of faculty members in my entire life." The manner in which she dealt with the scandal may well have cost the chancellor her job; she resigned shortly before the mandatory five-year review of her stewardship, announcing somewhat gratuitously that she never again would serve as the head of a university.

Patients' reactions to the accusations of egg theft would be as searing as the chancellor's allegation that the doctors' behavior was "depraved." One patient labeled what had been done to her as "rape on a genetic level." In an odd contrast, while the fertility scandal was preoccupying the media, two UCI faculty members—one a physicist, the second a chemist—were awarded Nobel Prizes. The assistant executive vice chancellor attempted, with a notable absence of success, to smother the fertility clinic problems with the Nobel Prize blanket: "The fertility scandal," William Parker proclaimed, "was three jokers screwing around here for three years. The Nobel prizes was scholars working here for three decades."[1]

The Challenders, the initial complainants, lived in a small house in Corona, California, an upper-middle-class city of about 55,000 residents, with the Temecula Mountains rising beyond their backyard.[2] She is bubbly and gregarious, welcoming. He is more reserved—choosing his words carefully, appearing to be wary—but nonetheless polite. He gives the impression of a man not to be taken lightly, a man who speaks little, but when he does speak expects to be listened to and treated with respect.

Debbie Challender was born to Al and Betty Hager on the first of October in 1958 in Hawthorne, California, a Los Angeles suburb. Her father was an engineer at North American Rockwell. Her mother stayed at home and raised Debbie and her brother, born nine years earlier. Debbie attended Valley Christian, a nearby parochial school, and remains deeply devout. After high school, she qualified as a registered nurse at Cerritos College. She then went to work for Kaiser Permanente and, moving among different Kaiser sites, has been with the organization ever since, primarily as a pediatric nurse. Today she is a case manager in Kaiser's occupational medicine division at the Fontana, California, treatment center.

John is a native of Springfield, Ohio. His father was in charge of the motor pool at the Patterson Air Force Base in nearby Dayton; his mother worked as a cosmetologist. John moved to California in 1974, prodded by two weather-related incidents that occurred in close succession: first, his brother in California told him during a telephone conversation about taking a dip that day in the swimming pool; then John walked outside into the Ohio frost and found that someone unable to navigate on the ice and snow had crashed into his car.

The Challenders had met when John was managing and Debbie working at a Burger King outlet. She was only sixteen years old—he is ten years older—and it would be another four years before they were married, on June 23, 1979, in Orange, California. They set up house in Mira Loma and later moved to Riverside. There were some hard times: in 1987, John suffered a heart attack and lost the trucking company he owned. Seven years later the Challenders filed for bankruptcy, gave up the Riverside home, and moved to Corona. "I liked it there," says Debbie about Corona, almost invariably upbeat; John grants only that Corona was "a convenient place to live."

The couple first told their story about their experiences at the UCI fertility clinic during a June 6, 1995, press conference attended by nearly two hundred media representatives.[3] The Challenders had taken their complaint to Theodore S. Wentworth, a Newport Beach attorney with thirty-two years' experience. Wentworth told them that the only way they would get the university's attention was to initiate a legal action, to mount "a monetary assault." That action could take any of three forms: the Challenders could file suit as John and Mary Doe; they could file suit under their own names; or they could elect the second option and take steps to see to it that the media paid attention to their case. "The media was a tool that we could use or we could be carried with the tide," John remembers being told by the attorney. John believes that the media representatives understood perfectly well that the situation provided a good match between the reporters' goals—to arouse public interest and sell newspapers—and those of the Challenders—to secure justice and compensation for what had been done to them.

Wentworth sent the Challenders to Anne Ready in Santa Monica, who runs Ready for Media, "the west coast's most experienced media strategy and training firm," so that she could prepare them to deal with print, radio, and television reporters. The aim of Ready's agency, she says, is "to level the playing field by teaching [those who come for help] the media rules and how to play the game." A key theme is that persons being interviewed should provide answers that direct the interviewers to themes that are of concern to the client, though not necessarily issues being raised by the questioner. Mock interview sessions often are arranged for people scheduled to appear on talk shows. Ready is vague about fees. Clients usually are seen for about three to four hours and the charge, she says, can range from "hundreds to thousands of dollars."[4]

The Challenders were concerned, John remembers, that they would "muddle the message" and that people would say, "Look at that clown; he's scared to death." "Neither one of us wanted them to focus on the messenger," says John, "but on our message." In the three-hour session, Ready emphasized that "if you have a key point, keep it in your mind and be sure to repeat it again and again." She warned them to say things in short bursts: to create sound bites for the media. The Challenders were instructed "not to let the media lead you in a direction you don't want to go."[5]

Wentworth later would be criticized for prepping his clients and trying to make them more media savvy. His defense, in a letter published in the *Los Angeles Times*, focuses on his view of his clients' inexperience and the need to prepare them for what lay ahead.

It was obvious when I filed suit, the media would put a huge number of cameras and reporters in the face of the uninitiated family coming forward to seek justice. It seemed a compassionate move on the part of caring counsel to assist a vulnerable client with the media. They might well have camped out in their front yard with searchlights trained on their home if they did not come forward.[6]

"These were not acting lessons," Wentworth maintained. The Challenders needed to put their thoughts into short sentences and they needed to be able to talk on camera while listening to questions, sometimes through an earphone for satellite transmission. Wentworth thought he deserved praise, not condemnation: "Why criticize a thoughtful, considerate lawyer for adding some grace to the disgrace of a media frenzy, and the often callous questions posed to clients in a delicate but public matter?"[7] A defense attorney insisted that Wentworth's tactic would have backfired if his clients had had to face a cross-examination, though it would never come to that. A sharp lawyer would tell the jury that the former patients "can't be that upset if they need to go to media school to learn how to act."[8]

At the press conference, Wentworth announced that he had filed lawsuits on the Challenders' behalf against the university, the fertility clinic, and the three doctors who were partners in its operation: Ricardo H. Asch, José P. Balmaceda, and Sergio C. Stone. The suits alleged that the doctors had misappropriated the Challenders' eggs, embryos, or both and altered or destroyed evidence. The university, it was claimed, had failed to supervise the clinic properly and then had spent almost a million dollars to silence whistle-blowers who reported irregularities.

The Challenders said that they had learned of their problem in May 1995, when two newspaper reporters from the *Orange County Regis-*

ter—a man and a woman—came to their house bringing photocopies of the Challenders' medical records. The records showed that eggs taken (*harvested* is the term used in the world of reproductive medicine) from Deborah had, without her permission, been implanted in other women. "We were devastated when we learned of this terrible thing," Deborah Challender said. Her lawyer, attuned to the world of short takes, dubbed the doctors' behavior "embryo piracy." He noted that three months earlier university investigators had uncovered five other confirmed or possible instances in which the clinic doctors had used human eggs without the consent of their owners. He believed that there were another half dozen or so cases, an estimate that would prove to be well off target, nowhere close to the more than one hundred that were settled, with about a third involving egg and embryo misappropriations.

The Challenders told the media that the color copy of the records they were shown by the reporters had their signatures in black ink with an "X" in blue ink written in the box indicating their consent to a donation of the eggs. They stoutly denied that they had—or ever would have—selected the donation option. Besides, the form was dated September 9, 1991, and Deborah did not have her own embryos implanted until two months later. She said that it was unthinkable that she would give away eggs or embryos before becoming pregnant herself.

The seemingly straightforward lament of the Challenders would not go unchallenged, though their obvious anguish about the apparent misuse of Debbie's eggs seems altogether genuine. Armchair investigators pointed out that the evidence of unconsented usage was hardly foolproof. Debbie had signed the form and now was claiming that the other-colored checkmark had been made subsequently by someone else. But why had she herself at the time she signed the document not checked the box that disallowed use of her eggs? Besides, it is not unreasonable that different pens came into use during the same interchange. Skeptics noted that the Challenders would have two children if the procedure was a success, that John Challender had undergone a serious health setback, and that Debbie might not under those circumstances want to conceive and raise a third child.

For his part, Asch, the doctor involved in the case, initially accepted the Challenders' position at face value and interpreted it in terms of a conspiracy theory: "I believe Mrs. Challender. I'm sure she's right. I'm sure she didn't mark the 'X' there, and I'm sure someone in the university, someone in the center who was trying to hurt me, trying to set me up, did that."[9]

Several years later, Asch told a different story about the Challender mix-up and was adamant that their medical chart indicated their consent to donate. Asch portrays the couple's relationship as one in which John was uncaring and Debbie was cowering. "She didn't have the guts to recognize to him that she did consent to donation," he said. Asch claims that John rarely accompanied his wife to the clinic: "Her husband never came, never came, never was with his wife. I think the day of the procedure he didn't come to leave a specimen. I think she brought it with her. The guy never, never, ever showed up." Asch's impression of the Challenders contrasts sharply with the judgment of virtually all commentators on the case, who see them as true victims of unethical medical tactics. According to Asch, "The man never gave a shit about his wife. Those people are crazy. Those people are really crazy. They had twenty embryos frozen, something like that. They never asked for them." Asch, himself Jewish, also felt personally insulted when the Challenders showed concern that the eggs allegedly went to a Jewish couple: "These people, when they learned that the recipient of the egg was Jewish, they became crazy."[10]

That press conference in June 1995 opened what would become a long, drawn-out battle among clinic patients, the doctors, and the university involving a Pandora's box of ethical and psychological issues. John Challender's reaction was somewhat unusual in its unequivocal, emotional condemnation of the theft of his and his wife's personal property. Many men we talked with wondered what the fuss was all about. If the eggs and embryos were not going to be used—and there are thousands of such materials now in storage—why should there be any concern about their transfer to other women? Most men say that they would be willing to donate sperm freely and would be indifferent to the result of the fertilization of an unknown woman's ovum by their sperm. Almost all women to whom we talked took a much more condemnatory position on the matter, perhaps because the harvesting process is more intimate or because procreation is so much more closely tied to the emotions of the mother. This was a thread that ran through the entire fabric of the fertility clinic scandal.

The Challenders, who would celebrate their sixteenth wedding anniversary during the month of the press conference, had struggled with infertility for ten years. Debbie had been referred to the UCI Center for Reproductive Health by specialists at Kaiser Permanente, where she worked. She had been a party in a class-action suit against Kaiser: she doesn't recall the details except that "something happened up north," at Kaiser's headquarters, and that she had signed some papers to become part of the complaining group. To settle her part in the suit, Kaiser agreed to pay Debbie's UCI bill for three attempts at a viable pregnancy. She had become pregnant on the first try. Debbie stresses that she bears no ill will toward Kaiser for sending her to UCI: theirs was a "good deed"; they "did not know about the bad situations at UCI." That the Challenders were able to obtain fertility treatments without having to pay fees that typically average about $10,000 for one treatment cycle distinguishes them from the more usual clinic clients: the quite wealthy and those of middling wealth who make considerable sacrifices to secure infertility treatments. An article in the *New England Journal of Medicine* estimates that in cases where the woman is over forty the cost of in vitro fertilization (IVF) is between $160,000 and $800,000.[11]

Insurance companies paid for only 20 percent of the regimens at UCI that sought to overcome infertility, since insurers define the procedure as elective rather than necessary. A mid-1998 court decision that declared reproduction to be "a major life activity," however, may allow infertile women to receive treatment under the terms of the Americans with Disabilities Act (ADA).[12] At the beginning of 2002, 20 percent of the large insurance companies provided coverage for fertility procedures. Montana, Arkansas, Illinois, Ohio, West Virginia, Rhode Island, New Jersey, Maryland, Massachusetts, and Hawaii mandated such coverage.[13] Four states—California, Texas, New York, and Connecticut—require insurance coverage for infertility treatment, though they exempt small businesses, self-insurance companies, unions, and the federal government from this provision.[14] A study published in 2002 demonstrated that in the states with mandated coverage for in vitro treatments there is a higher level of usage of the procedure, a smaller number of embryos transferred in each attempt at pregnancy, and fewer pregnancies in which the woman produced three or more fetuses.[15] In California, insurance law states that infertility should be covered, but that coverage is not mandatory. The introduction to the California legislation notes: "Insurance coverage for infertility is uneven, inconsistent, and frequently subject to arbitrary decisions which are not based on legitimate medical considerations."[16]

The Challenders had started treatment in September 1991 with Asch, the clinic director and a world-renowned fertility specialist. Forty-six eggs were harvested from Deborah in November and twenty-one of these were fertilized with her husband's sperm. The process of securing the eggs had made Deborah sick, so it wasn't until shortly after Thanksgiving that five embryos were implanted in her fallopian tubes. A son, christened James Dominic and called J.D., was born August 24, 1992. He joined an older brother, John Robert, known as J.R., who had been adopted by the Challenders as an infant six years earlier. The Challenders had so wanted to be fully involved—to bond with—J.R. that they had arranged to be in the delivery room when he was born. The videotape of that scene shows Debbie and John both in tears; the child is handed first to her, then to his mother, who looks rather dazed as Debbie bends down to embrace both her and the infant.

During the Challenders' press conference, two-and-a-half-year-old J.D. swiveled in the clerk's chair, played with the telephone, and, when that got tiresome, dashed around the room, smiling and giving high fives to passersby before politely asking for help to unwrap a chocolate candy. Later, one of the plaintiffs' attorneys, acting as baby-sitter, played with toy automobiles with J.D. When one car banged into another, the attorney jokingly referred to a tactic that some lawyers were accused of employing to enlist patients who might have a case against the fertility clinic: "Remember," he told the boy, "when one car hits another, leave my card."[17]

The Challenders said that they had requested that their extra embryos be frozen in case they might want to use them later, a procedure that had been developed less than two decades earlier.[18] Their medical records indicated that at least three eggs were implanted in another woman. That forty-four-year-old woman, the Challenders learned, gave birth to dizygotic twins—a boy and a girl. It is not certain whether these children were tied to the Challenders: the birth mother apparently also received eggs from four other unconsenting donors.

The Challenders expressed strong feelings about the eggs that were used without their approval. "The embryos [they meant eggs] they stole, those were my babies," John Challender said. "They stole our children and put them into another woman." Deborah added: "Some tell us that it is impossible to have an emotional bond with embryos, but they don't understand." John preferred to know as little as possible about those other children that he believes might genetically be tied to him, though he thinks about them often and says that he does a double-take when he sees a child that looks like J.D., wondering if this might be his son or his daughter. But he fears meeting these other children. He told the media people that he was sleeping only three hours a night and was in no shape for the twelve-hour stretch that his job as a truck dispatcher demanded.

Debbie, for her part, ardently desires to learn if the twins are "hers" and, if so, she wants to establish some sort of relationship with them. "I want to see them," she says. "I have this need to see them. To hold them. To love them. To know that they're okay. I don't want them to say, when they're eighteen, 'You knew I existed and you walked away.'" She says that she desires to have the children as friends and "someday tell them the truth."[19]

The Challenders, both devout Christians, expressed initial concern that "their" twins were being raised by Jewish parents. John worried about "their spiritual welfare in the absence of Jesus Christ." Nonetheless, both Challenders emphatically state that they would never seek to remove the children from that other home.[20] John later would say that he was looking for a rabbi who could teach him something about Judaism: "I have no prejudices against them," he said. "The point is I'm so damned ignorant. I don't know anything about them. I want to extend a hand rather than going to battle." For his part, the Challenders' lawyer said that "only over [his] dead body" would there be a custody battle for the twins. "There are many beautiful stars in the sky and many beautiful religions. I cannot think of anything sillier than a custody battle over religious grounds."[21]

Nonetheless, the Challenders wanted the twins to be told that they are not genetically related to the couple raising them. John Challender believes that they also should be informed about the medical history of their biological parents, especially since he has heart trouble. But a biological connection to John is impossible since his sperm was never used to create an embryo for another patient. The exact source of the implanted egg is unknown—it is possible that it was Debbie's; it is also possible that it was inseminated by the recipient's husband.

The Challenders said at one time that they desired to carry out DNA tests to determine whether the twins are genetically connected to them, but attorneys presume that if they had gone forward with this request they would have been turned down by the courts on constitutional grounds. "Any time you suck blood from somebody, it does rise to the level of constitutional rights," one lawyer said. "It's an invasion of your privacy. Probably the most important thing I have is my body, and when somebody starts sticking needles in me, they're invading that." Other lawyers noted that no case of this type has ever come before American courts. In the end, the DNA tests never were made.[22] The Jewish couple, who had been close personal friends of Asch, refused categorically to recognize any obligation to the Challenders. "My clients have no interest in a public debate regarding a very private matter," their attorney, Steven Militzok, announced. "My clients have their children's well-being to consider." But the Challenders' lawyer remained unimpressed with this rationale; indeed, at one point he suggested that the recipients of Debbie Challender's eggs might bear some responsibility for the allegedly improper swap, that they should have taken care to learn whether eggs that they received came from "an appropriate source." Following a meeting between the attorneys for both couples, Wentworth could offer only an irritated comment on Militzok: "You just wanted to punch him." Militzok merely repeated his earlier sentiment that his clients "are truly among the most aggrieved victims of this tragedy."[23]

The Challenders' enthusiasm for DNA testing may also have been dampened by a shrewd question put to them by Hattie Kaufmann during a CBS *This Morning* television show: "Has it gone so far that when you ever look at your son, that you have now at home, and wonder, 'Is he really mine? Could this embryo have come from someone else? Has it gone that far?'" Debbie answered that zinger for the couple: "Oh, that question is in our mind. I mean, we—in our heart, he's ours, no matter what. But, yeah, we do have that question."[24]

Perhaps most to the point was the conciliatory observation by Andrea Shrednick, a medical psychologist at the University of Southern California who conducts therapy sessions with infertile couples: "One side feels robbed, and one feels cheated." She hoped that the matter could be handled in a non-adversarial manner; after all, "they did not steal from one another, they had this done to them. They were *all* victims. Once you get into name-calling and a tug of war, nobody's going to win, least of all the child."[25]

A month later, in July 1995, the daily *Orange County Register* again focused on the cross-religion issue. The *Register* would thrust its way deeply into the scandal, both uncovering and reporting stories, often to the dismay of university administrators. It would win a Pulitzer Prize for investigative reporting, carrying more than 230 stories on the subject in 1995 alone. It also earned the George Polk Award for medical reporting[26] and the Roy W. Howard Award given by the Scripps Howard Foundation to honor public service reporting.

The paper ran a banner headline: "Fertility Scandal Begets Religious Anguish." It reported that the Challenders had repeated their concern that "their" twins would not go to heaven. The *Register* offered the results of a survey of experts regarding the status of a child born to Jewish parents but created by the egg and sperm of non-Jews. These rabbinical opinions spanned a wide range, though the majority view appeared to be that of Rabbi David Bleich of Yeshiva University in New York, an Orthodox Jew and one of the faith's leading authorities on medical ethics. "The birth mother is the mother," Rabbi Bleich maintained. But then he retreated into the kind of reasoning that, at least in caricatures, often makes rabbinical thought so charming—and elusive: "There's an open question that there can be more than one mother. It may be necessary to have a type of quasi-conversion in order to establish full Jewish identity." A local rabbi also was perplexed about the religious status of the children: "You can argue both sides," said Rabbi Marc Rubenstein, and then did so: "The person who delivers the baby is considered very sacred. But the egg itself is considered sacred also." Other rabbis noted that Jews accept the biblical edict to be fruitful and multiply and that, particularly with the "shortage of Jews in the world," any reasonable method of high-tech fertility was to be encouraged. On the other hand, a Hasidic rabbi insisted that Jewish law prohibits egg donation and allows in vitro fertilization only between a husband and wife. His colleagues of less orthodox persuasion disagreed with him: "There was no licentiousness nor adultery," said one, and he believed that Jewish doctrine on forbidden unions did not apply in this case since the biological parents were not Jewish or subject to Jewish law.[27] The most pragmatic advice came from a rabbi who had consulted what he considered to be an authoritative source. It was all "halachically [according to Jewish law and custom] simple," he said, sending interested readers to their dictionary. What the twins ought to do is to undergo a "symbolic conversion" to wipe out any doubt.[28]

For ethicists, both sacred and secular, a core problem concerned the separation in fertility clinic procedures of lovemaking from baby-making. Robert Snowden, a British sociologist, has called in vitro fertilization a "mechanistic, objective and biological matter, disembodied from the union of persons and passions." Has something of inestimable value been sacrificed, he asks, when children can be regarded as a commodity created in a laboratory rather than as a product of affection or, at least, interaction between their parents?[29] In the 1950s doctors often allowed an infertile husband to operate the syringe that would implant donated semen in his wife's uterus so that he could say, "I impregnated my wife."[30] Some ethicists recommend that the fertilizing sperm of the husband be collected by means of coitus interruptus, rather than from what they regard as a raw act of masturbation.

For their part, officials at the Irvine campus of the University of California, an institution then employing 8,000 persons and serving 17,000 students, refused comment on the Challenders' press conference, announcing that they did not believe it was seemly or fair to issue a public statement on a pending lawsuit. They did declare that the university had terminated its relationship with the fertility clinic at the end of the previous week. A medical school spokesperson later would parry attempts to discuss with us her role in the fertility clinic case. "It would be too painful," she said. Her predecessor, who had quit just before the scandal became public, had indicated that she was pleased with neither the way the university handled the situation nor the part that she as its employee was obligated to play.

While the local media focused on details of the Challenders' situation, the national television shows, often skipping very lightly over the facts, sought to arouse emotional responses in viewers. Oprah Winfrey in her September 5, 1995, program began with a barrage of overblown rhetoric: "It is an extraordinary tale, all the makings of a terrifying science-fiction thriller." "Is it a high-tech baby kidnapping too bizarre and horrifying to be real?" she asked. Later in the program the story became "unimaginable" and the program's presentation, notably sketchy, was heralded as "the first in-depth" coverage. Oprah observed that she normally tried to put herself in the position of guests such as the Challenders but that it was proving "hard to even comprehend what that . . . feels like, that somebody stole your eggs." "Can you imagine, audience, what this is like?"

The fertility clinic clients were described in breathless terms: "Their desperation was almost suffocating as each quietly prayed that medical magic could give them what nature could not." Oprah escalated the "horror" of the case by having John Challender say in response to a leading question that he feared that some of the couple's embryos had been sold and shipped overseas.

Other television overviews of the fertility scandal offered more informed and revealing insights. On ABC's *Prime Time*, Diane Sawyer, after pronouncing that a woman's eggs represent "her most valuable thing," settled down into a serious review of the problems at the UCI fertility clinic. She asked rhetorically: "Was Asch so blinded by his success that he didn't care when he was playing God?" The clinic patients Sawyer interviewed most often declared that arrogance underlay Asch's actions. "He wanted to win a Nobel Prize," it was said. "He wanted to be number one." Confronted by these charges, Asch, who also was on the program, shrugged resignedly and told Sawyer that the remarks were prompted by jealousy—indeed, perhaps by racism, presumably referring to his Latino and Jewish background. "They are trying to deteriorate my reputation," said Asch, reaching for a word that was a bit beyond his bilingual talents. "To humiliate me."

Films were shown of the walls of Asch's office, decorated with pictures of infants, many dressed in appealing costumes, visions that must have teased and tantalized new and in-process patients. Sawyer also interviewed a male nurse who had worked at the UCI fertility clinic and reported that he had found evidence in the wastepaper basket by the Xerox machine that convinced him that something improper was going on. But he said that he could not persuade anybody in power at the university to take his complaints seriously.

Sawyer confronted Asch with a number of tough allegations. He deflected or denied all of them. "How did it happen?" he was asked in regard to unconsented egg usages. Two things are important to know, Asch answered. "I didn't do it. And I have never intentionally asked anyone else to do it." He pointed out that dealing with consent forms was not part of his job, and that the nurses who handled the consents for the clinic did not work for him, but were university employees. He refused point-blank to answer any questions about Teri Ord, the skilled embryologist Asch had brought with him to California from their laboratory in Texas. Asch and his wife had been best man and matron of honor at Ord's wedding to an Irvine clinic fellow. Later, there was a serious falling out, perhaps because the doctors had not rallied to Ord's side when the medical school declared her unable to keep her position because she did not possess an advanced degree. She had accused Asch of knowingly giving eggs from one patient to another without the owner's consent after Asch implied that the situation might be of her making. After she and her doctor-husband had twin babies, she scornfully denied that Asch and his wife had been the children's godparents.[31]

Asch scoffed at patients who suddenly had expressed a compelling interest in their embryos. "They keep them frozen for eight years," he said, "and then suddenly, now, they are concerned about them." He said he did not understand why anyone would be bothered that his or her genes might show up in another person's child, calling this "an obsession." He declared that genes are not very important, that they play little or no role in most skills and traits that humans exhibit. Sawyer noted at this point that Asch's own child was adopted.

Asch says that Sawyer set a bad tone for the interview when her first question, before the show had even started, was about Asch's adopted son. When she asked why they had adopted, he remembers explaining to Sawyer, "We wanted to give someone who wouldn't have a chance in life a chance." Asch also recalls telling Sawyer: "I know that any child in my family, my social enclosure, my environment, with the teaching that we give to our children, is going to be a fine person because of the love we give them."[32] Asch observes that when Sawyer asked him about genetics he didn't "know where she was going." His remarks on camera would later be edited so that he appeared to be discounting the feelings of patients who claimed they had been deprived of a biological child.

Finally, Sawyer asked Asch how he would like to be remembered when his career was completed. "I will be remembered," Asch replied, "for all the good things that I've done in my life." Then he added, after a longish pause, "And for all that I *will do* in my life."

In Mexico City, several years later, Asch voiced his regret about the decision to talk with Sawyer. He says he reluctantly agreed to the television show, against his wife's advice, partly because his lawyer wanted to meet the celebrated interviewer. Asch describes Sawyer as a "very charming lady" who told him that Saddam Hussein was the only person who had been displeased with an interview that she conducted. Asch considers himself to be the second person on that list.

Scrutiny of the fertility scandal by Maria Shriver on *Dateline* had a notable twist. *Dateline* showed clips of both Asch and the Challenders from a feature called "The Baby Business" that had been filmed three years earlier, before the scandal erupted and after their son J.D. had been conceived. The Challenders had very different things to say about Asch at that time. They were voluble about his abilities: "God blessed Dr. Asch," said John. "It was a miracle," Debbie added. "He's the greatest physician: this man is Superman."

The program also indulged in the usual hyperbole to arouse audience interest, emphasizing the "sudden twist" that the earlier story had taken and how so many women had been "betrayed." Shriver and Ronald Brower, Asch's lawyer, both solemnly agreed that Asch was extraordinarily bright. Having forged that accord, Shriver then wanted to know how so intelligent a man could not have seen to it that no one "stole" eggs from unconsenting patients. "Took," the lawyer corrected, "not stole." "All right, took or stole" was all that Shriver was willing to concede. The lawyer then repeated Asch's claim: it had been done without his knowledge and, most certainly, without his approval.

Shriver's coverage of the clinic three years earlier, rather eerily, had taken up precisely the question that had now become so important. "Do you worry about your responsibility for the eggs that you harvest?" Shriver had asked Asch then.

"I worry, perhaps that's my problem; I worry about everything," Asch responded. He said he worried that his laboratory might catch on fire, that someone might come into the clinic and steal the embryos. He was plagued by constant concern for the well-being of those in his care.

Shriver then wanted to know: "Do you worry that eggs might get mixed up?"

No, he did not worry about that, Asch replied. He "had set up specific standards to which that is impossible."

"It isn't impossible," Shriver retorted in top combative cross-examination form.

Asch conceded that, of course, it was not "impossible" that eggs might get switched, but he said pleasantly enough that he "had minimized the possibility to a point where it is extremely unlikely."

Shriver also interviewed Teri Ord. Ord said that she had never seen the consent forms that were used in the clinic. But she claimed that she was well aware of wrongdoing. Shriver wanted to know why she had not told Asch about the problems. In her position, Ord answered, you do what you are told, you don't go running to your boss to tell him about something that you presume he knows perfectly well.

Dateline could not resist a common ploy of investigative television when it came to finishing its well-packaged look at the UCI fertility scandal. A reporter with a hidden tape recorder, posing as a prospective client, went to the clinic in Mexico City where Asch was working and asked him about the expense of a fertility procedure. Asch offered a very wide range of figures, adding that the precise cost depended on particular circumstances. He then assured the ersatz patient that he would be taken care of by the eminently skilled staff at the clinic. Later, as Asch and a colleague left the clinic, he was badgered by a *Dateline* reporter who threw accusations at him and then thrust a microphone in his face, asking if he cared to respond. Asch walked steadfastly onward as the reporter continued her tasteless—and eminently unfair—harangue. It was a tactic used not to acquire information but to make the show look as if it were relentlessly in pursuit of the truth and that Asch, by his silence, was admitting his guilt.

Other issues also made headlines during the weeks after the Challenders went public with their case. Arthur Caplan, the director of the Center for Bioethics at the University of Pennsylvania, said, "If you were looking for moral catastrophes, I guess this is the *Titanic* out on the bioethics ocean."[33] Caplan pointed out that theological considerations were but "one of a host of potential problems when you use reproductive materials without consent—you are stirring up a moral pot that can boil over in all sorts of unanticipated ways."[34]

The *Register* quoted Elizabeth Bartholet, the Morris Wasserstein Public Interest Professor of Law and an expert on reproductive medicine at the Harvard Law School: "The area of reproductive technology," she observed of the $2-billion-a-year industry, "is just miles out in front of the law. There's almost no law and people are out there wildly experimenting with . . . the purchase and sale of eggs."[35]

When initial details of the scandal began to appear, the Challenders took a moral high road, saying that they had gone public very reluctantly and only because the issues were so important. They insisted that they would not appear on news shows or deal with magazines that pay for stories, but would talk only with the mainstream media. Money, they told a reporter, was the last thing on their minds. Later, when they settled their case for $450,000 (minus Wentworth's contingency fee and expenses), they repeated their belief that cold cash could not assuage their hurt. "It doesn't resolve it," John Challender said. "You can't put a dollar figure on what happened. A million doesn't undo it. Two doesn't. Three doesn't. The money is secondary."[36] Their attorney echoed these sentiments, noting that the couple had sued because "our technology has surpassed our society's ethics. We need to explore the ethics of what is happening with assisted reproduction, and we filed suit in order to force the university to have a dialogue about it."

Financial considerations did not remain in last place forever for the Challenders, however. When in late 1998 we made contact with them after repeated unsuccessful attempts to set up an interview, they said that, on the advice of their attorney, they would not meet with us unless we paid them a percentage of the income from any book that we might write or gave them $75 an hour. We agreed to the second option, spent about an hour with them in their still unfurnished house built four months previously in a posh Riverside neighborhood with money that they had received from the fertility clinic lawsuit.

Looking back on the case during our interview, the Challenders noted that "for the most part, the media was extremely ethical, courteous, and considerate." John emphasized that the couple had drawn their strength from the fact that they were not fabricating anything: "The media," John observed, "only grows fangs when someone is hiding something." He had been particularly angered by the attempts of the university to cover up its actions and its failures to act: he stressed that he cannot abide dishonesty.

John and Debbie had come to differ amiably in their opinion about Ricardo Asch. John now said that he thought that Asch was insufferably arrogant. "I would have walked out after the first time I met him. It was only because of her that I stayed." He said he was particularly irritated when Asch flat out told Debbie, "You will be pregnant," especially since this pronouncement came in the wake of ten years of his wife's unsuccessful attempts to conceive. The remark indicated to John that Asch was too impressed with himself, believing and boasting that he was superior to the other doctors with whom they had worked. Asch might have said, John offered, "I think I can help you"; that alone would have been a bold statement.

When we asked John why he thought that Asch had done what he had to them, he suggested that "he was a showboat, he liked the attention and notoriety, liked wealth and power." These traits, he observed, were not necessarily despicable but, when combined with arrogance, they can be deadly. John told the man who had portrayed the physician in the television drama about their case that he was "underacting," that Asch was more villainous than he'd been portrayed. The actor's answer was that showing Asch as John saw him would not be credible to the general public and would be regarded as overacting.

For her part, Debbie Challender continued to say that she was quite taken with Asch, a gender distinction in judgments about the man that we often would encounter. For one thing, she pointed out, she had spent an adult lifetime working with physicians, and for her their arrogance was neither an uncommon nor an unexpected trait. "I thought he was nice and charming," she said. "I didn't have a problem with him."

The Challenders maintained that they had never doubted that they would prevail in their lawsuit. John used an analogy to the sales work that he now does for a trucking company. There is what we call an "assumed close," he said, a point at which you are pretty certain that the deal is done. He thought throughout the fertility clinic case that theirs was an "assumed close." Debbie added that the Challenders' stability as a family rooted in religion eased the difficulties of their unfamiliar situation as courtroom plaintiffs and momentary media celebrities.

Finally, we wanted to know how the Challenders saw themselves. Debbie said that she believed that she was a strong individual, her strength gained "from faith in God and the fact that I love my family with all my heart." John demurred at the question and Debbie said that she'd answer it for him if he didn't mind. That was all right, he agreed; she could try but he would retain a veto right. John, she offered, "is very strong"—then she turned to him—"can I say opinionated?" Certainly, he told her, "There's nothing wrong with that. That's a compliment."

The Challenders, before the in vitro fertilization process provided them with a child, were part of the estimated 8 to 15 percent of American families—more than five million couples—that are labeled "involun-

tarily infertile." To be placed in that category a couple must fail to conceive after a year of regular sexual intercourse without the use of
contraceptives, must not have had a prior conception, or must not have
been able to carry a pregnancy to live birth. Involuntary infertility has
two components—the physical incapacity to procreate and the psychic
wish to do so.[37]

There is considerable dispute about the personal and marital consequences of infertility. Most studies agree that infertile couples do about
the same as most people on standardized tests that measure specific personality traits. The psychologists Robert Edelmann and Kevin J. Connolly, for instance, indicate that, on the basis of a study of clinic patients,
"an infertile population demonstrates the spread of scores on psychological tests that is typical of the normal population,"[38] though they grant
that it is possible that only well-adjusted couples get as far as seeking
medical help in their efforts to conceive.[39]

But there also is research suggesting that for some couples involuntary infertility creates personal crises and is psychologically threatening
and emotionally stressful.[40] Infertility is said often to produce feelings of
frustration, anxiety, and depression and to create guilt because it offends
the religious tradition wherein children are seen as a blessing from
heaven and barrenness as a divine curse or punishment.[41] That humans
"replenish the earth" is God's command (Genesis 1:20). Infertility also
may undermine sexual pleasure because each act of intercourse becomes a reminder of procreative failure,[42] though when a low sex drive
is reported by an infertile couple, it is uncertain whether that is a cause
of the infertility or a consequence of it.[43]

The wife's emotional state is more inclined than her husband's to be
affected by infertility, since she is more likely to be regarded by her family and friends—and herself—as having failed in the most important
achievement possible for women. Even if the failure to conceive lies with
the male—a matter true in about 40 percent of infertility cases[44]—wives
often seek to deflect insult to their mate's virility by offering vague explanations for their childlessness. Sometimes wives will imply that the procreative difficulty lies in what they jokingly might label their own
"plumbing."

When Debbie Challender gave birth and dropped from the roster of
the infertile, she joined a growing number of couples who with the aid
of new medical techniques have been enabled to procreate. These tech-

niques, standing "at the end of the fertility career path," have produced an increasing bounty of babies.[45] In its annual report for 2002, the Division of Reproductive Health in the Centers for Disease Control and Prevention noted a 27 percent nationwide growth in "fertility-enhanced births" in 1998 as compared to two years earlier. Three hundred fertility clinics had reported that their clients underwent 81,899 procedures and had about 20,000 live deliveries. Some 56 percent of the clinic deliveries were multiple births, compared to 3 percent of regular births.[46]

Fertility-enhanced births burst upon the scene in 1978, when Patrick Steptoe and Robert Edwards succeeded in accomplishing the first induced human pregnancy, which resulted in the birth in Oldham, England, of Louise Joy Brown (who works today as a nurse).[47] A year later, Elizabeth Carr became the first IVF child born in the United States. Carr remembers only one occasion in which she was teased about her IVF birth. During a soccer game, a teammate shouted: "You stupid test-tube baby! You can't kick! They didn't put that in the petri dish!"[48]

The production of the egg (or, in medical terminology, the oocyte) was not stimulated by artificial means in these early procedures, and only a low rate of pregnancies was being achieved. This led to techniques that allowed the harvesting of many more eggs than would be produced in a normal female cycle. Once those techniques had been discovered, the question arose about what to do with "extra" ones; this was the matter at the core of the Irvine fertility scandal. Eggs that have been retrieved must be used because attempts at freezing eggs have overall been unsuccessful. Egg cryopreservation is a difficult process because the internal structure of the cell is so delicate that ice crystals that form during freezing puncture and destroy the egg when it is thawed. Embryos can be saved for future use, though many clinics limit the options: either implant the embryos or destroy them. Three of four frozen embryos show some cellular damage and the likelihood of pregnancy is lower with the use of such cryopreserved embryos.[49]

Few, if any, people in the fertility business take the position that extra embryos ought to employed for any purpose—such as research and the impregnation of another woman—without the informed consent of the donor. But those in the business are well aware that many couples give clear signals of indifference to the fate of their unused eggs or embryos. At UCI, there was a yearly fee of fifty dollars for embryo storage. But often nobody got around to sending out the invoices, and even when bills were sent, a large number of couples never responded.

The Mt. Sinai Medical Center in New York City charges a quarterly fee of $500 for embryo storage, hoping that the high tariff will push former patients toward making a decision about what to do with their reproductive materials. Many patients are reluctant to see their substances destroyed because they regard them as possessing life (much as those who are against abortion view the fetus). Others ultimately donate the materials to laboratories that use them for stem cell research. Some patients are willing to donate the eggs and embryos to other couples, but they may insist on meeting those couples and maintaining a relationship with any children that may be born.[50]

That Asch himself, or at least some of his coworkers, was well aware of the issue of informed consent is evident in the detailed attention paid to the question in scientific articles that the Irvine fertility team published in medical journals. In one piece, of which Asch was senior author, Balmaceda second, and Teri Ord third, it is noted that donated oocytes were used in a gamete intrafallopian transfer (GIFT) procedure to impregnate six patients who had premature ovarian failure (POF), a condition defined as cessation of menstruation prior to the age of forty, which affects about 150,000 American women.

The first successful in vitro fertilization implantation and embryo transfer for such patients had been carried out in Australia in 1984, though only one of the seven patients bore a child.[51] Asch was aiming to better the Australian success rate; his team's use of GIFT procedures resulted in four pregnancies in a group of six twenty-six- to thirty-five-year-old nulligravidas (never before pregnant) women with premature ovarian failure. This is the description of part of the experimental method:

> Oocytes were obtained from patients in our GIFT program who altruistically donated the extra oocytes not used for transfer. A separate legal consent form was signed prior to the procedure by both the recipient and the donors. The donation was anonymous and nonfinancially reimbursed. The results of the donations were not given to the donors.[52]

Asch also was well aware that women not undergoing fertility treatment could readily be recruited for oocyte donations. The sociologist Roberta Lessor in 1993 was the lead author on an article in the journal

Fertility and Sterility that lists Balmaceda and Asch among the four co-authors; the article reports on a project to determine the social and psychological traits of oocyte donors. Ninety-five women were recruited during a two-year period from the middle-class neighborhoods surrounding the medical center in which Asch's clinic was located. Potential donors were solicited by advertisements inserted in the area's leading newspaper. The ads showed a mother and a baby and asked if a woman under thirty-five would like to help an infertile woman to have a child through egg donation. It was emphasized that this was not a project involving surrogacy; that is, the volunteer would not herself carry the child.

Sixty-nine of the women volunteering were deemed acceptable and sixty of them actually provided oocytes. The typical donor was twenty-six years old, married, with one or two children, and was deemed by testing and interviews to be free from psychopathology. The donors had on the average completed two years of college, worked at least part-time in a white-collar job, and were said to show "high energy." Members of the group in general did not endorse "traditional female role stereotypes." Most said that their motivation was the desire to give another woman a chance to have a baby.

The recruitment project had been conducted in part because the development of embryo cryopreservation methods had markedly reduced the availability of donated oocytes. Women who undergo fertility treatment generally have their extra embryos frozen in case treatment fails or for future family planning. "Increasingly," the article notes, "oocyte donation programs are turning to the volunteer donor, . . . women who come forward to participate."[53] A newspaper report puts a human face on the process. It tells of the egg donation of a thirty-three-year-old nurse and mother of three children. She had been moved by the decade-long struggle of her sister to conceive; she notes that eggs discarded through menstruation need not go to waste. Then she grins shyly and says: "I hope they tell the recipient that I have really dry skin."[54]

A British study also used media publicity to recruit volunteers to donate eggs. Twenty London women came forward to undergo ovarian stimulation and oocyte collection that resulted in the production of 182 eggs that went to thirty-four recipients. In addition, fifteen fertility clinic patients agreed prior to their treatment cycle that they would donate a maximum of six oocytes if they produced more than twelve. Members of this group provided ninety oocytes to sixteen recipients. There is some dispute among ethicists whether these donations represent adequately free choices, since the women might not be willing to say "no" because they would be turning down requests from those who would be providing their treatment.

The donors in the British study by a large majority said that they did not believe they should be paid for what they had done. They were divided, however, about whether the recipients of the eggs should to be told who the donors were: 87 percent of the volunteers but only 45 percent of the patients at the clinic thought that it would be a good idea to provide this information to egg recipients. Beyond that, thirty-two of the thirty-five women said that they would be willing to donate oocytes again.

Those of the clinic patients who donated their excess eggs had a 47 percent pregnancy rate, a rate higher than that for the other patients in the clinic, but this was likely related to the fact that successful pregnancy is statistically tied to the number of oocytes that a patient produces.[55]

Recent campaigns to recruit egg donors have focused on advertisements in college student newspapers. One advertisement in the paper of an elite institution specified the traits being sought in donors, but did not set out the proposed payment. There was hardly any response. When the half-page advertisement, which included an illustration of a stork bringing a baby, was repeated, this time stating the reward, there was an enthusiastic response. This is what the advertisement in the papers at Stanford, Yale, Harvard, Princeton, Pennsylvania, MIT, and Cal Tech proclaimed:

EGG DONOR NEEDED

LARGE FINANCIAL INCENTIVE

Intelligent, Athletic Egg Donor Needed
For Loving Family

You must be at least 5'10"
Have a 1400 + SAT score
Possess no major family medical issues

$50,000.00
Free Medical Screening
All Expenses Paid

Source: John Boudreau, *Orange County Register*, 28 February 1999;
Stanford Daily, 18 February 1999.

The money is defined as compensation for their time and trouble, not for their ova. In 2002 the U.S. Congress appropriated one million dollars to publicize the donation option for couples producing "surplus" eggs.[56] Critics of such tactics see it as but another instance of the commodification of contemporary life, which is now working its way into the trade for human body parts and products.[57] The American Society for Assisted Reproduction warns that "financial payments should not be so excessive as to constitute undue inducement."[58] But how would society expect to determine the amount of money that is "excessive" in regard to persons with different means and different desires, much less to measure "undue inducement"?[59]

Given these conditions, why would Asch use the eggs of patients such as Debbie Challender to implant in other women (presuming, of course, that he did so)? Was it merely because it seemed the path of least resistance, the easiest thing to do? Did he not understand why anybody would object? Did he believe that there was no reason for patients to be concerned about their "excess" oocytes being used for an admirable end?

Sir William Osler, the preeminent medical figure of the nineteenth century, thought he knew what produced the attitude that would allow a doctor to overrule ethical imperatives. Osler believed that medical practitioners were prone to arrogance because their work often lacked leavening influences. "No class of men needs friction so much as physicians—no class gets less," Osler wrote. He declared that "the daily round of a busy practitioner tends to develop an egotism of a most intense kind, to which there is no antidote. The few setbacks are forgotten, the mistakes are often buried, and ten years of successful work tends to make a man touchy, dogmatic, intolerant of correction, and abominably self-centered." According to his biographer, Osler, commenting on the conflict between service and self-serving behavior, "even seemed to go so far as to think that a man could not make more than a bare living and still be an honest and competent physician."[60]

Women who donate oocytes often point out that they are acquainted with an infertile couple and that this influenced their decision. Contrary to the Challenders, whose "donation" was involuntary, altruistic donors do not desire to have subsequent contact with either the recipients of their donation or offspring of the process. About one in four said that she never thought about the child conceived from her egg donation;

others expressed rather low-keyed kinds of interests: "I would like to know if it's a boy or girl and if he or she looked like me," or "I don't think of it in a negative or longing way. I just wonder if it worked and hope that the recipients are happy."[61]

In part because it is a relatively new phenomenon, the in vitro fertilization procedure has not as yet been embedded in a cushion of legal dictates that specify what is acceptable and what illegal. Ad hoc kinds of conclusions about in vitro fertilization usually are based on laws and standards that were established in regard to abortion and surrogate parenthood procedures; sometimes, however, there are no parallels between in vitro fertilization and earlier kinds of reproductive processes, and in this gap lie the problems of fault and responsibility in the UCI fertility clinic scandal.

Meanwhile, throughout this country as well as in others whose citizens had come to the UCI fertility clinic, infants manufactured there by one means or another grew, romped, cried, smiled, and undoubtedly brought a great deal of pleasure to their once-infertile parents. How it went wrong is the story to be told in the following pages.

CHAPTER 2

The Seeds of Discontent

■ The 1986 recruitment of Ricardo Asch, M.D., by the medical school at the University of California, Irvine, was the opening act for the drama that in the end would force Asch and his closest colleague into exile, one to Mexico and the other to Chile, and would come close to sending Sergio Stone, a doctor who worked with the pair, to prison. Asch possessed superstar qualities that led UCI to recruit him. He was a preeminent physician in fertility medicine, one of the world's best-known and most highly regarded figures. He regularly traveled nationally and internationally to deliver lectures and present demonstrations. Particularly important for the university's scholarly reputation, Asch published solid research articles in first-rate scientific journals. Physicians at medical schools in the United States are expected to treat patients, to teach and supervise medical students, and to carry out and publish benchmark research, preferably research that is heavily funded so that the university can siphon off a portion of the grants to meet overhead expenses (and, typically, a bit more than that). Doctors who can effectively meet such stiff requirements are in heavy demand.

The fact that Asch appeared to be a medical money-making machine was perhaps the most appealing attraction he had for the university. UCIMC often seeks out partnerships with clinics specializing in such fields as dermatology, ophthalmology, and neurology to improve its image and to increase profits. Some faculty at the College of Medicine have expressed concerns over sweetheart deals with specialty practices that are favored over other medical care areas because they bring in patients who personally or through their insurance can handle large costs. Chronically posting financial losses, the medical school and its associated hospital had become a drain on the funds that the state legislature provided for the university system. At the same time, the UCI hospital had an honorable reputation as a place where indigent patients could receive state-of-the-art medical treatment. Often it was the only hope for members of minority groups, many of them illegal immigrants, who needed care. But the load of unreimbursed treatment made running the medical school and hospital an accountant's nightmare. Asch looked as though he could be of great help. The fertility treatments that he offered were very expensive. The medical school is located in an affluent area; Asch's clients would possess the wherewithal for procedures that generally were not covered by insurance policies. Bringing Asch on board was like getting a dazzling $15-million-a-year superstar first baseman who would entice into the stadium additional spectators whose entrance and parking and feeding fees would more than compensate for the stellar performer's salary.[1]

The university and American Medical International, one of the nation's largest hospital chains, joined forces to lure Asch from his position at the University of Texas Medical School in San Antonio. Sergio Stone had first been offered the opportunity to establish a fertility center, but he backed off from the task. "I had a choice," he reflects today. "I could be trained [in fertility medicine] and run a Mickey Mouse program or I could bring in the best."

Asch was the best—or, most certainly, one of the very best. Thomas Cesario, the dean of the UCI College of Medicine, looking back, observes: "Asch had all the trappings of a distinguished person—a high earner who would act as a magnet to attract patients."[2] Note might be made of the order in which Cesario enumerates Asch's appeal.

Newspaper reports heralded Asch's arrival on the local scene with heady delight, while the university sponsored a picnic to celebrate the arrival of this trailblazing fertility wizard. Stone would laconically recollect those times: "There were some balloons" is the way he now puts it.[3]

Asch declared that his new base at UCI offered "a place where I can do everything I want to do. Research, see patients, and really be on my own with a lot of freedom." He may have overestimated the last: the university could look the other way, and did so for some time, but it had to take action when accusations of irregularities became public knowledge and the media played it up big. Asch also expressed his pleasure with the opportunity to attract clients in southern California. "The only way to do research is to have a lot of patients," he observed.[4] He then added, seemingly gratuitously and a bit ominously, "Unfortunately, we need patient consent [for research]."

Asch had been accorded a tenured faculty position carrying an annual base salary of $120,900, but that was a relatively minor portion of the amount of money he would earn from his work at the university. He was permitted to bring his own team to UCI, including his partner Balmaceda, the biologist Teri Ord, and an assortment of academic fellows, medical residents, and graduate students. Ord, uniformly praised for her meticulous record-keeping, did not have the formal educational background for the level of work she was doing—and by all accounts doing very well. When she resigned late in 1994, she said that she had left because of what she vaguely identified as problems with the clinic doctors. One of the clinic workers we interviewed said that Ord often complained about what she saw as the inadequate pay she got for the skilled work she was doing. Ord's husband, Pasquale Patrizo, who many considered Asch's protégé, apparently was not received warmly by Stone and Balmaceda, which might have contributed to Ord's disenchantment.

Asch's first clinic location was at the American Medical International facility in the Garden Grove medical center, a few miles west of the main UCI hospital. Asch and Balmaceda worked there from 1986 until 1990. About two-thirds of the cases of unconsented egg transfer were connected to treatments at Garden Grove. Asch and Balmaceda also formed a private partnership in the late 1980s, the Center for Reproductive Health (CRH), also at Garden Grove; in 1989 they opened another fertility clinic, which was affiliated with the university, at Saddleback Memorial Medical Center in Laguna Hills. Additionally, Asch and Balmaceda provided treatment and procedures separate from the partnership in Italy, Brazil, Argentina, and Guatemala.

When the Center for Reproductive Health closed its Garden Grove offices in 1990 and moved to the new Pavilion II building in the UCI hospital complex, things were going very well. The center was, as one observer noted, "prestigious and lucrative."[5] Asch supervised the clinic at the UCI Medical Center (UCIMC) and Balmaceda oversaw the work at the Saddleback site. Stone, who joined in the partnership at this time, was never deeply involved in the fertility procedures. His energy was more, though not entirely, devoted to academic pursuits rather than work with patients; on the latter front he performed surgery at several local hospitals.

Jane L. Frederick, a 1984 University of Southern California medical school graduate who had just completed a four-year fellowship at USC, was hired by the partnership to assist at both the UCIMC and Saddleback locations. She split her time about equally between the two facilities and was appointed an assistant professor in the UCI College of Medicine.

Frederick remained on the side lines as the fertility scandal unfolded. The university agreed to defend and indemnify her, alone among the CRH physicians, from the multitude of lawsuits brought by former clinic patients. In time, she was removed from the lawsuits when no evidence of wrongdoing on her part was demonstrated. She was not fired from the university, although her academic appointment expired soon after the news of the scandal surfaced. When an attorney advertised in the local newspaper for clients who had been treated by Asch, Balmaceda, Stone, and Frederick, her attorney obtained a printed retraction from the newspaper, which admitted that there was no evidence she had done anything wrong. Nor was Frederick named in the federal indictment for mail fraud against Asch, Balmaceda, and Stone.

Somewhat later, the university took action against Frederick on the ground that she had prescribed an unapproved fertility drug, hMG (human menopausal gonadotrophin) Massone, to clinic patients. The case was never resolved formally because Frederick's appointment expired before a university-appointed committee could make a ruling.

Frederick, however, sued for defamation. Joseph Hartley, one of her attorneys, during a deposition of Sidney Golub, the university's executive vice chancellor, showed that the allegation against Frederick had been pushed by Golub on the flimsiest of evidence. That evidence involved notations on several patient charts of use of "hMG" and on one record in particular the further notation, in brackets: "[See Dr. Asch]." Hartley pointed out that the term hMG could have been used in a generic sense, and that it was not usual for the doctors to indicate use of the FDA-approved Pergonal by its trade name. He stressed that if a patient had been given an unauthorized drug, she most likely had gotten it from Asch, and that Frederick was but the doctor on call during subsequent stages of the patient's treatment. Finally, Hartley wanted to know why Golub had not picked up the telephone and asked Frederick personally what the notation signified before he commenced a formal university investigation.

The manner in which Golub was deposed in the ensuing litigation reflected the belief of university officials that they were being badgered (as they sometimes were) by outsiders who did not appreciate their higher calling. There was, for instance, a testy interchange when Hartley asked Golub to estimate the date that he had reached one of the conclusions in the Frederick case:

HARTLEY: What you believe were allegations that Dr. Frederick had prescribed hMG Massone. But can you fix it to any—to being closer to any particular date? Any family members' birthdays, Easter, Passover. Anything like that?

GOLUB: Mr. Hartley, is there a reason that you make reference to Jewish holidays?

HARTLEY: Not particularly. I have a whole list of things that I go down.

GOLUB: I'm just struck by the fact that it's the third reference to Judaism since I've arrived.

HARTLEY: Nothing in particular.

GOLUB: I didn't know if there was something of interest in this area for you.

HARTLEY: Besides Arbor Day I can't think of any other holidays that occur in the springtime, except for my birthday. I doubt that you celebrate that.

GOLUB: I don't think so. Don't even celebrate mine.[6]

Frederick lost the defamation case because the California civil code protects statements made in the course of an official investigation. She was held responsible for court costs of $674. (Currently, she is a private practitioner in Laguna Hills, California, with the clever e-mail address of ivf@havingbabies.com.)

Troubles surfaced very early at the clinic in its new home in the Pavilion II building. Some patient payments were missing, and Asch reported that money had been stolen from his wallet. Then, in December 1991, there was a reported theft of $4,600 from the clinic, of which $3,400 had been in traveler's checks and the remainder in cash. The university's auditor, Bruce Murdy, was brought in to investigate. Nerves were on edge because there was no evidence of a break-in, which naturally fueled the rumor that each incident was an inside job.

Murdy produced a four-page report early in 1992. He pointed out that a great deal of cash was coming into the clinic and that control of its whereabouts and disposition often was haphazard or nonexistent. Patients from states other than California and from abroad often paid in cash or with traveler's checks, with payments running from three thousand to thirty thousand dollars. Checks sometimes were incomplete, with the payee left blank, and money would accumulate at the clinic until the completion of a treatment series. These series ran approximately three weeks and involved anywhere from fifty to seventy patients, with an average payment of seven thousand dollars from each. A treatment series therefore could produce as much as half a million dollars.

The audit report recommended the establishment of more formal cash control and record-keeping procedures, including the use of a daily journal to track the flow of money. The clinic did have a "day log" in which physician fees were recorded, but there was no place where the amounts due to the medical center or to the anesthesiology department were listed—and both of these groups wanted to be sure they got what was owed them.

The audit also recommended tightened security. The reception area was pinpointed as the most vulnerable spot in the clinic. The campus police suggested that security glass be installed to protect staff members, that there be alarms hidden on the desks where financial transactions occurred, and that a partition be installed that would keep outsiders from watching money being handled and placed in a drawer. There was nothing in the report even to suggest that any greater problem than the money losses existed at the clinic.

Fingers of suspicion about the missing money had been pointed at Toula Batshoun, the clinic manager. She was thirty-four at the time and had worked for Asch since 1986, when he arrived in California, and she was in a particularly good position to have stolen the cash. But no proof whatsoever tying her to the theft was ever forthcoming. Batshoun admitted at the time of the audit that she had falsified a personal insurance billing to avoid paying the deductible on her family medical policy. There also were rumors that Batshoun had committed perjury when giving a deposition in 1990 in order to help Asch fight a malpractice suit, though details of the case, if it truly existed, never have been released.[7]

Batshoun maintains that she told the auditor about improper use of eggs by Asch and that she offered to supply documents both to him and to other university officials to support her claim.[8] She says that after the audit, in March 1992, she confronted Asch personally and showed him forms that indicated he had used eggs without the patients' consent.[9] She claims that Asch shredded the documents and threatened her with physical harm. Batshoun went on extended sick leave soon after the audit was finished and apparently was forced out of her job in early 1993.

Batshoun, who has repeatedly refused through her attorney to discuss with us her experiences at the clinic, later filed a lawsuit against the university. She claimed that she was subjected to retaliation, wrongfully terminated, and slandered. She specifically alleged that she had been falsely accused of attempting to sell documents to UCI for $27 million.[10] The suit was dismissed with prejudice (meaning that it could not be refiled).[11] She remains a controversial figure. A clinic nurse, for instance, had told other employees that Batshoun was paying personal bills with clinic credit cards. Stone described her as "a different bird" and said that he had tried to get her fired from the first day he had encountered her. Asch insists that she "was a crook" and that "nobody trusted her." He claims that she stole fifteen hundred dollars from his office and twelve thousand dollars from the front office.[12] Another serious charge against Batshoun involved a patient who had checked "no donation" on the consent form. Asch maintains that Batshoun altered the consent form and then appropriated the eggs for use for her best friend.

Rumors continued to swirl around the clinic in the wake of the audit. Some employees said that patients had paid for their treatments with jewelry and had agreed to donate eggs in order to have their cases handled by the fertility doctors. These innuendos and allegations triggered another internal audit. At the request of the university, in November 1992 David Swanberg, a certified public accountant, initiated this second review.

Swanberg found that the way cash was handled at the clinic still was unsatisfactory. His recommendation was that money be dealt with by an employee who had no responsibility for accounts receivable or for insurance billing, which would make it more difficult for a single person to manipulate the books. He told the employees that they should keep cash, checks, and credit card payments in the safe that had been installed after the initial audit.

Swanberg also discovered that the fertility clinic physicians maintained two separate bank accounts. Each day's receipts were deposited in a California bank. But then the money was transferred to a Shearson Lehman Brothers investment account in Boston. This arrangement raised a red flag for Swanberg, but the doctors told him that the Boston account offered superior interest. Swanberg suggested that a local bank be used, but his recommendation was never adopted. From his viewpoint, canceled checks would be more readily recoverable and careful auditing more feasible if a local bank was involved.

Only one "unusual" item was specified in Swanberg's report. A refund check for an out-of-state patient had been written on May 11, 1992, and cleared by the bank in July. The check, according to Swanberg's audit, had been stolen and ended up at a local business that had no affiliation with the clinic. Asch says he became aware of the missing money when an Arizona patient, whose sister served as her childbearing surrogate, telephoned because she had received a billing on a paid account. He believed that the check had been stolen by Batshoun and cashed at the company where her husband worked.

Swanberg also identified problems with the fertility clinic's billing of insurance carriers. Some billings did not have the required signed patient authorization and there was an occasional failure to enter the amount that had been charged to the insurance company. Swanberg noted that "the insurance billing should correctly match the procedures and attending physician names appearing on the medical documents." This implied that the diagnostic codes in bills to insurance companies may not have represented what was done, and what actually was done may not have qualified for insurance coverage. Egg retrieval procedures, for instance, are not covered by most insurance policies, and sometimes they were billed as cyst removals, which qualified for compensation.

Nineteen of the twenty billings that Swanberg examined were found to have problems: seven listed the wrong physician, seven had insurance claims missing, and a number indicated that the insurance companies were overbilled.[13] Patient charts also were found wanting. Employees proved unable to locate some missing files and patient records that were supposed to be confidential were not always kept in secured storage.

In contrast, the laboratory records kept by Teri Ord were reported to be in very good shape. Documentation of the contents of the liquid storage tanks that contained frozen sperm, eggs, and embryos were "well organized and meticulously [so]." Swanberg's formal report made no mention of unconsented use of eggs and sperm. But Batshoun had repeated to him her suspicion that Asch was employing eggs without patient consent, though she did not provide specific documentation.

The claim regarding failure to obtain consent for egg use was reinforced in a conversation between Swanberg and Norbert Giltner, the clinic nurse. Giltner is one of the more enigmatic figures in the fertility clinic scandal. It is difficult to distinguish whether it was ethical impulses, a certain pleasure in intrigue, or what many saw as his strong personal antipathy toward Asch that motivated his actions. He would back away from aggressive pursuit of the wrongdoing he believed was rampant at the clinic, explaining that he expected that nothing would be done about it. He requested another assignment, but then succeeded in being moved back to the clinic, despite his alleged awareness of what was going on.

Giltner reported that he first met for two hours with Swanberg to try to impress upon him, on the basis of documents he displayed, that there was unconsented egg use. Giltner described Swanberg's reaction: "He looked at me, like I'm an accountant. I have no ideas what to do with this."[14] But Giltner also later said that Swanberg had "acted most interested" in the information and indicated that he would include it in his report. He did not do so, but references to egg misuse appear in Swanberg's notes.[15] These were withheld by the university for years on the ground that its policies prohibit the disclosure of audit work notes.[16]

Finally, in 2000 Karen Taillon, an attorney representing Sergio

Stone, won a court victory that forced the disclosure of Swanberg's full report, both the formal review and the notes that supplemented it. The noted allegations that had not been allowed to surface—combined with testimony about discussions of this material—provided damning evidence that university officials definitely had been alerted to the unconsented egg transfers at the fertility clinic. The Swanberg notes in part stated:

> 4. Toula said that there were questions on eggs and embryos. Patient knows they don't have any eggs. They do not tell women that her extra eggs are being fertilized and implanted in another patient.
> 5. Consent agreements should be in the charts. "Give eggs to research." The [sic] actually give eggs to another woman.
> 6. Eggs are controlled by: Gil Giltner, RN and Biologist, Teri Ord, and Asch. Patient would not know. Women donated eggs would not know. Perfect match to a person they are giving it to. Quality of eggs. Gil knows the number of eggs. They report fewer eggs than what are retrieved.[17]

Despite the tortured phrasing and Swanberg's rudimentary comprehension of the situation, the notes allow no interpretation other than that Swanberg had been told and was conveying information that lay at the core of the scandal at the fertility clinic.

Since Swanberg conveyed the information in his notes to university officials, they had as early as 1992 at least an idea that something might be seriously awry at the fertility clinic. Swanberg maintains that he talked directly with Asch about the allegations and that Asch denied the charges. Swanberg also says that he discussed the charges with the executive managers at the hospital. Despite official denial, an internal university document shows that the egg allegations were taken up during a December 16, 1992, meeting involving Walter Henry, then the dean of the College of Medicine, Andrew Yeilding, the director of internal auditing, and James Heron, the director of finances at UCI.[18] A report of the meeting was sent to Mary Piccione, the executive director of the hospital, Diane Geocaris, counsel to the chancellor, and John F. Lundberg, deputy general counsel for health care. University officials maintain that they looked into the allegations of egg misuse after getting the report, and they concluded that there was not adequate ground to launch an official inquiry. It very possibly was their knowledge of these circumstances that prompted university attorneys to avoid any public trial of civil suits by fertility patients. They might not have wanted it widely known that they had failed to follow up satisfactorily the notice of wrongdoing that they had been given.

An internal document that surfaced in 2002 provides for some speculation on who knew what when. The investigative notes dated December 7, 1995, reportedly written by a university auditor, include an interview with Diane Geocaris. Geocaris's calendar, the auditor observed, indicated two meetings in 1992 to discuss fertility clinic matters, but both had been marked canceled in her appointment book. It may have been this situation that prompted Geocaris, according to the report, to go "into a rage" and say, "[I'm] not taking the fall for this. I'm tired of pissant people not doing their jobs and trying to pin the blame on me. I didn't know anything about any fucking eggs until 1994." Though Geocaris claimed to have received only "juicy" items of gossip by e-mail, her June 29, 1993, e-mail response to a colleague regarding a fertility clinic patient complaint shows early knowledge of other types of clinic mishaps, despite her insistence that her first recollection of the case was in 1994.

Swanberg's formal report concluded with an enthusiastic endorsement of the operation of the fertility clinic: "Practice physicians are credited with developing state of the art in vitro fertilization techniques that are emulated by other physicians throughout the world." The problems uncovered presumably were regarded as minor aberrations. Later auditors would express dismay at the shallowness of Swanberg's work. A normal report, they maintained, should catalog the strengths and weaknesses of an enterprise and specify clearly any serious difficulties that had been discovered.

Supplementing Swanberg's notes was a lawsuit filed by Patricia Haynes and her husband, Edward, claiming that university officials had known and failed to take action about inappropriate egg hijackings well before the Challender case became public. The Hayneses stated that they were anxious that eggs they believed had been taken from Patricia were apparently missing. She said that she had filed a malpractice claim with the medical school in February 1993; the school said it forwarded the claim to Lundberg, the university's Oakland-based counsel, with a copy going to the Professional Risk Management group in Arlington, Virginia, which was responsible for dealing with claims against the university. Lundberg denies awareness of the Hayneses' claim until a year later, when matters had already begun to unravel seriously at the clinic.

Lundberg angrily denies that Swanberg had told him about the wrongdoing concerning eggs. He says that the allegation makes his "blood boil" and suggests that for some reason, which he cannot fathom, the notes themselves were "cooked," backdated to make his office look negligent. But he offers no explanation for why the Hayneses' claim, which he says he first saw in 1994, was not turned over to the clinical investigating committee when it began its work in November 1994. Notes from a closed regents' meeting in June 1995 reveal that Regent James Holst questioned Lundberg about how much he knew in 1992. Lundberg replied, according to the report, "[I have] no recollection of communication from internal audit—continuing to search memory."

Dr. Stanley Korenman of the UCLA medical school, who later served as chair of a clinical panel looking into fertility clinic affairs, says today that he had no knowledge of the Hayneses' suit. Had he been aware of it, his group would have inquired further: "It would have been an important avenue to investigate." He adds that "Haynes's claim could have shown us that in 1993 university officials had responsibility for what was going on, and they did not awaken to that, or they were awake and decided to bury it. I don't know."[19]

In 2000 Melanie Blum, the plaintiffs' lawyer, filed a class-action lawsuit against the university for negligence, illegal conversion of eggs and embryos, and a multitude of other matters. She believes that it was the pressing need of the university to keep Swanberg's testimony from the record that led to out-of-court settlements. She claims that the university outside counsel had contacted her in 1996, asking what it would take to avoid deposing Swanberg. She maintains that the lawyer was "distraught" and "desperate." He finds her comments "ridiculous." But the university did settle, deeming it the wiser action, given the uncertainty of a jury response.[20]

Swanberg's upbeat formal report notwithstanding, the problems at the clinic did not go away; indeed, soon after the atmosphere took on an even more contentious tone. Debra Krahel, an administrator, moved to the front of the firing line. Krahel, thirty-nine years old at the time, had attended college at Arkansas State and Wichita State, graduating with a degree in speech pathology. Her brown hair, meticulously styled, and dark eyes lend her an aura of intensity. She grew up in California's Central Valley, and her mother, Shirley Frey, one of the first women to run for sheriff in California, is said to have instilled a deep sense of values in her daughter.[21] Krahel is the mother of four. Her husband, Bill Krahel, developed the first ear thermometer; the later sale of his Thermascan Company made the family financially secure.

Krahel had been recruited by the UCI Medical Center in September 1993 as senior associate director of ambulatory care, a job that involved the management of a division with a $50 million budget. She presents herself as a poised professional; she is strong and assertive, and she emphasizes that she is committed to maintaining a high standard of personal and professional ethics.

Krahel says that when she was hired she was told by the administrators at the hospital that they sought continued growth and upgrading. "I was given a lot of promises about autonomy and building a community network and the latitude I would have in management."[22] She reported directly to Mary Piccione, the chief hospital manager, and Herb Spiwak, the deputy director.

The Center for Reproductive Health represented only a small part of Krahel's realm of responsibility. But within three months of her hiring, Krahel became concerned about the clinic's financial operations and what she viewed as a notably vague management agreement between the hospital and the clinic doctors. When she voiced this concern to Piccione and Spiwak she was told, she recalls, that Asch had a "special arrangement" and that she should focus on other aspects of her job. But Krahel's concerns about the fertility practice escalated when she discovered that clinic invoices showed that revenues generated were not being reported to the hospital. There also was a matter of unauthorized purchases of office and medical supplies: "They could have been running three or four clinics with the amount of supplies they had," she says. Krahel again notified Spiwak of these problems, and again was told, she says, that "these are world-renowned physicians; leave them alone, let them do what they'll do." Krahel remained uncomfortable, feeling that she might be liable for the wrongdoing—and that most certainly the university and the hospital would be.

In January 1994, according to Krahel, she discussed her suspicions with Marilyn Killane, the fertility clinic office manager. Fifty-six years old at the time, Killane had about twenty years' experience in the medical field and had been working for three years in the fertility clinic at Cornell University when she was recruited by Balmaceda in 1992. Balmaceda and Asch had bypassed hospital and university procedures to hire her, although Asch denies any involvement in her recruitment. Killane, with a marked New York accent and rather tough demeanor, was generally viewed as an "abrasive but dedicated employee."[23] Patients appeared to be turned off by her businesslike demeanor. One told us: "She was so cold and mean, I just couldn't believe she dealt with patients." Another said: "She seemed very sour to me and chronically depressed. She had a grudge against the world."

Killane made one patient, who had undergone several procedures with Asch, and who held a teaching position at the university, pay for her treatment despite her insurance coverage. "Killane," she said, "was the meanest bitch I have ever encountered. The woman had me in tears. I was crying in frustration because I felt that I had come up against a wall and she wouldn't move."[24]

Killane offers a very different take on her relationships at the clinic and with its patients. She says that when she was hired she learned that the permanent position she had been offered was not available because Toula Batshoun had not yet resigned. She was told that everything would be cleared up in a few weeks, but it was another six months before she officially was named office manager.

She immediately became disaffected with the way the clinic was run. "I was pretty knowledgeable about how things were done," she notes, "but here it was completely run different [from Cornell], and I was having major problems with it. It was really hard for me to grasp it, and yet I thought I knew what reproductive health was about."[25] Killane also had a more personal reason for her disenchantment. Her daughter was hired in 1993 as a part-time clinic worker to help upgrade and computerize the facility's billing and records. Then her daughter was fired by Asch, who offered no reason for her dismissal.

Killane felt personally vulnerable because of what she saw as large amounts of cash being handled without satisfactory accounting. She worried that her predecessor had been dismissed for appropriating clinic funds. A confrontation with Asch, she says, dramatically escalated her concerns. He accused her of taking money from a patient whose check had bounced and who had thereafter paid $2,355 in cash to cover part of the cost of treatment. Killane says that Asch retracted his accusation when she produced a receipt that he had signed. Asch granted that he might have carelessly left the cash in his car. Killane thought that he acted "very pompous" and commented derisively, "That's my month's salary."

Killane told Krahel that the clinic doctors were receiving from patients cash payments that were not entered into the records, and that the doctors sometimes would walk out of the clinic with considerable amounts of cash. She also maintained that insurance companies were being billed improperly. Krahel says that she viewed this information with some reservations because she was uncertain about the clinic office manager's reason for talking with her. She also was wary because "Marilyn [Killane] probably wasn't the best office manager I had ever encountered."[26]

In February 1994, a month after their first discussion, Killane provided Krahel with written material to support her claims. She also showed her a vial of hMG Massone, which had not received approval from the Federal Drug Administration for use in the United States. Killane said that Asch was bringing the drug back from Latin America and billing it as Pergonal—its approved counterpart here. Krahel at once reported the matter to Spiwak. "Herb," she remembers saying, "we have a real monumental problem here, and I think that the UC Regents are at risk with what's happening if the patients find out and realize that they are being given something that's not Pergonal." Spiwak's response, according to Krahel, was "get rid of Marilyn, she's a problem, get her out of here." Krahel was shocked. "I was dumbfounded. I'm seeing the problem as being the doctors. I think if I would have played along with him, he would have said 'fire her' and would have left the whole thing alone."[27]

Spiwak finally told Krahel that he would ask the university's internal auditors to conduct another investigation. Two weeks later, Krahel again expressed her concern about the unauthorized drug use, this time to Thomas Garite, the chair of the obstetrics and gynecology department. He told her, she says, that doctors are allowed to bring in drugs and prescribe them regardless of what the FDA says. Krahel then took her case to Philip DiSaia, the chief of the medical staff, who also seemed uninterested. She claims that she was at the time severely reprimanded by Piccione for discussing these matters with medical faculty chairs. Krahel put into writing her understanding of what had gone on between her and her boss: "Mary advised me that I had loose lips and should keep the facts about Reproductive Health to myself. Mary instructed me to let Herb handle everything and that I should defer everything to Herb. *Mary advised me to forget about all of this* [emphasis in original]."[28]

The tension between Krahel and Spiwak began to escalate. In a subsequent meeting, he accused her of being uninformed and of misleading staff members regarding financial aspects of the hospital's operation. She claims that Spiwak became "very irrational" and "loud" and finally ordered her to "get out of [his] goddamned office!" Krahel later would maintain that when Spiwak moved toward the office door he "bumped" into her and that the whole episode left her "very shaken and fearful." She said that "Herb's volatility caused me to feel extremely vulnerable," and she thought that if she continued to disagree with him she would be in jeopardy of physical retaliation. In later statements, she amended Spiwak's angry dismissal by asserting that he said "Get the fuck out!" and alleging that he had "battered and assaulted" her when he bumped into her.

Spiwak grants the confrontation, but remembers it as a great deal less heated. He remembers being very frightened as Krahel raged at him. He says she "exploded" as soon as she came into his office, asking, "Why are you doing this to me?" In Spiwak's view Krahel was "totally incompetent" and "a good schemer."[29]

Krahel told Carol Chatham, who worked with her, that Killane was nervous and frightened because of problems at the clinic. Chatham had been hired as a temporary employee by Krahel in November 1993, with the understanding that she would be given the position of administrator of health services. Her work placed her in close contact with what was going on at the fertility clinic, and she says that its affairs took up a large portion of her time. She found herself settling employee squabbles there and dealing with daily demands by the physicians. "I was constantly checking with the nursing staff and I made two or three runs through per day. I had break-ins, files missing, deliveries that had eggs in them that were broken open and were sitting on docks." These statements, notes one of the fertility doctors, are questionable, given Chatham's limited job responsibilities at the clinic. He maintains that the likelihood that eggs were haphazardly placed anywhere in the medical center is preposterous. Chatham learned that few medical center employees wanted to have anything to do with the reproductive health unit. Her staff had warned her about it, she says, but she at first had no idea of "just how bad it could be."[30]

Chatham was given the assignment to find another position for Killane, a matter complicated by Killane's insistence that she could work only in a reproductive health unit. Besides, Killane's job behavior posed a problem in relocating her. Chatham remembers that Killane "spent a lot of time going back and forth to Human Resources, internal audit, and training seminars. She had doctors' appointments. She was sick." Chatham remembers trying to train Killane to use the automated billing system and being told that it was all too boring. Chatham says that Killane would "read the newspaper, bring a book to read, and get coffee."[31]

Spiwak had responded to Killane's charges about the fertility clinic by asking the university's Human Resources Department to deal with a "labor relations problem," an indication that the allegations were to be viewed as a disciplinary issue. Killane had been defined as a troublemaker. Mary Piccione, for instance, called her a malcontent, and Piccione would be quoted by another employee as saying: "[Asch] is a big person and we need to be sure of the facts. This is just a disgruntled employee."[32]

In early March 1994, again at Spiwak's request, another internal auditor, Robert Chatwin, began an investigation of the clinic. Chatwin had worked at UCI for eight years, primarily at the medical center. What began for him as a routine matter soon turned into something of a personal crusade. Chatwin, raised in Glendora, California, is an earnest, conservative man who became absorbed in the web of intrigue that the fertility case presented. In most cases, an auditor's job demands meticulous attention to mundane details. Chatwin, aged forty-four at the time of the scandal, had attended Citrus Junior College, then California Polytechnic University in Pomona, before he transferred to the University of Southern California business school. During his last semester at USC he went to London as a Mormon missionary for two years. He comments wryly, "The British didn't care much for the religion, but they were very nice to me."

Killane, in a written statement to university officials March 15, requested protection as a whistle-blower, contrary to her earlier statement that she was interested in pursuing neither a Workers' Compensation stress claim nor whistle-blower status. She sought whistle-blower protection, Killane wrote, because of her "alleged allegations towards" the three clinic physicians. These allegations mentioned nothing about egg transfers; rather, they focused on use of a non-approved drug, diversion of cash, and "harassment and discrimination by physicians towards me."[33] The Human Resources Department, Killane believes, was set on discouraging her whistle-blower application: "They gave me these articles to read how [whistle-blowers] lost their jobs, ruined their lives, what happened to their lives. They said whistle-blowers are very recognizable because they always carry around stacks of documents. It's true. That was me. It was very intimidating."[34]

The California legislature had enacted whistle-blower legislation that became effective in May 1993. It forbade punitive retaliatory actions against persons who formally identified themselves as motivated by the desire to right a significant wrong in their work environment. Violators of the protective provision could be fined up to $10,000 or be sentenced to a one-year jail term—or both. The whistle-blower proving retaliatory actions could sue and, if successful, receive attorney's fees and actual and punitive damages.[35]

When the smoke cleared, some mild consensus emerged that Killane's status as whistle-blower was the most legitimate when compared to the other women employees who ultimately claimed that status. In part, this seemed to be because she confined her allegations almost exclusively to the prescribing and distribution of hMG Massone and not to the larger issues of unconsented egg transfers. As early as 1996, Sidney Golub, UCI's executive vice chancellor, would single Killane out for praise during a state senate hearing:

> I want to acknowledge the brave act that triggered this entire episode. Yesterday, I was able to publicly thank Ms. Marilyn Killane since others had revealed her identity despite her whistle-blower status. She was the . . . one who first alerted us to the financial irregularities and the use of non-approved drugs, and she provided key information in many of the investigations. We owe her a debt of gratitude for her efforts.[36]

For her part, though, Killane hardly took any pleasure in such plaudits. "I feel like I have WB carved right here," she told a reporter, touching her forehead.[37]

Meanwhile, Chatwin continued to probe into clinic activities. He found Asch uncooperative, despite his initial assurance that the auditors could have complete access to the clinic operations and its records. Chatwin's repeated written requests for particular documents were ignored by Asch and, as he kept at his task, he began to focus primarily on the illegal prescribing of hMG Massone. But he also started to hear rumors of improprieties that involved eggs and embryos. On April 12, 1994, he discussed the allegations with Nurse Giltner, who turned over laboratory reports that appeared to support the rumors.

Chatwin transmitted a copy of his preliminary findings to the university attorneys at the end of April.[38] He believed that he had uncovered substantial evidence of serious wrongdoing at the fertility clinic and he recommended that university officials seize relevant patient records. The audit office also recommended that a letter be sent to seven clinic employees that would guarantee them protection from any retaliation if they would cooperate with the ongoing investigation.

On May 9 Chatwin provided a written update to the chancellor's office offering additional documentation of the allegation that eggs had been used without patient consent. This report included copies of clinic records that identified specific questionable egg transfers. Chatwin, talking with Krahel, made it clear that he would take a direct reporting path to the main campus and would not share any information with Piccione or Spiwak. He feared that they might undermine his work.

But then Chatwin's plan to continue pressing the matter came to an abrupt end. The university later would declare that the auditors continued their work, but Andrew Yeilding, head of the auditing staff, insists that Diane Geocaris, the chancellor's attorney, told him to stop pursuing the inquiry, "that the auditors should not go back to Dr. Asch and press him for any additional records at this time."[39] Internal notes indicate that a university auditor determined on the basis of an interview with Geocaris that she believed UCI internal auditors were eager to "get" Spiwak and Piccione. The chief auditor would later tell the *Los Angeles Times* that he believed that the university ignored the information his staff had uncovered.[40]

Meanwhile, efforts to locate another position for Killane had gotten nowhere, and she was told at the end of May 1994 that she would have to return to the fertility clinic or she would be fired. The day that Killane was scheduled to resume her old spot, however, Krahel received both a fax and a phone call from Asch in Mexico City saying that he would not tolerate having Killane work in the clinic. Stone also requested that Killane not be reinstated because of what he called "her inability to work with the professional personnel and the staff." Killane had filed a written complaint with Human Resources in February that Stone had engaged in harassment and sex discrimination. She says Stone would yell at her and refer to the staff in derogatory terms. Asch says that Stone "really pissed her [Killane] off so bad that this lady wanted to have vengeance." He described one incident that struck him as cartoonlike: the wall between his office and Stone's was moving because of their screaming.[41]

Killane's complaint was investigated by UCI's Office of Affirmative Action and Equal Opportunity. The final report found "a dichotomy" in views; faculty reported high morale and high revenue and attributed both to the clinic's success rate in patient treatment. The CRH staff, in contrast, reported poor to terrible morale and complained about understaffing, unresolved conflict, unclear roles and responsibilities, verbal abuse, poor communication, and unethical and illegal conduct by a few individuals in the unit. Because of her legally protected status as a whistle-blower, Killane had to be placed on administrative leave rather than dismissed.

There were some attempts during the following month by hospital administrators to appease the disgruntled employees. Krahel was transferred for reasons that she says were not explained to her. The new position carried the same salary, but it represented a significant reduction in supervisory responsibilities. Krahel strongly objected, but she says that Piccione told her: "Don't challenge my decision. Do you want another chance or not?" Piccione said that the transfer had nothing to do with the business of the fertility clinic: she defined it as a favor to Krahel to keep her from being fired because of complaints from several physicians about her performance.

In July, after she had heard from Chatwin about the alleged unconsented egg transfers, Krahel raised the topic with Giltner. He showed her cryologs that indicated that in 1991 Asch was making transfers of both eggs and embryos without consent from the "donors." The charts also failed to indicate whether precautionary testing for HIV and hepatitis B had been done. Krahel noted that "most of the transfers were occurring between young women producing viable eggs and older women who were post-menopausal. The doctors were giving eggs and sometimes embryos from these healthy patients to sterile patients."

Giltner told Krahel that he had provided the same information to Swanberg during the 1992–1993 audit. Krahel says: "I asked Norbert [Giltner] if you knew in 1992, when this series happened, why are you talking to me now about this? I was livid. He said, 'Oh, I talked to the auditors.' Then he leans back and says: 'What the hell are we going to do about it?' Just like that. 'You'll get fired like everybody else.' I said, 'I will do something, regardless of whether I get fired or not.'"[42]

Krahel's mistrust of the university administrators continued to grow as the investigation stalled and the clinic doctors went on about their business. Her doubts about the integrity of the internal inquiry prompted her to schedule an off-site meeting with Chatwin, to which she wore a concealed microcassette recorder. She later laughed at her foolishness when she explained how easily the red light on the recorder could be spotted through her scarf when she leaned over for a package of sugar. At the time, her feelings of paranoia were inflamed because she believed that she was being followed. Several weeks later, after a heated meeting with Chatwin and Andrew Yeilding, Krahel concluded that the auditors' intentions were above reproach.

Later in July, Krahel sent an eight-page report to Chatwin that detailed what she believed she knew of inappropriate activities at the hospital and at the fertility clinic. She complained that the hospital administrators had misrepresented what her job would be when they hired her, had failed to develop performance goals for determining her annual bonus, had attempted to retaliate against Marilyn Killane, and had given directives to cover up the problems at the fertility clinic. She also spelled out her concerns about possible retaliation against her by the hospital administrators:

I realize that the [*sic*] my complaint may be viewed by some as disgruntlement; however I feel that I have the support of a number of physicians who have witnessed this regime and have grown tired of the absence of growth, clinic support performance, and lack of overall administrative function. I am fearful

that this complaint will jeopardize my continued employment,
yet I am compelled to go forward.

Taking the advice of Chatwin and Yeilding, Krahel concluded her typed
letter with a handwritten note asking for protection under applicable
federal and state whistle-blower laws.

Krahel also continued her own investigation of possible clinic
wrongdoing, despite warnings to her by the internal auditor that she
should not contact clinic patients. On July 27, 1994, she telephoned a
former patient whose eggs she believed had been used without her consent. She says that she asked the patient if she could locate an up-to-
date embryo donation consent form. "My husband and I would never
do that," Krahel remembers the woman saying. She then asked if she
needed to do anything about the seventeen embryos that she believed
were in storage; she later asked for literature on research, indicating that
she might be willing to donate some embryos for that purpose. Krahel
maintains that at no time did she suggest that the women's embryos
had been given to a patient who had borne a child. She recalls that she
told the woman she had looked at the wrong column, and that it now
was evident that she had not consented. "I hung up the phone and I sat
there for what seemed forever, but over an hour, and I cried. I sobbed."
The emotional impact of that experience continued to haunt Krahel,
who cried again, a year and a half later, when she talked about the
episode.

Krahel also contacted her predecessor, Stephanie Ander, to inquire
whether there had been earlier problems at the clinic. Krahel reports
that Ander said, "So you've tripped across the missing eggs." Ander denies making such a statement and maintains that she was unaware of
any problems with eggs and embryos when she was at UCIMC.[43] Ander
had worked at the hospital from January 1991 to February 1993. She
told investigators that during that time she had gone to Spiwak to discuss clinic problems. His response had been: "I would just like to close
the whole fucking thing down." She apologized for the language but
observed that she had but repeated a "common term Herb used." The
implication seems to be that Spiwak was out of sorts with the fertility
operation and its rogue procedures but felt compelled by hospital imperatives to put up with it.

Piccione meanwhile had begun the process to terminate Krahel, claiming that Krahel was responsible for inciting a conspiracy against the management of the clinic. On July 25 Piccione met with Christine Taylor, the university's director of employee and labor relations, to discuss her intention to fire Krahel. Taylor then told Piccione that Krahel had asked for whistle-blower protection. Two days later, acting on the advice of the counsel in the University of California president's office, Piccione placed Krahel on administrative leave. Krahel says that Piccione telephoned this information to her and that when she asked for an explanation the line went dead.

Chatham, who later received whistle-blower status, was fired on the same day as Krahel. She was summoned to Spiwak's office, where he told her that he had a letter he wanted to read to her. It stated: "Your services are no longer needed at the Medical Center." The termination was to be effective immediately. Chatham was both shocked and embarrassed. "My eyes were starting to fill up and I was trying to control it. Then I see Rita Pitts, the head of Human Resources, and she walks over and asks for my badge, papers, and keys."[44]

Chatham was escorted to her office, to collect her personal belongings, and then out of the building. She was certain that she had been fired because of her association with Krahel. "They never condemned my job performance. I spent months going back over it; thinking, what did I do wrong? I didn't do anything wrong. I didn't do anything wrong."[45]

Debra Krahel feared for her personal safety. She had made copies of many documents and given them to her mother for safekeeping. "It's like I was obsessed with the thought that I was going to be dead and no one would be able to convince anyone of this," she said. Krahel was certain that she and Chatham were being followed because they were in possession of information that could destroy Asch. "It was really weird," she recalls. "Our neighbors said there was a van sitting outside of my house for three hours and when I came home it drove away. My attorney said that I was just paranoid, but now everyone believes that we probably were followed." Krahel offers no explanation of what might possibly have been learned by tracking her movements, or why the van would park in front of her house while she was absent and then leave when she returned home.

Meanwhile, the university chancellor decided not to take the auditor's advice to initiate an independent investigation and referred the charges against the fertility clinic to the UCI Medical Center. Dean Thomas Cesario then discussed with Asch the issue of non-approved drugs and egg and embryo misappropriation. He told Asch that he knew of the accusations, but did not know their source; he possessed only "bits and pieces of information that had filtered down."

On July 26 Asch and his attorney proposed a resolution of the issues. Asch offered to resign from the medical staff if the university would agree to halt all further investigations. This tactic would leave Asch's reputation untarnished; outside agencies were not to be informed that he had departed under pressure. Wilkening rejected the proposal, and a university attorney, Paul Najar, added: "There was never any suggestion that the university not comply with its legal obligations. There were only questions over which agencies they were legally obligated to report to."[46] The following month the university informed the California State Board of Pharmacy that Asch had used a non-approved fertility drug. But no other agencies were contacted at this time.

On September 10, 1994, Debra Krahel, Carol Chatham, and Marilyn Killane, represented by counsel, filed an Improper Governmental Activities complaint against the university. They alleged, among other things, that human eggs had been used at the fertility clinic without proper consent. The university response, oddly (since the information was included in the 1992 Swanberg report), was that these were "new" allegations and that they required the formation of new investigatory panels. A reasonable interpretation is that the university's reaction was prompted by a new player, the women's attorney. By the end of the month, the university decided to establish three panels to look into the fertility clinic operations: a clinical panel to examine its medical practices; an audit panel to probe fiscal matters; and a human resources panel to scrutinize management's actions.

KPMG Peat Marwick, the powerhouse accounting firm, was hired early in October to carry out the audit probe. Its fee would be $128,481. The company assigned Michael Hamilton, a senior partner, and Carolyn Beaver to the case. Hamilton and Beaver scrutinized twenty-eight patient medical charts from the clinic, thirty-four more from UCIMC, and twenty-five CRH patient ledger cards that included billing logs. They also interviewed Asch, Balmaceda, Stone, and twenty-five other persons.

Eleven specific fiscal improprieties had been alleged. Among other things, the doctors were said to have failed to report cash payments to the university, submitted false insurance claims, and misappropriated hospital property. Accusations against the hospital administration included failing to maintain financial and operating controls, awarding contracts that were economically unsound, and discriminating against patients without financial resources.

Late in October, Charles Wiggins and Allen C. Snyder, law professors at the University of San Diego, were employed to investigate management practices. They interviewed thirty-one people and investigated ten allegations related to management and employee issues.

At about the same time, Yeilding received a phone call from Sandra Lier, UCI's associate vice chancellor for administration and business. She told him to cease all audit activity at the medical center. The auditors were puzzled; they insisted that they were just as capable as the outsiders of reviewing the allegations of financial improprieties. Chancellor Wilkening commented later that she did not know who had approved the cease order to the internal auditors and that she thought it inappropriate.[47] It may be that, unbeknown to the chancellor, her colleague had decided that she did not want investigators stumbling over each other and that a review by outsiders would carry much less risk of appearing tainted.

Settlement negotiations got under way in early November 1994 between the university and the three whistle-blowers. That a settlement offer was considered four months before the investigation into retaliation was completed could be seen as an effort by UCI to contain a potential scandal.

The Clinical Panel, appointed on November 2, included three prominent University of California doctors: Stanley Korenman, professor of medicine and associate dean of the UCLA Medical School; Mary C. Martin Cadieux, director of the in vitro fertilization program at the University of California, San Francisco; and Maureen Bocian, director of the division of human genetic and birth defects at UCI. The doctors were not paid for their work, which involved the review of twenty-eight patient charts and a variety of other documents.

This panel was charged with looking into thirteen medical-related allegations raised by the whistle-blowers. Several involved standards of patient care, including the improper sale and distribution of non-approved drugs, the improper use of human sperm, and the failure to be

respectful to patients. Part of the alleged misconduct in the whistle-
blower complaint was described in these words:

> Clinically, Dr. Asch in particular has conducted himself in a way
> that demonstrates disregard for the dignity and rights of patients
> by scheduling patients for procedures and then delaying or can-
> celing the treatment in order to pursue his own entertainment.
> For example, Dr. Asch has kept patients and attending staff
> members waiting for hours to permit him to watch sporting
> events [on television]. At times, patients have been anesthetized
> while waiting for Dr. Asch to shift his attention from a sporting
> event to the scheduled procedure. Dr. Stone also failed to accord
> minimal respect to the rights of patients, failing to communicate
> with them and engaging in abusive and hostile tirades. On at
> least one occasion, a CRH staff member was requested, on the
> spot and without any screening, to donate sperm to fertilize a
> CRH patient's embryo.[48]

According to UCI officials, this panel's investigations involved "interviews of dozens of witnesses and the review of thousands of documents."
The investigators encountered many of the same problems that had be-
deviled their predecessors. Only bits and pieces of the records they
wanted to see were made available to them. One of the group said later,
"Every single chart we wanted was gone—either missing or stolen."[49]

Charts had begun to disappear from the clinic as early as 1991.
Those that were found often were incomplete and sometimes misleading.
In several instances charts did not indicate that patients had agreed to
the use of their eggs, though later—after the panel's report was completed—it was said that the patients had provided verbal consent.

Whether the panels had been appointed in a timely fashion or only
after the events were getting beyond the university's ability to contain
them became a further matter of dispute. Official university statements
said that the three panels had been created in "late September," although Golub claimed that the "panels began their work in October
1994." But one of the three was not appointed until November. A letter
to state senator Tom Hayden from Stanley Korenman, a member of the
Clinical Panel, defended the timeliness of the university's actions, noting
that "investigatory activity began within three weeks of receiving the

allegations."[50] A more accurate reading of the record shows that his panel was appointed almost two months after the third whistler-blower complaint had been lodged.

As the panels began their inquiries, the roots of the scandal were spreading. In December Debra Krahel, concerned that the university was intent on covering up misdeeds, telephoned Arthur Caplan, the bioethics expert. He referred her to Gary Ellis at the National Institutes of Health (NIH). On December 20 Krahel met in Philadelphia with Ellis, Caplan, and four other NIH officials. For Krahel this was a milestone: somebody with some clout finally was listening to her. She provided documents relating to unauthorized egg transfers. After the meeting Ellis said, "The story was one of such egregious activity that even if only a part of it were true, I knew we had to take it seriously."[51]

CHAPTER 3

Coincidence, Contrivance, and Confusion

■ The inquiry into the problems of the Center for Reproductive Health began to pick up speed and focus some twelve months after Krahel's initial complaints to Spiwak. The January 26, 1995, site visit of Gary Ellis of the federal National Institutes of Health was particularly ominous for the university. Ellis played it low-key when he visited the campus, saying that he was merely checking the medical school's compliance with research protocol requirements. The university spokesperson claimed that the visit was a routine matter as well. But the administrators at UCI knew that Ellis's arrival on the scene was a threatening development. That he was accompanied by two specialists in fertility medicine indicated that he was taking Debra Krahel's allegations very seriously.

The two specialists were Alan DeCherney, a past president of the American Society of Reproductive Medicine, and Alta Charo, an associate professor of law and medical ethics at the University of Wisconsin. DeCherney found nothing amiss. He said that he had examined "thousands" of medical log entries at the clinic and saw nothing to arouse concern. He told Ellis that the records were "meticulous" and that he disbelieved the charges. Why, he asked rhetorically, would these renowned doctors misuse eggs and embryos? They had no reason do to so.

Nonetheless, DeCherney was not completely satisfied. He had once heard a lawyer compare medical records to a checkbook: "With so many entries, how could there be no mistakes?" the attorney asked. DeCherney began to wonder if the scrupulousness of the records might not itself be evidence of tampering and manipulation. He was aware of chitchat at fertility conferences that questioned the striking success of Asch's efforts. The back-stabbing might have been the product of professional jealousy; but it also could be a warning signal, an indication of wrongdoing. Similar rumors of unreasonable success triggered by unacceptable practice had been tied to the Cornell University clinic, which would become involved in the UCI scandal when it was learned that embryos had been shipped to it from UCI for use in research.

DeCherney's views notwithstanding, the federal site visit team expressed serious concerns about the clinic's research practices, patient care, and oversight. Ellis warned the university administrators, "We have a pretty good idea of what's going on and you will hear from us soon." He was annoyed at Vice Chancellor Golub's repeated question: "Do you have other sources of information?" "They were truly puzzled about how we discovered the research issue," Ellis remembers.[1]

Faced with the potential loss of $13.5 million in research funds from the National Institutes of Health, the university initiated another inquiry into scientific misconduct at the fertility clinic. For his part, Ellis was convinced that the university was intent on dodging its problems, and he believed that the administrators were playacting when they asserted that research misconduct was a newly discovered fertility clinic issue.

A few weeks later all research at the clinic was halted by university orders. The ob/gyn department was charged with making certain that nothing was done to sidestep this command. The university took possession of whatever patient records it could locate, despite the complaint by at least one of the doctors that this action interfered with patient care. A security guard was posted at the clinic, and it was ordered that a nurse would first have to copy any charts that were requested before handing them over to a clinic doctor.

* * *

Meanwhile, the Clinical Panel turned in a report that sustained four of the nine charges against the doctors. The panel noted that the physicians had declined to provide satisfactory documentation to justify suspect donations, and it concluded that there had been at least two cases of unconsented egg or embryo transfer. The report declared that Asch had kept patients anesthetized while he attended to other, unrelated matters, and that screening procedures for patients and for egg donors were inconsistent and not well documented. It also charged that Asch dispensed, imported, and shipped a non–FDA-approved fertility drug.

The panel found that Stone had not participated in any wrongdoing. Strangely, and much to Stone's dismay, few people seemed to care or pay any attention to the findings. He was exonerated on the charges that he had failed to respect patients and that he had engaged in abusive and hostile tirades. The panel cleared all three doctors of several of the more frivolous and outlandish allegations. It found no evidence that the clinic had operated an unlicensed sperm collection bank, or that a staff member had been requested to donate sperm to fertilize a patient's egg.

The hospital managers got a clean bill of health from the panel. They had not, it said, tried to cover up problems, a finding that was relayed to Piccione and Spiwak by the chancellor.

The university apparently placed considerable faith in the Clinical Panel report, though it continued to drag its feet about informing the patients whose eggs had been used.

Debra Krahel, pleased by the findings, pressed forward. "I felt very strongly," she said, "that the patients have a right to know, but the flip side is the reality that so many lives would be disrupted." This posed a dilemma about the proper course to take. "You look at all the emotional heartache and everything else and that's what the university played on." Krahel believes that the UCI administrators had continually insisted that the patients had no need, much less a right, to know details of possible egg theft.[2]

The university appeared to have decided that for the moment there was no point to rippling calm waters. Officials also undoubtedly were aware that to wade into those waters could stir up a tidal wave of lawsuits that would cost much money, time, and prestige. There was a lot of self-interest and self-protection on that high moral ground the university sought to occupy.

Then the university began another round of talks with Asch about possible settlement routes. University officers said that they wanted the doctors to resign, to provide access to their records, and to give permission for the university to contact patients. The university insisted the settlement include the right to report misbehavior to appropriate government agencies and to go forward with its own investigation.

Asch refused to agree to these terms, continuing to insist that the matter be kept under wraps. When news of the negotiations leaked, Chancellor Wilkening explained: "We contemplated a settlement because it became clear that separating this group of physicians from the university as soon as possible was in the best interest of the UCI faculty, students, and the patients."[3] This statement fit the strategy of denying the depth of the difficulty unless pushed into a corner where such denial no longer was sensible. In truth, the fertility clinic problems had little, if any, impact on UCI students and hardly any on all but a few faculty. Damage had already been done to the patients. It is not unreasonable, therefore, to conclude that it was primarily in the best interest of the administrators that the matter be settled as expeditiously and quietly as possible.

University officials also were haggling with Killane, Krahel, and Chatham over their claim that they had been subject to retaliation for their whistle-blowing. Killane argued that as a consequence of her exposure of clinic wrongdoing, she was labeled a liar, she was threatened with dismissal and ultimately demoted to "paper clip jobs," and her career was ruined. Krahel claimed that her forthcomingness had resulted in a transfer and then in her dismissal.

For their part, university officials were faced with the vexing problem of distinguishing between retaliation for whistle-blowing and just desserts for poor job performance. Killane had been regarded by some as a troublemaker and Krahel as an unsatisfactory employee. The university Human Resources Department says that soon after her arrival on the job, there were reports of Krahel's poor job performance, an assessment seconded by Piccione, who maintained that Krahel did not work well with others. But Krahel's personnel file contained no information about any deficiencies in her job performance, though Piccione put on record a critical review several months after Krahel was forced to take a leave of absence.

* * *

Adding considerable fuel to the situation was the report by Charles Wiggins and Allen C. Snyder, professors of law at the University of San Diego, regarding hospital management practices. They had been hired in October 1994 by Paul Najar, a university lawyer, after Najar had attended a bar association presentation on negotiation by Wiggins that he found impressive.

The pair, both in their late forties, looked into ten allegations related to management and employee issues, with particular focus on the whistle-blowers. They also were asked to adjudicate questions regarding the alleged retaliation against complaining employees. The three women who had received whistle-blower status charged that Piccione and Spiwak had "engaged in secretive, retaliatory, and abusive management practices to protect their activities from scrutiny or accountability from above or below."[4] This issue, however, at least according to Piccione and Spiwak, was not touched upon in the initial Wiggins-Snyder report, but was added only after the university administrators asked the attorneys to attend to it. When we interviewed him several years later, Snyder did not remember such a sequence of events and believes that, perhaps, the pair was asked to elaborate on a few minor points they had made in the report.[5]

Other issues that Wiggins and Snyder scrutinized were charges that Piccione and Spiwak were inaccessible to hospital staff members, and that both Spiwak and Piccione failed to take timely action to deal with complaints about the running of the fertility center.

The Wiggins-Snyder report, eight months in preparation, presents Debra Krahel's allegations at considerable length, so that there develops a cumulative force about them. Each allegation is followed by a review of information considered relevant and by a conclusion that evidence for the accuracy of the charge is inconclusive.

Take, for example, Krahel's position that she had been specifically told by Spiwak to get rid of Killane, to fire her or transfer her to a job that could in short order be eliminated—along with Killane herself. The investigators found it reasonable that Krahel might have interpreted what Spiwak, "a loud man," had said as conveying that message, but they decided that Krahel may well have misunderstood Spiwak's aggravation to be directed at Killane rather that an expression of his desire to "get rid" of the fertility clinic. They were obviously put off by the shouting match between Krahel and Spiwak, but they did not find sufficient material to support a harassment charge. The "bumping" episode when Krahel left Spiwak's office was first said to be a possible assault and battery, but then the lawyers concluded that it had been an inadvertent outcome of a hostile encounter. Nor did they find that Krahel had been unreasonably silenced; indeed, they suggested that the effort might have been to have her direct her energies, which were regarded as less than adequate by her superiors, to doing a better job on what she was supposed to be doing and to cease complaining about the fertility clinic (or, in the investigators' words, "to leave the CRH resolution to the authorities she had informed.")[6] The investigators also found that the management team had responded to Krahel's complaints about trouble in the clinic in a reasonably timely fashion by calling for the internal audit.

Nor were the law professors much impressed with the complaint that Spiwak had coerced employees to care for his dog, though they granted that such a request from a superior to an inferior might seem to be an order. This interpretation was undercut, however, by witnesses who said that they hadn't at all minded dog-sitting Spiwak's hound. There was, however, more sympathy for Krahel's complaint that she had not been evaluated in any formal way until well after the clinic scandal began to unfold. The investigators were annoyed that the medical school officials seemed so adverse to putting things in writing; perhaps they wanted to make it difficult for anyone to find a paper trail.

By far the largest segment of the Wiggins-Snyder report was devoted to the question of whether there had been retaliation against Krahel because of her whistle-blowing actions. Here again there was a great deal of equivocation and considerable annoyance at what the lawyers perceived to be the atmosphere of the hospital. "If UCIMC were a place where differences could be settled by reason, not power," then a dispute between Krahel and another employee could have been resolved readily, they argued, defining the ambiance of a very large operation by a very small segment of it.[7] They noted that "why personal antipathy between two senior managers was converted into a terminal ground for Krahel is equally mysterious."[8] That sentence of course presumes a causal chain that most certainly had not been and would not be established conclusively.

The report did say that

in large part Krahel had been put on leave (only because she could not have been terminated) in substantial part because she openly criticized policy and practices at a large, public institution. UCIMC does not allege that what Krahel said was false or if false, was said in bad faith. The mere fact that she questioned what senior management said seems to have been translated to mean that she did not "fit" within the organization. This reveals the limit of debate and discussion allowed within this large, public institution. When people disagreed, they seemed to resolve disagreements based on power and position, not on the weight or wisdom of argument.[9]

The report then dealt with allegations that Krahel was a poor employee by observing that she was an argumentative individual who had found herself in a frustrating position. "She is a strong, assertive, opinionated person," the report observed. In her previous job, she had been able to give orders; now she found herself lower on the totem pole, and she had balked at having to take orders. She was not used to "implementing other people's directives." In short, Krahel was not a person "notably suited to play this role," which was, however, the role that she was being paid to play.

The investigators granted that there was considerable difficulty "in separating the displeasure based on actual job performance [from Krahel's] whistle-blowing." But Wiggins and Snyder did it nonetheless, with—as we shall see—formidable consequences for those who suffered from their speculative conclusions.

Wiggins and Snyder's conclusion was a tough pronouncement, particularly for an academic world in which more rabbinical postures and euphemistic terms are used when intramural squabbles are reviewed. They could not resist, for instance, falling back on their knowledge of criminal law to observe that if an assault charge could be proven against Spiwak for pushing Krahel (they did not believe it could), it could lead to a $10,000 fine, a year in jail, or both.

The later negative evaluation of Krahel's performance struck Wiggins and Snyder as having "the distinct aura of self-serving justifications for questionable practices and decisions." Adding it all up, the investigators decided that the whistle-blowers had been subjected to "verbal abuse, baseless criticism, job transfers, and ultimately were dismissed," presumably because of what they had said about the clinic's illicit activities.

These comments and conclusions came from a pair of outsiders, faculty members at the private University of San Diego Law School, a solid but much less prestigious venue than the campuses of the University of California. Perhaps this accounts for the odd repetition of the words "public" and "large" to describe UCI in the report. But however much such turf considerations infiltrated the investigators' language, there was power in their conclusion that university administrators had dealt with the whistle-blowers in an out-of-line manner and that their leadership style tilted heavily toward the authoritarian, if not tyrannical. This conclusion, of course, stems in some measure from Wiggins's expertise in the use of negotiation tactics to settle differences. But to say, as they did, that decisions were made in terms of "power and position" rather than "weight or wisdom of argument" is merely a way to condemn those decisions. In a hierarchical situation, decisions—good, bad, or indifferent—almost invariably are made on the basis of power and position.

Wiggins and Snyder could not have known that their report would be employed as the basis for summarily firing Piccione and Spiwak, which occurred on June 22, 1995. Told on the telephone that this had happened, Snyder spontaneously asked, "Didn't they afford her a hearing?" In a somewhat more formal discussion in his office, he addressed the same matter, first noting that he was talking "not as a lawyer, but as a human being." "Nobody should have been fired on the basis of that report without the opportunity to respond to it," he said, after carefully negotiating his exact wording; he specified that the form that such a hearing might take was a matter that would need further consideration. He said that the Wiggins-Snyder report was not an adequate reason to fire the two managers, though it could have been used as a "pretext" to do so.

Snyder is well aware of and not unsympathetic to the fact that Piccione and Spiwak had taken over a debt-plagued operation and with hardball tactics had turned it around financially. The San Diego team, however, found their management style too harsh. They had not warmed to Spiwak, who challenged them to do what they would and was neither sufficiently subordinate nor conciliatory. Snyder, when asked, said that he had not known that Piccione had relied upon advice from university attorneys when she made the fertility clinic personnel decisions. Had he been aware of this, Snyder said, he would have pursued the matter further with the particular attorneys. Piccione had not been represented by counsel at the Wiggins-Snyder interview, unaware that her job would be tied to the contents of the report.[10]

Finally, Wiggins and Snyder, in writing, offered us the following summary statement: "The University did what it did. Whether they were correct or not is beyond our charge. We did the best we could to discover event facts, differences of opinion or view, and to draw inferences from what we learned. We made no recommendations—and we were not asked for any."[11]

The university meanwhile continued to negotiate secretly with the whistle-blowers. Agreements signed between March and May 1995 said that sums were being awarded to them for "alleged personal, emotional and/or physical injury and distress." The word "alleged" is odd, though perhaps only part of a stratagem to avoid further legal entanglements. But the university, as always, admitted no wrongdoing on its part.

The ultimate agreements with Krahel, Killane, and Chatham included negotiated wording regarding how university officials would respond if asked for reference letters. The university would not, the parties decided, mention either whistle-blowing or alleged incidents of retaliation. That this arrangement might harm a prospective employer—and that it was less than honest—did not seem to be of concern to the university.

The university issued a press release noting that the settlements had been "amicable," a judgment that hardly reflected the sentiments of the three women who wondered why they had not been allowed to retain their jobs or been placed in equivalent positions so they could keep their income and benefits. The same question was asked by Gray Davis, then lieutenant governor and a university regent—but an answer was never publicly forthcoming.

That the amicability of the settlement was a shared viewpoint was pointedly contradicted by the whistle-blowers in comments to the press after they had been released from their no-talk agreement in June 1995. Krahel noted of an interview the whistle-blowers had given to a *People* magazine reporter: "He kept telling us to smile. And I kept saying, 'This is nothing to smile about'—because it isn't. And he said, 'But, hey, it's all over now.' And I said, 'No, it isn't. It's only just begun.'"[12]

Krahel believes that the settlements were hastened because she hired Gloria Allred as her attorney. Allred, a flamboyant character, is known to publicly crucify those who differ with her clients on matters of fact or interpretation. Krahel feels that the university caved in: "they agreed to everything."

Krahel was paid $450,000 as compensation for the alleged retaliation, $33,000 for the balance on her employment contract, and $11,000 for vacation time. She also was given insurance benefits for eighteen months. Killane received a lump sum payment of $112,480.67, plus eight yearly payments ranging from $23,000 to $29,000—a total of $325,436.94. Chatham received $98,930.67. The three women were given a total of $918,367.61 to compensate for their treatment by the university.

UCI officials later would describe the settlements as ending "any liability the university had for claims of retaliation and to avoid litigation." The settlements specified that the money paid would "forever" protect the university and related entities "from any and all charges, complaints, controversies, damages, actions, causes of action, suits, rights, demands, costs, losses, debts and expenses of any nature whatsoever, known or unknown, suspected or unsuspected."[13] The university, in essence, presumed that the whistle-blowers would take their money, go away, and, above all else, shut up.

Settlements with whistle-blowers can be a mixed bag. Some see them as right and just: a way to punish wrongdoers and reward those in the right. Others fear that the prospect of financial gain can promote a spate of greed-prompted tattling. In the fertility clinic scandal, financial reward clearly seems not to have prompted the women who were, in a sense, later bought off. But clinic employees who subsequently filed lawsuits seem to have been rather less than altruistic: the scent of gold was heady. Toula Batshoun, for instance, now maintains that she was the initial whistle-blower but that she "never received a penny." Another employee, Linda Martin, has insisted that she was unreasonably defined as a troubled employee when she reported fertility clinic problems.

The settlements included confidentiality clauses that prohibited the whistle-blowers from discussing terms of the agreements and matters pertaining to the fertility clinic. The university maintained that these restrictions were included to protect the integrity of the continuing investigation and the privacy of patients. Krahel's confidentiality clause, like the two others, stated:

Debra Krahel and her attorneys and agents represent and agree that with the exception of any judicial civil matter where disclosure of this Agreement is ordered by the court, or where disclosure is compelled by law, they will keep the existence, terms, and conditions of this Agreement, the settlement, any matters pertaining to Krahel's complaint of unlawful governmental activity ("whistleblower complaint") any and all actions by [redacted in our copy] and the University in accordance therewith, strictly confidential, and that they will not disclose, discuss, or reveal any information concerning this Agreement or the matters referenced above, to any other persons, entities, or organizations except Krahel's attorneys or personal financial or tax advisor, all of whom will be informed and bound by this confidentiality provision. Krahel is to advise the University, in writing, of any request or demand for disclosure in any legal proceeding immediately upon learning of it so that the University will be afforded a full opportunity to intervene to object and to take any other action necessary to protect the confidentiality of this Agreement. In response to any inquiries about this instant matter or its resolution, Krahel and her attorneys and agents may say: "THE MATTER HAS BEEN RESOLVED IN A MANNER SATISFACTORY TO ALL PARTIES CONCERNED."[14]

Krahel was also forbidden to make "any disparaging statements to any person or entity about the University and/or its officers, faculty members, management, and employees." The university magnanimously agreed that, in the spirit of things, it would not publicly disparage Krahel.

There was a penalty for failing to abide by these provisions. If Krahel was found to have "knowingly and intentionally" violated the agreement, she would have to pay the university "liquidated damages" of $100,000, an amount described for legal, albeit not commonsensical, reasons as "not . . . a penalty" and "not punitive in any way." The sum was said to be a reasonable estimate of the amount of "actual damage" that the university would suffer by disclosure.

One might suspect that the confidentiality requirement sought to keep the public in the dark about the manner in which the university had spent taxpayer money. The ingredients that produced the "reasonable estimate" of the damage if they spilled the beans must have been wildly speculative; it seems more likely that the amount was determined to be sufficient to keep the women silent—that is, a gag.

As the scandal escalated, the newspapers soon learned of the confidentiality clauses and trumpeted what they had found out. On the UCI campus, Jon Wiener, a well-known history professor, wrote in the *Chronicle of Higher Education* that he considered the "secret expenditure of public funds to assure further secrecy" intensely disturbing, "deeply objectionable," and "indefensible." Regent Gray Davis called for a comprehensive review of the situations of whistle-blowers on UC campuses. Davis noted that the amount paid to the three UCI women represented 87 percent of payments to whistle-blowers during the previous five years on all University of California campuses put together. Figures showed that thirty-three UC employees had filed whistle-blower complaints in the preceding half-dozen years. Ten, including the three fertility clinic women, were given money, and only four of the settlements included confidentiality clauses.

Next to surface, in April 1995, was the KPMG Peat Marwick accounting report. The auditors declared that fertility clinic doctors had failed to report cash payments to the university and had filed false insurance claims. They found no evidence to substantiate charges that had been leveled against the managers of the center, including allegations that Piccione and Spiwak had engaged in economically wasteful and legally questionable practices; had misused university property and nonlicensed operating room facilities; and had sought to cover up their own misbehavior by maintaining that the whistle-blowers were disgruntled employees.

In typical fashion, the university sought to keep a lid on these findings. In April 1995, for instance, Debra Krahel's attorney received a stonewalling letter from the university's legal council:

I am unable to provide any additional information about the investigatory findings or actions taken by the university because of the privileged and confidential nature of the results. Because the CRH will no longer be located at the university, the UCIMC, or affiliated with the university we will not be able to audit any of the center's procedures.

In time, much of what the university originally held to be protected and private information would, under pressure, be disclosed. The initial stonewalling response naturally triggered anger: Krahel, her confidentiality clause notwithstanding, felt that she had an obligation to the patients. She called the local newspaper with a two-word declaration of war: "Fire away!"[15]

The university continued to negotiate with the doctors, seeking to contain the damage. A possible deal was again stalled by Asch's insistence that all further inquiries would have to be halted if he agreed to resign his position. The university, in reply, demanded that Asch vacate the clinic premises by five o'clock P.M. on April 28, 1995.

The battle over the clinic's records intensified. On April 26 Asch and Balmaceda arranged to have frozen embryos as well as lab records, embryology reports, charts, and computer materials moved from the clinic. The frozen embryos and sperm were taken to the California Cryobank in Los Angeles. The doctors intended to reopen their clinic in rented space in a seven-story office building in Tustin, a few miles from Irvine.

The university immediately accused the doctors of stealing "evidence." These "dramatic events," its spokesperson proclaimed, had occurred "without warning." The university responded to what it labeled the clinic "break-in" by dispatching security officers to seize what might have been left behind. It was never reported what the officers found; it is likely that their pickings were slim.

Reports about the "confiscation" of the charts are puzzling and in some regards contradictory. Administrators accused the doctors of stealing these records, although executive vice chancellor Golub three months earlier had informed the federal authorities that the university had obtained custody of all patient charts. Golub also wrote that the records at the Saddleback fertility clinic had been obtained, though in the same letter he said that the hospital attorney there had refused to comply with the university's request for the records unless he had Balmaceda's consent. It is arguable whether the university had the legal power to take possession of the records; it later adopted a new oversight policy that required physicians covered by university-paid malpractice insurance to provide access to patient charts upon request.

Asch may have been busy during the period trying to clean up what might have been damning bits of paper trail evidence. He is said to have telephoned patients during April and May to ask them to sign consent forms for eggs that allegedly had been used by mistake. Jon Petrini, a Bakersfield attorney, informed the university that his client had been contacted by Asch on May 12 about a retroactive consent. Linda Rolette, an investigator said to be working for Asch's attorney, was reported to have visited a patient's home on Asch's behalf to obtain a signed consent form. A San Diego couple said that Asch scheduled a meeting with them in the spring of 1995 at his Del Mar home to obtain a signed, predated consent form. Asch allegedly told the woman that her eggs had been given to someone in Mexico. The couple's attorney described the conversation: "[Asch] said that there had been some trouble, some confusion about one or two of her eggs. Dr. Asch asked her if she hadn't signed a consent form to donate and she said absolutely not. In fact, when they signed the consent form they said they did not agree to be donors."

The couple claim that Asch informed them that the women in Mexico had given birth, though he was not certain whether the child was a product of the San Diego woman's eggs.

In mid-May 1995 the university filed a lawsuit requesting a temporary restraining order to safeguard and preserve fertility clinic research records and medical equipment that it said belonged to it. It also sought damages from the physicians for the intentional destruction of documents and evidence and for stealing property valued at $53,000. It subsequently was discovered that the equipment was not missing but had been overlooked in an inventory, though the university did not publicly acknowledge this error.

The following day, the UCI executive vice chancellor declared that dozens of interviews and hundreds of documents showed no evidence that any patient's health had been put at risk. Earlier, the university had argued in court that the doctors' research transgressions, if proven, "would call into serious question the accuracy and integrity of defendants' research" and could "shed grave doubt on the quality of any medical treatment based on that research."[16] This dire and rather senseless allegation was subsequently dropped, since it is apparent that a failure to obtain human subjects' approval hardly is likely to raise "grave doubts" about the "quality of any medical treatment" carried out during research.

The university, sensing what might happen if it opened that Pandora's box, still had not contacted patients, either to determine if they had consented to the use of their ova or to inform them of their possible victimization, though for almost a year it possessed incontestable proof of unconsented egg transfers. Were the university administrators still hoping that the whole business would somehow go away, or that they could concoct a story that would get them off the liability hook?

In their defense, university officials claimed that they were attempting to gather a team of skilled experts, including a psychologist, to deal with patients when they finally learned what had gone on. They insisted that the need to take such a step was more important than any haste in dealing with patients. Maureen Bocian, a member of the Clinical Panel, portrayed the concern as an ethical dilemma. "If one is accused of stealing a car, the next step is to call the owner," she said. "That's easy. But you just don't call someone and ask if they know where their embryos are."[17]

The analogy is strained. No one asks someone whose car has been stolen if he knows where the vehicle might be. Nor does it seem unreasonable to tell a woman forthrightly that there is evidence that her eggs have been used without her consent. This, it turned out, is what was done in the end—and without the involvement of a psychologist.

The university again failed to take account of the media in its calculations—and of the persistence of Debra Krahel. A May 19th headline in the local newspaper proclaimed: "Fertility Fraud: Baby Born after Doctor Took Eggs without Consent." The newspaper had talked with additional patients who confirmed that they had not consented to egg donations.

Krahel, after seeing the newspaper report, contacted a former CRH patient and told her: "I can't disclose who I am but if you investigate your medical chart you will find out it [egg theft] applied to you."[18] The university, learning that Krahel was talking with patients, wrote a letter telling her to keep quiet or pay the stipulated $100,000 fine that was part of her settlement agreement.

Matters were moving inexorably forward on other fronts as well that day. The clinic doctors were placed on paid leave from the medical school faculty and were told to stay away from the university pending the completion of investigations. This action, Wilkening noted in a press release, "was necessary in light of new information concerning allegations against physicians in the Center for Reproductive Health." There were no details about what the allegations might have been, but it is safe to assume that they were the prods of the press about unconsented egg transfers.

Asch resigned from the medical staff of UCIMC less than two weeks later, though Balmaceda and Stone hung on to their jobs. Asch explained his action in a letter to another doctor on the faculty:

I find myself filled with sadness as I sit down to write a letter, which a few months ago, I would never [*sic*] thought I would be writing. However, after many hours of reflection and after consulting with family and friends, I have made the most difficult decision of my professional career. Because of our personal and professional relationships, and because you recruited me to UCI, I feel that I should explain to you the intolerable circumstances which have brought me to this decision.[19]

Asch went on to castigate the university for its failure to take responsibility for errant employees, for violating patient confidentiality, and for inflicting severe emotional stress on his family. He emphasized his devotion to his work and the high quality of care that he provided patients. He denied any wrongdoing: "I emphatically and categorically deny each and every allegation of wrongdoing leveled against me. I can only assume that these allegations were the result of misinformation and rumor." Later, he came to believe that patients were driven by greed, a desire to cash in on what they would allege had been done to them.

Some days later, Asch told a press conference that he had been the object of an attempt at blackmail. A letter had come to him, Asch said, signed by "Malcolm X" and demanding $100,000 from each clinic physician. He passed copies around:

My dear fellow Doctors,
Shocked. I was stunned too when I realized the significance of the number of *documents* in my possession. [W]hile I am studying the papers to understand the implications of all of them, I have enclosed a minute sample to show you guys that your games are up. I was tempted to act like a good citizen and turn over this *gold mine* to the L.A. TIMES and other national news media to expose your long over due outrageous excesses. But, I decided that a piece of the action may be a *better option*. This is an important project for me. I want [you] to know that I [am] capable of breaking laws, as much as I am capable of abiding by them.

I had a lot of difficulty figuring how much this is worth to all of us involved. However, I came up with a price which I must warn you, I am pretty firm on. I am billing each of you *$100,000*. Not bad considering the fact that your careers and probably your lifes [*sic*] are in jeopardy.

I am not a career criminal, but, I have taken major precautions, enough to shield myself in case any of you decide to act *stupidly* or *foolishly*. For all your sakes, I hope you guys play ball.

I will contact you soon to tell you how [the] *money* will be collected.

Your Pal,

Dr. Malcolm X

The letter, while bordering on the literate and presumably spell-checked on the word processor where it was generated, indicates that the writer was at least somewhat deluded. Use of the term "career criminal" and the observation that "this is an important project for me" are slight clues to the writer's background and mentality, as is the use of such "fancy" words as "implications" and "minute" to describe the sample of "incriminating" documents that the writer enclosed.

Asch and his lawyer said that the letter had arrived at the clinic a week or so before and that it included twenty-five pages of one patient's medical record. Lloyd Charton, Asch's civil attorney, offered his view for the media: "It's very simple. An individual who had access to the clinic understood that Dr. Asch is internationally renowned . . . [and] decided if they threatened to wrongly accuse Dr. Asch of activities that they knew he didn't conduct, he might pay them some money to keep quiet. Dr. Asch basically made it clear that his position was to jump in the lake."

Did this mean that Asch had been contacted further and had told the writer that he or she was—to change the metaphor—barking up the wrong tree? His lawyer's attorney-like statement of his client's innocence reduces his "explanation" to the ludicrous: "if they threatened to wrongly accuse Dr. Asch of activities that they knew he didn't conduct, he might pay them some money." It is very unlikely that the letter writer, whether the correspondence was a hoax or a serious blackmail attempt, "knew" that Asch was innocent.

The university on May 25 amended its lawsuit to include five charges of unconsented egg and embryo transfer. The amended complaint also accused the clinic physicians of conducting research using human subjects without having obtained proper consent and of distributing a non-approved drug. No explanation was given for the failure to include these well-known allegations in the original court filing.

The university's agreements with Asch and the clinic were officially terminated on June 2. The chancellor announced, as she had several times before, that the scandal now was under control.

But another storm broke when the media on June 6 reported details of the whistle-blowers' stories. University officials found themselves having to acknowledge the confidential settlement arrangements.[20] The wording of their press release, as always, downplayed the significance of what had gone on. The university, it said, had "reached amicable settlement agreements" with the three women. The adjective, as noted earlier, was not accurate. "I never wanted a settlement," Killane responded. "I wanted a job. If this is called justice, [they and] I don't live on the same planet." Wilkening's position was characteristic: "Settlements," she said, "are the last way we have to make whole someone, an employee who has suffered some problems." The implication, of course, is that the university was being a generous benefactor.

In the California legislature, state senators were finding the fertility clinic business disturbing, particularly the university's handling of it. Senator Tom Hayden, the well-known 1960s radical—the *New York Times* once labeled him "the single greatest figure of the 1960s student movement"—convened his Select Committee on Higher Education in mid-June.[21] Hearings on the fertility clinic, Hayden declaimed, were to protect the public interest and to comprehend and prevent "reproductive anarchy." The committee had the media's attention and gave the politicians a chance to occupy the high moral ground.

Testimony before the committee during its nine-hour hearing resembled a grade-B made-for-television movie. Hayden opened by chastising university administrators, one of his favorite targets, for their slow response to the whistle-blowers' complaints and their lack of oversight. "University officials tend to isolate the breakdown as a merely localized phenomenon, involving only a handful of 'bad apples,'" Hayden asserted.

Hayden mocked university clichés regarding "self-regulation" and "faculty integrity" and added caustic comments on what he saw as the discrepancy between what actually went on at the university and the language deployed to describe these matters to outsiders:

> This regulatory model is based on an idyllic academic model far different from the competitive culture of academic entrepreneurs. . . . Self-regulation can become no regulation, until it is too late. The UCI Medical Center was expected to critically oversee the very enterprise which it was uncritically promoting as the prestigious vanguard of fertility research and treatment. Amidst heady hopes for academic prestige, even a Nobel Prize.

Patients and whistle-blowers told their stories to a sympathetic committee audience. Krahel, released by the university from the constraints of confidentiality at Hayden's request, took credit for uncovering the unconsented transfers. Her story had escalated; what had gone on was "rape":

> Words can't describe the outrage my co-whistle-blowers and I feel while we witness evidence to the series of biomedical rapes that occurred while the institution turned its back and argues still over who owns the medical charts. A year ago, I looked at a cryolog. Without alarm, I called a patient. I spent about three hours confirming the birth of a baby boy nine months after an alleged unconsented transfer of a young couples' embryo. The information was available to any administrator that bother[ed] to ask questions and to listen.

The internal auditors Robert Chatwin and his boss, Andrew Yeilding, appeared voluntarily at the hearing, though they had been told by university officials that it would be better if they stayed on the sidelines. Chatwin said that the egg issue had been raised with the managers of the medical center in late 1992 and that the information he provided in his July 1994 update to hospital management, doctors, and university counsel confirmed the charge.

During a phone conversation with Hayden the evening before the hearing, Chatwin had characterized that July meeting with university officials as a "milestone," but now he downplayed its importance. Tom

Hayden joked about the new twist: "So it was somewhere between a milestone and a routine meeting."

The three doctors had been subpoenaed to appear before the committee. Balmaceda and Stone read prepared statements that criticized the university for its handling of the affair. Balmaceda asserted that the "investigations met none of the legal standards for due process, let alone decent fairness." Stone similarly testified that "the university has abused its authority, has not followed due process, and has sued me concerning matters that I have no involvement in whatsoever." Neither doctor would comment on specific allegations.

The committee members obviously were irritated by Asch's and Balmaceda's refusals to talk about eggs and embryos and frustrated that they could not force them to respond. Asch and his wife remained in a small anteroom, secluded from the press and spectators. His attorney had told him that he was in danger of being ambushed and advised him to remain silent. His only response to the committee was a "No" when he was asked if he would testify voluntarily. The committee was unwilling to compel testimony for fear of jeopardizing possible later criminal proceedings. Hayden, visibly out of sorts, sparred verbally with Asch's lawyer. Then, in a petty retaliatory move, he required Asch to remain at the hearings throughout the remainder of the day, despite Asch's repeated requests to be excused. At the end, Hayden snapped, "I think Dr. Asch will be taking the 7:00 plane back to where it takes him." Off-camera, an unidentified committee member added sarcastically, "Argentina."

Mary Piccione, the executive director of UCIMC, making her first public appearance since the scandal had erupted, denied the charge that she had retaliated against employees. In a quavering voice she insisted that Krahel and Chatham were "opportunists." She told the committee that "never has somebody so heartbreakingly attacked me."

Herb Spiwak supported Piccione: "All I can say is I believed there was one whistle-blower. I think the other two people were poor performers cloaked as whistle-blowers in that they were about to lose their jobs." Executive Vice Chancellor Golub obliquely made the same point, praising the "brave act" by Killane but not mentioning the other two women. "Ms. Killane is a consummate health-care professional," Golub said, "who from the beginning put the well-being of patients ahead of her own career and personal goals. She deserves our respect and admiration."

University officials rejected any suggestion that they had engaged in a cover-up and defended the speed and the quality of their investigations. They implied rather broadly that they believed that the senate committee members were engaged in political posturing and sanctimonious self-righteousness. Afterward, off the record, a university official lambasted the legislators for what she saw as its "self-aggrandizing, chest-pounding behavior." She also deplored the accusatory rather than adjudicatory posture that she believed the committee had adopted.

The record provides some justification for these judgments. Senator Bill Leonard asked, "Has anyone called the cops?" Senator Quentin Kopp declared that the university lawyers were "not very vigilant." Hayden and Jackie Speier, another legislator, repeatedly wanted to know why no one had bothered to inform the patients. Hayden remarked that a university call to the Challenders within minutes of their being contacted by the press was "a coincidence, a connivance, or a confusion." He left little doubt that it was the second of the three c's that prevailed. Another committee member, Steve Peace, in his first contribution to the hearing, groused about what he saw as a corrupt relationship between the university and "these people," presumably meaning the doctors. Accusations thrown at university representatives, who often seemed unwilling or unable to provide forthright answers, occupied at least an hour of the hearing. Finally, Hayden, saying that his temper was high and his patience waning, brought the hearing to an end.

A later letter from the committee to the UC Regents would accuse UCI officials of making "misleading statements and omissions" that impeded satisfactory investigation of the fertility clinic scandal. Hayden indicated that the management audit had convinced him that the problem at UCI was systemic, marked by secrecy and an absence of accountability.

The hearing and subsequent comments made it obvious that UCI administrators had better launch some good-faith efforts if they were going to clear their own and their institution's names. Golub took a somewhat plaintive and self-pitying position: "We are not liars. We have told the truth as we saw it. Truth is an evolving thing in this." Wilkening wrote a letter to the *Los Angeles Times* defending herself and the university, choosing to ignore the striking inadequacies of what she called the careful and arduous endeavors the university had adopted to deal with the fertility clinic problem.

What seems to be escaping note is that the university, since early 1994, has been carefully, arduously investigating what went on at the Center for Reproductive Health to determine how it could have happened and how to prevent future unethical behavior. We have persisted, throughout considerable embarrassment to the university, because it is our moral and ethical duty.

Later, Richard Atkinson, the president of the University of California system, felt compelled to put an official seal of approval on Wilkening's handling of the matter. For some, his words were as ominous as those of an American president about to unload a cabinet member, trying to appear uninfluenced by external pressure. Speaking at a meeting of the Board of Regents, Atkinson said: "Chancellor Wilkening has been responsive and effective in the issues associated with the Center for Reproductive Health. My judgment is that Chancellor Wilkening has exhibited integrity, tenacity and outstanding leadership in guiding the campus through this difficult set of problems."

There are some who believe that Wilkening was unreasonably criticized for the way issues were handled, but exceedingly few who then or today would agree with Atkinson's judgment; his remarks could be seen only as a gesture seeking to close ranks and control damage. For Atkinson, at least in public, it was not the steward of the ship who was at fault but rather the rats that had gotten on board.

Mary Piccione and Herb Spiwak were terminated eight days after the senate hearing. Ironically, just a few days before Piccione and Spiwak were fired, Executive Vice Chancellor Golub (obviously not in communication with the chancellor) sent both of them admiring letters on university stationery, praising their performance during their state senate testimony. The one to Piccione read:

Dear Mary:
    I am sorry that I did not have a moment to talk to you after the hearings. I wanted to express my concern and affection. I know this entire affair has been a horror for you. I want you to know that I admire what you have accomplished under trying circumstances. You are a real pro. With warmest best wishes, Sid.[22]

The letter to Spiwak had the same tone, and noted as well: "I thought you handled yourself very well. The entire affair was a nightmare but none of it can take away what you have accomplished."[23]

Piccione and Spiwak were notified by the chancellor that their dismissal was based on their poor oversight of clinic activities, a failure to remedy business problems at the clinic, and their "unacceptable management style," which had created "a climate of fear." The Wiggins-Snyder report was used to support the charge that the hospital administrators had ignored or quashed findings in internal audit reports.

The firing of Piccione and Spiwak in many ways is the most disturbing aspect of the fertility clinic scandal. They were seasoned professionals in hospital management, experienced in handling crises. Their performance record while running the UCI hospital, an enterprise in deep financial trouble when they took over, was exemplary. That financial crisis had peaked in 1988–1989, right before Piccione was hired. The hospital showed a $11.6 million loss and had to borrow $56 million from the university's working capital loan fund. The Board of Regents was believed to be seriously considering closing the facility. Within three years of Piccione's hiring, the hospital was showing modest yearly gains, and the $56 million loan had been repaid.[24]

Before Piccione and Spiwak arrived on the scene, the medical center had been devastated by dumping, that is, the referral by other hospitals to UCI of patients who were unable to pay for treatment: "They come here after they've been everywhere else, and we can't turn them away because we have a conscience," a UCI emergency room doctor said. "So we take them in here and they become our red ink."[25]

Piccione and Spiwak tightened up procedures. They both received excellent marks in all their evaluations. Neither had very much to do with the fertility clinic; it accounted for less than one tenth of one percent of hospital revenues. They were aware that in the labyrinthine structure of the medical school the private clinics constituted fiefdoms. "We were essentially the landlords of the private clinics," Piccione notes, "and at UCI the clinics had a long history of turmoil and tension."

Piccione and Spiwak were vulnerable because, as is usual in their business, they had no contracts; they had pretty much expected to spend the remainder of their careers at the facility.

Their firing apparently had been a precipitate response by the chancellor. Wilkening perhaps overspoke at the regents' meeting when she adopted a tough posture to try to demonstrate that she was in command. She said that she was reviewing charges; "upon completion of my review, I will not hesitate to take appropriate action." Soon thereafter, Piccione and Spiwak were fired. This was despite the observation of one regent, Tirso del Junco, that everyone involved in the fertility clinic "fiasco" would be given due process and that part of such a procedure would involve a hearing.[26] Golub struck the same note, a false note as it turned out. "Simple fairness requires that all respondents be given an opportunity to reply to the conclusions of the report," he said.[27] Wilkening echoed this sentiment: "I will not rush into decisions that concern people's lives, their privacy and their right to due process."[28]

During a special faculty meeting to discuss fertility clinic issues, the chancellor was asked why she had not placed Piccione and Spiwak on administrative leave. Her response was a non-answer: "I spent two weeks to a month thinking about what I would do. The medical center is a major enterprise and if I was going to take some action, I needed to think about what was going to happen."[29] Another time, Wilkening responded to the allegation that faculty morale was poor by saying, "A mentor told me morale in universities is always bad. Universities tend to have critical work forces."[30]

Thorstein Veblen, with his mordant cynicism, may well have provided the most accurate interpretation of the dynamics of the firing of Piccione and Spiwak when he published *The Higher Learning in America* almost a century earlier:

> The case is not unknown, nor is it altogether a chance occurrence, where such an [university] executive with plenary powers, driven to uncommonly fatuous lengths by this calculus of expedient notoriety, and intent on putting a needed patch on the seat of his honor, has endeavored to save some remnant of goodwill among his academic acquaintance by protesting, in strict and confidential privacy, that his course of action . . . was taken for the sake of popular effect, and not because he did not know better; apparently having by familiar use come to the persuasion that a knave is more to be esteemed than a fool, and overlooking the great ease with which he has been able to combine the two characters.[31]

On the same theme, Scott Sagan has discussed "the politics of blame" in regard to the space shuttle *Challenger* launch decision. Leaving managers twisting in the wind, he notes, is the best of all possible outcomes because the cure is easy: fire and retire managers, and go on. The focus on managers effectively kept the public from wondering who put Christina McAuliffe (or Ricardo Asch and José Balmaceda) there in the first place.[32]

Piccione, in the first and only interview that she has granted, told us (and Spiwak shared the same memory) that Wilkening had summoned her and informed her that she and Spiwak were being let go because they had been lax in their oversight of the hospital and had demonstrated "an unacceptable management style."[33]

Wilkening indicated, Piccione and Spiwak say, that she had regarded the Wiggins-Snyder report, which had set out these charges, as a "piece of garbage" and that she was about to "throw it into the wastebasket." But the *Orange County Register* had called and said that it had a copy of the report and was going to feature it the next day. Wilkening felt that she had to take drastic action or she would be blamed for being unresponsive. "Things are getting hot," she said. She asked Piccione to submit her resignation: "Resign and disappear." When Piccione refused, she was told that she was fired. Piccione tried to defend her record, but Wilkening replied: "It doesn't matter if it's true. This is political; it's not about the truth." Piccione adds: "These are not her specific words, but it is damned close." No mention was made of a full and proper hearing.

We told Piccione that her statement was, to our minds, a very strong condemnation of Wilkening and asked her whether she really wanted us to quote her. She thought about it for several moments—she is a woman who is careful with words, though she also is, among the numerous persons we interviewed, the one who showed the least self-pity. Then she answered: "Well, that's what she said. You can use it." A month or so later, in the only interview he has granted, Spiwak verified the incident. He said it occurred when he and Piccione, uncertain whether they were meant to leave their offices immediately, revisited Wilkening. Wilkening told him that she would try to protect his job (she didn't succeed, presuming that she did try), but that Piccione had to go.

We enclosed Piccione and Spiwak's statement in a letter to Wilkening at her home in Arizona, asking for any response she might have. She did not respond.

* * *

When UCI in 1989 hired Piccione, then fifty-three years old, the *New York Times* noted it as the first occasion in which a woman had obtained a top administrative post in a University of California teaching hospital. Her starting salary—$125,000—made her the highest paid female administrator in the entire university system. Ten years later she was earning $176,000. Her successor, Mark Laret, would be paid more than $250,000.

Piccione was born in New York City to parents who had immigrated from Sicily and met and married in Manhattan. They were very poor, but in time her father, Frank, came to own a large fish store in Brooklyn and another in the Bronx, which he subsequently gave to his brother. Her mother, Catherine, made silk flowers for dresses. Her father died from a heart attack when Mary was fourteen, and she believes that this led her unconsciously to choose a career in the medical field.

Piccione received all her degrees at night school because she wanted to pay her own way. She got a bachelor's and a master's degree in English literature at St. John's University and a master's of public administration at New York University. Her first major medical position was a nine-year stretch at the Maimonides Medical Center, where her most satisfying job was working in the Coney Island adjunct hospital as the administrative coordinator of a coronary drug project that involved eighty hospitals and was sponsored by the National Heart Institute. The research, involving male subjects aged thirty-five to sixty-five who had had one heart attack, required them to follow a protocol that might prevent or delay a subsequent attack.

Ernest Grief, her mentor, encouraged Piccione to take a one-year residency in hospital management, and he invited her to accompany the doctors on rounds so that she could learn about various medical conditions and practices. Her next job involved one year at the NYU School of Dentistry as assistant director of the clinic; she then spent a year at Roosevelt Hospital. After that, she became the first woman to receive an administrative post in the State University of New York hospital system, working for eleven years at the Downstate Medical Facility in Brooklyn.

A headhunter had recruited Piccione for the Irvine job. Her first inkling of serious trouble at the fertility clinic came when Spiwak, the assistant she brought with her from New York, where they had worked together, told her that Krahel had come to him with her complaints. She immediately ordered an audit; she later suspended Krahel on orders from central administration. She notes that she herself could not have known what went on at the fertility clinic because she did not have access to the medical charts there. She had heard only that Asch was "a genius." When the Krahel issue surfaced, she felt that she had "responsibility without authority."

Her knowledge of specific difficulties at the clinic had come much earlier, when Stephanie Ander, one of the hospital workers, complained that jewelry was being accepted as payment for treatments. Piccione learned of the unconsented egg transfers in summer 1994 during a meeting with the medical school dean, a university administrator, the UCI lawyer, and two auditors. She remembers responding that the situation was "horrible" and that "something must be done about it." She assigned the person in charge of quality assurance at the hospital to look into the matter and called the senior university lawyer to tell him what she had found out. This attorney, when things began to heat up, advised Piccione that she had no need of her own lawyer. She also recalls another UCI attorney, Diane Geocaris, screaming at her, "You are all hiding things."

Several hospital colleagues took issue with Geocaris's accusation that Piccione was burying fertility clinic issues. Asch says that the first time he heard of the egg rumors was from Piccione, whom he characterizes as the "most sincere and honest person" at the hospital. Piccione, Asch remembers, was a typical New Yorker who would look into your eyes and tell you exactly what she thought. "She was ruthless, but good. She was always busy." During a conversation with us years later, Asch reflected on the clinic events and commented about Piccione: "That's a person I would love to talk with."

In July 1994 Piccione was told to take a hands-off position on the clinic because the university desired an independent scrutiny of the operation. Eleven months later she was fired.

Piccione notes that when the Wiggins-Snyder report first was submitted it had no conclusion; the chancellor had urged the writers to add recommendations. She feels that she was set up. "I should have resigned then," she now says.

Piccione recently had been deposed in a case involving the Garden Grove fertility operation. Walter Koontz, a plaintiff's attorney, told her that Jack Peltason, the chancellor who had hired and admired her, had known about the egg issue by at least the early 1990s, and that was why he had never publicly defended her: he wanted to stay removed from the conflict. She tells of seeing Peltason at a campus concert recently and deciding to let bygones rest. When she greeted him, he told her how good she looked and that she was lucky to be rid of the mess at the hospital.

Since being terminated, Piccione says that "life has been a struggle." The Laguna Beach house she lived in burned down during a fire that ravaged the community and she "lost everything." She had almost connected with a good health care job but the offer was withdrawn when she refused to end her lawsuit against the university—a suit that, in the end, she lost because without a contract she had no claim on continued employment or due process.

How would Piccione summarize what happened to her? "I loved to do what I was doing. Work was everything. . . . I may be a cynical New Yorker, but I believed in justice. My worst memory of what happened was that there was no justice."

Herb Spiwak, Mary Piccione's assistant, is a tall, thin, balding man, who was forty-two-years-old when he joined her in taking over the UCI Medical Center. Like Piccione, he came from a working-class background. He was born in Brooklyn, New York, and his father, Sol, drove a cab for most of his life. His mother, Helen, stayed home, raising the kids. Spiwak was educated in public schools in Queens and received a bachelor's degree in history from Queens College. He then studied, in his words, "in a slowish way" for an M.P.S. (Master of Public Service) at the New School for Social Research in Manhattan. His thesis was a case study of a hospital business office. While he attended night classes he worked during the day, first at the University Hospital in Brooklyn, then at the State University of New York Downstate Medical Center. He started in the business office there and rose to be chief financial officer.

It was at Downstate that Mary Piccione singled Spiwak out "as a sort of a protégé." He emphasizes that she has always worked in the public sector, and that she is "one of the most honest people I've ever met." Spiwak spent thirteen years at Downstate before coming to Irvine with Piccione. He never thought about the need for an employment contract: "People stay forever. They usually have to pry you out of those jobs."

Spiwak believes that a key event in the loss of his job was the failure of David Swanberg, the internal auditor, to testify at the state senate hearing. Swanberg, he believes, knew about the egg situation years before and would have supported Piccione and Spiwak. He also believes that Robert Chatwin, another internal auditor, confided to Debra Krahel unsavory tidbits about the clinic that he had uncovered because nobody else would listen to him, and that Krahel then used these bits of information to propel herself into whistle-blower status to avoid being fired for inadequate job performance.

Spiwak has no hesitation in judging Asch. "You can quote me," he says. "He was the biggest pain in the ass I ever met in my life. Whenever he screwed something up—equipment, personnel—he wanted us to fix it."[34]

Spiwak's suit against the university for his dismissal got nowhere because there had been no contract to breach. Allegation after allegation was thrown out until only the charge of defamation remained. At that point the university filed a SLAPP (Strategic Litigation Against Public Participation) suit against Spiwak, claiming that his court filings were frivolous and that he ought to pay all the litigation expenses and an additional penalty. He notes with a wry smile: "Thieves fall through a skylight while they are robbing a place and they get compensation. Not us." He withdrew his suit.

Piccione's and Spiwak's lawsuits accused Wilkening of making public statements that were "lacking in professionalism, integrity, decency, respect for process, and respect for law." Piccione said that the university had exposed her to "hatred, contempt, ridicule, and derision" and argued that the firings were carried out to support Wilkening's pretense that she was behaving diligently and with dispatch.

Like others, Spiwak feels that he was made a scapegoat for the publicized failure of the university to take a tough position against what was going on at the fertility clinic. He points out that neither the head of the obstetrics department, Thomas Garite, nor Walter Henry, then the medical school dean, drew a word of censure, though they both had the information and the power to bring the practices at the clinic into fiscal and ethical alignment. He recalls that he had been given the job of closing the fertility clinic down. "Why did they trust me then?" And, "Later, they needed someone to blame besides themselves." He also observes that whistle-blowers are typically paid off only when what they tell about leads to the recovery of money. Why, he asks rhetorically, did the university give so much money to the three women unless it was an attempt to buy their silence?

Spiwak recalls with some bitterness being told by a university attorney during a deposition well after he had lost his job, "You guys got fucked. I apologize for having to put you through this." He had been cleared of any wrongdoing by the Clinical Panel and the Peat Marwick inquiry. It was the Wiggins-Snyder report, which sat around unnoticed for about half a year until the newspapers got their hands on it, that dictated his doom. He repeats Wilkening's words that what was going to happen to him had nothing to do with justice; it was a matter of politics.

A news story following the termination of Piccione and Spiwak reported that Alan Hoffer, chair of the education department at UCI, was quitting that job because he had lost confidence in the chancellor and believed that she had bungled the fertility clinic scandal and other explosive matters. "The way they deal with things lacks kindness and humanity," Hoffer declared. "There's no collegiality. Rather they've developed the environment of a cutthroat business."[35] A more biting comment came from an internal auditor who sought to summarize university tactics: "First, lie, and if that doesn't work, delay. If steps one and two fail—redact."

On the other hand, Ralph Cicerone, who was dean of the physical sciences department and later would succeed Wilkening as chancellor, let it be known that he thought the firing of Piccione and Spiwak showed strength and demonstrated that the chancellor was taking charge. "This is the kind of decisive action that is going to move things forward."[36] Subsequently, as we shall see, Cicerone as chancellor would have the opportunity to display similar "decisiveness" and, some would say, to demonstrate convincingly a failure to appreciate that decisive action is not necessarily the same as well-informed and fair action.

Wilkening said the terminations were intended to "send a signal that violating whistle-blower protection laws would not be tolerated at UCI." But neither Piccione nor Spiwak was aware of the whistle-blowers' status; both could point out that personnel moves were recommended or cleared by university lawyers.

The dismissal of Piccione and Spiwak was criticized by the UCI Department of Human Resources. An eight-page report by four members of the department claimed that the Wiggins-Snyder report was "a gross mischaracterization of relevant facts and an unsupported condemnation of actions taken by medical center administrators." They repeated the accusation that Krahel was an incompetent employee who wrapped herself in "the protection of a whistle-blower flag." The report slammed what it called the "apparently unchallenged acceptance" of statements by Krahel.[37]

The seven-person internal auditor staff also took a direct hit when Andrew Yeilding, the group's chief, was demoted for reasons that never were made clear and many believe were insubstantial. Yeilding had been employed at the university for twenty years and had been head of the auditing operations for twelve. He is described by fellow auditors as the "best boss," "stable as a rock, calm, unassuming, intelligent, and well-read." When Yeilding told his family of his demotion, his father replied, "Good for you. Who needs all that pressure?" Yeilding seemed to agree. Wilkening maintained that the move was made to "strengthen the office," based on its failure to respond to Giltner's 1992 report of egg misuse. Patrick Reed, head of the systemwide University of California auditors, insisted that Yeilding's demotion had no connection to what had been going on at the fertility clinic. What was being sought was "a fresh perspective and a broad-based background." Many onlookers saw the action as another instance of scapegoating. Debra Krahel, almost predictably by now, shared her indignation about Yeilding's treatment in the letters-to-the-editor column of the *Los Angeles Times*:

> I am enraged over the University of California's decision to demote internal Auditor Andrew Yeilding. This act of reprisal is consistent with the retaliatory nature of the university's present regime. Any honest, upstanding employee that refused to compromise his personal integrity to protect the actions of inept superiors is certain to face demotion, termination and the university's continued attempts at discrediting his or her character.

Meanwhile, the search for evidence of clinic wrongdoing intensified. At 6:30 in the morning on September 19, 1995, an estimated fifty enforcement agents, with an alerted press in tow, raided the homes and offices of the fertility clinic doctors. The task force included agents from the FBI, the IRS, the U.S. Customs, the U.S. Postal Inspectors, the California Medical Board, and the UCI police department.

Searches were focused on Asch's former home in Newport Beach, Stone's home in Villa Park and his office at Fountain Valley Hospital, and clinic offices at UCI and Saddleback Memorial Medical Center. The cache being sought comprised patient records covering the period from January 1989 to December 1994; vials of hMG Massone and documents related to its use; drug order forms, invoices, and shipping records; large amounts of currency and safe-deposit keys; insurance billings; appointment books; calendars; ledgers dealing with medical appointments; and materials concerning medical fellows from foreign countries. A spokesperson for the raiders told the press that "the [doctors'] attorneys are keeping us from full and unfettered access."

Asch's criminal lawyer (he had different attorneys for different facets of the case) denounced the search as unnecessary, saying that Asch on two occasions had offered to provide documents to federal authorities. Stone's attorney said she had never received a request for documents: "The action was highly inappropriate. It could have been done in less dramatic ways and possibly was done in this way for show." Her last point seemed on target, given the hour and the presence of the media to record what went on.

A friend and colleague of Stone's said that sixteen agents, wearing bulletproof vests, rushed into the house yelling, "Nobody move." They separated all members of the household and then began grabbing things mentioned in the search warrant. At first, they acted as if they were raiding the hideout of a Mafia drug lord, but their attitude softened after a few hours. They departed at 2:30 in the afternoon, having seized computers, numerous papers, and all the cash they had been able to locate. Stone's mother-in-law was visiting from Chile at the time; the agents took the money in her purse.

The major quest was for egg logs. Federal authorities had offered Stone immunity from prosecution if he would hand over these records. Stone says woefully that he was unable to take advantage of this escape route and believes that had he produced the information he would still be on faculty at UCI. Stone said that he never had access to the egg logs, and that Asch had removed them from the clinic when he first learned of possible problems, either in June or July of the previous year.

Soon after the scandal became public, Asch had begun to liquidate his assets. He first sold his two-million-dollar Del Mar property and shortly thereafter the one-million-dollar house he owned in Newport Beach. He then left for a speaking tour in Mexico and Europe, with his lawyer noting that his client had not departed the United States permanently. "He still resides in the U.S. and his family is still here and he has an Orange County residence. He is planning on returning," the lawyer said.

But Asch did not return. By October he had settled in Mexico City. About the same time, Balmaceda left the United States to visit his mother in Chile, saying that she had health problems. Before departing, Balmaceda sold his million-dollar home in Corona del Mar. Both doctors were on paid leave. Asch could not be terminated without the university going through the elaborate procedures needed to fire a tenured employee; Balmaceda's contract still had time remaining. The university did cut Asch, Balmaceda, and Stone off from the incentive pay members of the medical faculty receive that is based on estimates of what their practice would generate.

The UC Regents, annoyed at keeping doctors on the payroll who were not even living in the country, in January 1996 took the unprecedented move of cutting off the salaries of Asch and Balmaceda. Regent Howard H. Leach explained the breach of usual procedures: "If the gentlemen want to come back to U.S. jurisdiction to sue us, I'd welcome that." The Office of the President issued a press release to justify the Regents' action:

> Ordinarily if a faculty member under disciplinary review is placed on leave with pay, he or she is available to cooperate with the university administration and Academic Senate in the investigation of the challenged conduct. In this case, Drs. Asch and Balmaceda have left the country and the Regents have taken appropriate action.

Asch filed a lawsuit arguing that the university had violated his rights by stopping his salary without following proper procedures. The doctors also went to court with a demand that the university cover their legal fees. Asch wanted $700,000 that he claimed he had paid attorneys and he estimated that in the future the sum could be as high as $25,000 a month. The university argued that it was not responsible for these fees because the physicians had acted outside the scope of the terms of their employment when they engaged in the unconsented use of patients' eggs and embryos.

In March 1996 a Superior Court judge ordered the university to pay Stone and Balmaceda's defense costs in one case because the patient had been treated only by Asch. The university was not pleased. A university attorney noted:

> In all likelihood the decision is going to be the same or similar in most of these cases based on [sic], and I mean the reason is that it doesn't matter so much what Dr. Stone did, the services that he performed on this patient in this particular case, because he was partners with all the people in this, they all knew what was going on.[38]

In view of the fact that attorneys are expected to put their clients in the best possible light and their opponents in the worst, this statement might be excusable. But it is a nasty piece of partisanship. Nobody had proved or even tried to prove that Stone in particular "knew what was going on." To allow an employee to incur costs related to suits dealing with matters in which he was not culpable seems callous. One wonders what the university's position would have been had the executive vice chancellor and the chancellor, who may well have known a good deal about clinic wrongdoing, been the objects of legal actions. Would the university have covered these administrators' legal costs? The answer has to be: Without doubt.

Settling Up

■ Amid the flurry of investigatory and legal activity surrounding the fertility clinic scandal, the university in April 1996 sponsored a three-day ethics conference, which sought, it was said, to encourage scholars, scientists, and clinicians to explore the challenges facing reproductive medicine. Attendance at the conference was by invitation and cost $275. Sixty-four participants registered. Six lectures were open to the campus community.

Its sponsors called the conference part of a healing process for the scandal-plagued institution. Thomas Cesario, the medical school dean, commented: "This has been a painful experience for us and we wanted to do something that was a positive thing for the field. We are victims, too."[1] Others viewed the conference as a public relations ploy. The university had paid a ten-thousand-dollar retainer the previous spring to Sitrick and Company in Los Angeles to advise it on "a general strategy" to deal with the flak from the fertility clinic problem.[2] Debra Krahel, who attended the conference by using the invitation sent to Gary Ellis at NIH, quipped: "I'm stunned by the hypocrisy. This is like Senator Bob Packwood hosting a conference on women's rights."[3]

Chancellor Laurel Wilkening, in her opening statement, noted the marked contrast between the university's apex—two Nobel Prize winners—and the problems with the doctors in the now-closed clinic. She explained that she had arrived on the campus only seven months before the whistle-blowers came forward. Adjudication of the case, she commented, was the courts' responsibility. Wilkening noted: "While UCI is certainly not proud to be the institution where such tragic ethical violations occurred—ground zero, so to speak, for fertility ethics—we want to play whatever part we can in contributing to the national discussion about these important issues."

University officials and conference participants avoided public mention of the three UCI physicians, acquiescing to Wilkening's admonition that the aim of the meeting was not to analyze what had occurred, but to move forward. The experts at the conference agreed that the proclamation by Dr. Edward Steptoe in 1978 after the birth of the first IVF baby that assisted reproduction was free from ethical problems was shortsighted.[4] But few solutions were offered about how to avoid future incidents of wrongdoing. Edward Wallach, a physician from Johns Hopkins University, lecturing on ethical issues, described the fall into deviant behavior as a slippery slope. After the first innocent step, he noted, doctors are easily propelled downward into other illicit behaviors. Wallach dramatically declared, "We have met the enemy and he is us." Other guest speakers reminded fellow clinicians ad nauseam that their goal was "first, do no harm."

During a question-and-answer session, Debra Krahel demanded to know how university administrators planned to deal with the institution's accountability. Outsiders were unaware of her role in the clinic scandal, but the sudden tension in the auditorium was palpable. Ron Miller, chair of the university's ethics committee, silenced Krahel when he caustically said, "I would like to get on to the specific issues of the talks." Conference participants during one afternoon breakaway session expressed astonishment at the hostile treatment of Krahel after she told her story to the group in more detail.

* * *

Ethical issues in reproductive medicine have long been debated, but with little result. Members of the medical and legal communities have few and vague guidelines on how to deal with egg and embryo transfers, multiple pregnancies, embryo storage, abandoned embryos, gamete donation, and assignment of parenthood. The UCI scandal brought to the foreground a host of dilemmas that previously had been by and large swept under the carpet.

Fertility specialists, who practice with little oversight and accountability, have been trusted to obey the law and abide by professional guidelines, but their autonomy creates numerous opportunities for errant activities. Accusations and rumors of unconsented "egg snatching" have been in the air since the development of IVF.[5] In *The Mother Machine*, Gena Corea tells of several Massachusetts doctors who conducted an "egg hunt" as part of a fifteen-year research project. They allegedly took hundreds of eggs from poor women receiving charity medical care and employed questionable consent procedures. Landrum Shettles, a pioneer in IVF, caused an uproar in the 1950s when he commented that "nice little old ladies" frequently ask where he obtained human eggs for his experiments. He had replied: "Most of them I just poached."[6] This comment, albeit spoken in jest, reflects the cavalier attitudes researchers may develop toward women's bodies.[7]

Fraud in reproductive medicine has ranged from false advertising to faked research results. Michael Soules, director of the Division of Reproductive Endocrinology and Infertility at the University of Washington, specifies four areas of concern. First, patients are often subjected to extensive and prolonged tests that may be unnecessary. Second, some treatments that have a low likelihood of success are overused. Third, treatments are employed beyond their known efficacy. Fourth, practices are extended beyond the patient's optimum years for achieving a pregnancy.[8]

Experts agree that infertility treatment in the United States represents the Wild West of medical practices. Jonathan Von Berkom, codirector of Reproductive Genetics In Vitro, suggests that "things are done in this field that would never, ever be done in any other field of medicine without review or without big studies that look at efficacy or safety."[9] The thin line between treatment and experimentation in reproductive medicine also may lead to questionable activities.

Most of these issues surfaced during the conference. But the time and the setting precluded any significant progress toward their resolution. Without first establishing what had gone wrong, a subject that was ignored, it was difficult to get much of anything done. Had someone directed the conferees' attention to UCI issues and then generalized and expanded that inventory, the table might have been set for a focused consideration of solutions. But that was never done—and the conference took its place among the innumerable scholarly boondoggles so well depicted by David Lodge, the satirical British scholar, in *Small World: An Academic Romance.*[10]

Federal prosecutors were determined to hold someone accountable for the well-publicized UCI fertility mishaps. After several years of investigation, they presented a case to a grand jury. On April 25, 1996, Sergio Stone was indicted on ten counts of federal mail fraud.[11] Nora Manella, a U.S. attorney, stated: "Health care fraud is the Justice Department's number one white collar crime priority, and false billing schemes are among the most common forms of health care fraud. Today's charges should stand as a reminder to all health care providers that dishonesty in billing practices can lead to criminal prosecution."[12]

According to the indictment, Stone had "knowingly devised and intended to devise a scheme and artifice to defraud insurance companies and obtain money from insurance companies by means of false and fraudulent pretenses, representations, and promises." Prosecutors called the alleged fraud a massive scheme. Stone was accused of billing insurance companies for the work of other qualified physicians when he was working alone or with trainees.

On June 27 Balmaceda was indicted as a co-defendant and declared a fugitive—a warrant was issued for his arrest. The indictment listed twenty counts of mail fraud that included both Balmaceda and Stone. Balmaceda's attorney insisted that his client would be willing to return from Chile and face charges, but he explained that he "doesn't want to suffer the same indignities as poor Dr. Stone."[13]

On November 14 Asch was indicted on thirty-five counts of mail fraud. The indictment accused him and his partners of mailing more than $66,000 worth of fraudulent insurance bills, in amounts ranging from $925 to $3,224, for physicians who allegedly assisted in surgery but were not listed on the operating room record. The assistant surgeons listed on the billings included Asch, Balmaceda, Stone, Jane Frederick, Lila Schmidt, Mark Denker, and Pasquale Patrizio.

Asch's criminal lawyer announced that his client would surrender to face the charges: "I believe he will get bail and stand trial. We look forward to a trial."[14] But Asch reportedly insisted that certain conditions be met before he would surrender. His demands included an opportunity to testify before the grand jury, a complete disclosure of all charges against him, and a predetermination of the amount of his bail. This request was viewed as unreasonable and never seriously considered.[15]

At a pretrial hearing, Wayne Gross, an assistant United States attorney, skirmished with Judge Gary Taylor over the point of filing as many as twenty counts of mail fraud. Taylor is the epitome of a desirable judicial figure. His distinguished manner and no-nonsense approach in the courtroom have earned him a solid reputation among lawyers who point out that he gets the most important cases in Orange County. In this instance, Taylor, his court calendar in mind, questioned Gross about the benefit of filing so many counts and expressed concern that this tactic might extend a one-week trial to three or four weeks. Taylor asked, "If you can't get your conviction on your best five, do you think you can get a conviction on twenty?" Gross insisted that twenty counts were necessary to show the billings were more than an aberration. He also assured the court that no additional charges would be filed against Stone, but implied that further charges could be forthcoming against Asch and Balmaceda.

Judge Taylor inquired about the status of Asch and Balmaceda. Gross replied that the doctors were considered fugitives and that extradition papers had been filed. After the hearing, Gross indicated that efforts were under way to ensure that the doctors returned to the United States, but he refused to comment on the specific process. The manner in which these judicial maneuvers played out is taken up in each of the next three chapters.

More than one hundred lawsuits filed by former UCI fertility clinic patients flooded the courts. Lawyers saw deep pockets and advertised in local papers for victims, saying that they wanted to speak with anyone associated with any aspect of the clinic operation. Some lawsuits named as many as eighteen defendants, including, for example, Asch, Balmaceda, Stone, Frederick, Ord, Piccione, Spiwak, the UC Board of Regents, the UCI Medical Center, Cornell University, the University of Wisconsin, and Saddleback Memorial Hospital. The patients accused the defendants of negligence, fraud, conspiracy, battery, infliction of emotional distress, and racketeering. They were said to have "intentionally or negligently sold, donated, converted, misappropriated or destroyed eggs" and deliberately overstimulated women's ovulation in a calculated scheme to steal their eggs.

In an effort to hold the fort, the university on February 2, 1996, sought a protective order to halt the release of information concerning fertility clinic affairs. Fifteen plaintiff lawyers were present to oppose the motion. The judge questioned whether such a gag order was in the best interests of patients or merely an effort to keep the liability of the regents in check. The university lawyer insisted that his client had "a right to have a fair trial," which might not be possible if "sensitive documents" were released to the public. The court denied the university's motion.

The gratitude patients feel toward fertility specialists is profound when treatment results in a birth. If the process fails, however, couples may become enraged, directing their anger at the physician.[16] Many CRH patients expressed anger and a range of other distressed emotions. Elizabeth Shaw Smith voiced her fury over Asch's alleged actions: "I feel they used me. They manipulated my body and stole my eggs and my money."[17] Kimberly DuBont, who was treated by Asch in 1990, believes that the possibility that a child was born from her missing eggs "would be the worst of all." She stated: "It would kill me. I would feel totally empty inside. I can't imagine anything worse. All of this is as awful as it can be now. I hate to say it, but I'm learning to expect the worst."[18] Nancy Vanags expressed similar feelings after learning that eighteen of her eggs may have been implanted in at least three other women. She called the situation deeply traumatic: "It's hell. I know no other way to describe it."[19]

One woman sued, even though she had consented to donate her eggs. She had paid a steep price for the fertility procedure and Asch had told her that he would use her surplus eggs to help women unable to pay his bill; she claimed that he had charged the regular price to those who received her eggs. She remembers Asch patting her hand after she finished the harvesting surgery. "You have good eggs," she says he told her. "Good eggs."[20]

In several cases, a recipient may have received eggs from two or more sources; in such instances the genetic parenthood of the children would remain unknown unless the recipients agreed to DNA testing. One plaintiff's lawyer commented that it appeared that Asch had used oocyte and sperm to create a "tossed salad."[21]

In late October 1996 Wilkening announced that an initial three settlements had been reached with patients. Throughout the scandal, outsiders involved in clinic issues tended to see her as in over her head and guided (or misguided) by the cadre of university attorneys, who were trained to protect their clients and to emphasize strategy, not truth. Golub often stood between the chancellor and those concerned about stonewalling by the UCI administration. He generally was more articulate and quicker on the uptake than Wilkening; some would merely grant that he was more glib than she. Golub, in his early fifties, had been born in Hartford, Connecticut, and received his bachelor's degree from Brandeis. He earned his Ph.D. at the Temple University School of Medicine and then spent two years at the prestigious Royal Karolinska Institute in Stockholm. Golub specialized in cancer research and was a professor of microbiology and biochemistry at UCLA from 1971 to 1994; he also held high administrative posts there before coming to Irvine. He was seen at UCI (as were many UC administrators) as a man with his eyes on a higher perch, that of either chancellor or head of a medical school. After Wilkening resigned, however, the new chancellor quickly replaced Golub, sending him back to the faculty position he concomitantly held in the medical school. He left the university the following year to take a position in New York City with a private organization.

Part of the money paid out to patients came from a $94 million self-insurance fund that had been created in 1983 for all UC medical facilities. Claims up to $5 million could be paid from the self-insurance fund. In addition, the university carried policies with private insurers. The regents were not informed of malpractice settlements at the time of the fertility scandal, but they subsequently decreed that they were thereafter to be provided with details of all of the larger settlements.

Much dissatisfaction was expressed by the university faculty about what was seen to be an outrageous use of public funds to pay the whistle-blowers and fertility clinic patients. The chancellor sought to allay such concerns in a letter circulated throughout the campus: "The source of the settlement money was misrepresented in some of the press accounts as an additional cost to tax payers of California. But in fact the money comes from the long-established UC systemwide self-insurance liability fund. UC medical centers, medical schools and student centers pay premiums to the fund."[22] Since all the premium payers are tax-supported entities, it is difficult to discern precisely what point the chancellor intended to make.

By July 1997 fifty patients had settled. They were categorized to determine how much money they would be offered. Those deemed deserving of the largest financial compensation were women who were unable to conceive but whose eggs were taken and implanted in other women in procedures that resulted in live births. The settlements for these couples ranged from $500,000 to $690,000. University lawyers insist that approximately a dozen births resulted from stolen eggs, while plaintiff lawyers estimate the number to be closer to fifty. The mid-range settlements involved couples whose eggs or embryos had been used without consent but for whom there was no evidence of a live birth. These lawsuits were settled for $250,000 to $325,000. At the lower end were malpractice claims and cases in which genetic materials were unaccounted for or used for research.

All told, the university and plaintiff lawyers divided the cases into ten categories, with special circumstances determining for those within a particular category whether they would be paid amounts on the lower or higher end of the range. These were the categories, in descending order:

1. Eggs were taken; the recipient had a birth and the "donor" did not.

2. Eggs were taken; both the "donor" and the recipient had a birth.

3. Eggs were taken from more than one women and given to a recipient.

4. Eggs were taken from more than one woman but one of the "donors" had a birth.

5. Embryos were taken and given to another couple or to a research inquiry; no evidence of a birth.

6. Eggs were taken and given to a recipient who did not have a birth; the donor also had no birth.

7. Eggs were taken and given to a recipient who did not have a birth; the donor did have a birth.

8. Medical complications owing to complications of treatment.

9. Eggs or embryos cannot all be accounted for.

10. Eggs were used in research.

None of the plaintiffs interviewed by reporters expressed any great pleasure about the money they had received, perhaps because they felt none, perhaps because they believed that it would be unseemly to appear satisfied with money after expressing so much anguish over what they had lost. The husband of one woman said that the money did little to assuage his wife's feelings. "She will never be able to forget about it," he said. "She breaks into tears and cries whenever someone reminds her about it." The couple still desired a child, but the husband indicated that they no longer were comfortable with any doctor practicing fertility medicine. "It's hard to trust again," he said.

Perhaps the most interesting aspect of the categories of financial worthiness lies in the larger settlements in cases in which the recipient of the eggs gave birth. This outcome, of course, was fortuitous, except in the sense that it might indicate that the eggs used were more vital. But there was no burden on the plaintiffs to show that they themselves intended to use these eggs or that other of their eggs were not available for subsequent use. Nor was there any consideration that, however inadvertently, having been a party to bringing happiness to another couple might be a satisfying rather than a devastating experience that merited higher financial recompense.[23]

Barbara Moore, the patient initially contacted by Debra Krahel when Krahel sought to confirm unconsented egg transfers, was part of the group of women who discovered that their eggs were implanted in other women who gave birth. Moore, who underwent treatment in 1991, says she was told by the doctors that clinic policy restricted the number of embryos transferred during a procedure to a maximum of four. She and her husband had decided to freeze any remaining embryos. Moore described her interaction with Asch in a written statement: "After the GIFT procedure was performed on me, Dr. Asch . . . told us he had harvested seven eggs, four of which were put into my fallopian tube. We were informed that the three remaining eggs were fertilized with my husband's sperm and frozen in an embryonic state for our future use."[24]

Moore believes that Asch deliberately deceived her because patient reports and research publications show that he often transferred more than four eggs or embryos. Moore also claims that Asch lied about the number of eggs he had harvested: "We have been informed that fourteen eggs were harvested, not seven," she stated. "We were further informed that three of the fourteen eggs were intentionally implanted in a different woman."[25]

Moore has indicated that even if a biological link were to be established with a child born from her egg, she and her husband would not disrupt the child's life. She expressed her feelings in a poignant statement to the birth parents: "At this point, the child is, like my husband and me, and possibly his birth parents, an innocent victim of a crime of the highest moral turpitude. My prayers now and for the rest of my whole life are for the child's happiness, health and most of all, that he will receive all the love imaginable from those that surround him."[26] The alleged recipient of Moore's eggs maintains that their son was conceived with an egg donated by a close family friend. The Moores received $600,000 from the university.

Live births that resulted from possible unconsented transfers often were difficult to confirm. Take, for example, the case of Susan Clay, a patient treated by Asch in 1993 at the University of California, San Diego. Though the unconsented transfer appears to have resulted in a birth, the recipient may have received five eggs from different women. And in another case, Deborah Beasley's lawsuit alleged that more than thirty of her embryos are missing and that she believes that a birth ensued from an unconsented transfer, although her $250,000 settlement indicates that a child was not born.

Much of what became known about the patients emerged in press reports that were supplemented by later hearing depositions. Diane and Grosvenor "Budge" Porter were among the couples who publicized their situation out of a desire to learn if a child had been born from her genetic materials. The Porters had grown accustomed to attention. As Diane explained, "My husband, being that he is kind of a public person in Nebraska and very well-known . . . [his life] has been kind of an open book because people have followed his story."[27]

Budge grew up in Cornhusker country and his family takes great pride in the three generations of Porter men who played football for the University of Nebraska.[28] But in April 1976 Budge became a quadriplegic when he broke his neck during a scrimmage. After years of therapy, he regained partial use of some muscles and now can walk short distances on crutches, though he remains primarily confined to a wheelchair.

Diane and Budge were introduced while the family was in California for a UCLA–Nebraska football game. She was a student at California State University, Fullerton, and worked at the hotel where the Porters were staying. Diane and Budge began a five-year long-distance relationship and were married in 1989 at the mission in San Juan Capistrano. They settled in Valley, Nebraska, a suburb of Omaha, with hopes of creating a large Catholic family.

Before the marriage, Budge had investigated the chances that he could father children. He was unable to ejaculate sperm because his vas deferens (the duct that carries sperm to the penis) was blocked; a series of operations had been unable to correct the problem. But the couple's hopes soared when a friend told them about a technique for extracting sperm developed by Dr. Sherman Silber, a urologist at St. Luke's Hospital in St. Louis. Diane says that by coincidence she saw a *Donahue* show around this time that featured Asch and Silber discussing the MESA (microsurgical epididymal sperm aspiration) procedure. "It gave us kind of a new hope," she says. "I was very familiar with UC Irvine being a very prestigious well-known university and hospital. So that gave me an extra good feeling about it, and, of course, Dr. Asch was real renowned, and Dr. Silber had many books and things published."[29]

In April 1991, at the age of twenty-nine, Diane consulted Asch; Budge was scheduled for a MESA series. The couple scurried about borrowing money. Budge's siblings contributed money they were slated to inherit from their grandparents, and Diane's sister offered her Visa card to cover the cost of a laparoscopy.[30] They also took a second mortgage on their house to help cover medical bills that would exceed $30,000. The pair were scheduled to undergo simultaneous surgeries.

Though Diane had some reservation about the clinic atmosphere, she remained confident that Asch's ability and skill would prevail. "The office was very busy and almost chaotic when you came in. And it seemed like they wanted to cattle call, get you in, check you out, get you out—and the next day to get you stimulated and get your eggs going."[31] Near the end of the drug treatment protocol, she began to swell; within three days she had gained at least fifteen pounds. When she arrived at the clinic for her regularly scheduled ultrasound, the technician became alarmed and alerted Asch, who decided it was time for the egg retrieval. She was told the sonogram showed that as many as sixty eggs were available. Asch reported that he had harvested twenty-three eggs and, according to Diane, he gave only a vague explanation of the discrepancy between the number originally detected and the actual number said to have been retrieved.

Meanwhile, Budge's sperm extraction failed, but the couple had made arrangements for donor sperm. They were giddily happy as the IVF procedure got under way. When four fertilized eggs were inserted by catheter into Diane's uterus, Budge joked, "Should we all have a cigarette now?"[32] The first IVF procedure was unsuccessful and the extra embryos were frozen for future attempts. Diane returned for an additional IVF, but still was unable to conceive. In 1993 a procedure by a doctor in Nebraska using Diane's eggs and donor sperm resulted in the birth of a daughter, Claire.[33]

Medical records show that four of Diane's eggs had been given to another woman, though the transfer did not result in a birth. Diane had never consented to donate her eggs. "There was no discussion on my husband's and my part about donating," she said. "I'm not Mother Teresa. I'm not that benevolent that I'm spending $30,000 so I could take eggs and spread them around." Diane was seeking treatments to "get a baby from Dr. Asch" and not "produce eggs for complete strangers."[34]

Asch admits that a mistake was made in the donation of Diane's eggs. "She signed 'no' for the donation of eggs and eggs were donated anyway," Asch said. He explained, in retrospect, "I should have known, and I regret in those few cases what happened. . . . There is nothing else to, you know, to assume whatever responsibility should be my responsibility."[35]

During the negotiations with the university, the Porters' suit was placed in a lower category because her eggs did not produce a child. "It was so ridiculous. They had a sliding scale," said Diane. "The categories were very cold, my husband and myself were very indignant. How can you say Diane Porter suffered on a scale of one to ten?"[36] The Porters agreed to an offer between $100,000 and $500,000, but refused to discuss the exact amount with reporters.[37] On the plus side, the Porters, who are considering having another child, can afford further fertility procedures with the six embryos that they had cryopreserved in 1991. "I guess that's one blessing from the money. It will afford us that, if we can get the nerve up to do it again."[38]

In another much-publicized case, Loretta and Basilio Jorge declared that her eggs, and possibly their embryos, were taken without consent in January 1989 and implanted in another woman. They demanded testing to determine if they are the genetic parents of twins born to the other couple. The Jorges say that as the "biological parents" they are desperate to know "their children." To confirm their suspicions, the Jorges arranged to have the children they allege are theirs secretly photographed and videotaped. After seeing the tape and a photo of one of the twins, Loretta Jorge stated: "That's the way I walked when I was a little girl. I know definitely the egg is mine. If this is [the result of implanted] embryos, definitely 100 percent I'm going to take those children. If it's [only my] eggs, I have to be more considerate."[39]

The birth parents, who believe the children are a product of their own eggs, are outraged that someone dares lay claim to their children and horrified at the prospect of a custody battle. The attorney representing the Jorges said, "The whole situation is horrible for everybody. It's a nightmare."[40] Such a case, according to John Robertson, a law professor and a leading expert in reproductive technology, presents a new challenge because there is no legal precedent and the situation involves "deep, intensely held values about personal identity, family, and morality."[41] The Jorges accepted a $650,000 settlement from the university.

Among the accusations of egg theft were some by women who claimed that while they were undergoing routine diagnostic procedures their eggs were secretly harvested. Merrill Mahon underwent fertility treatment in 1987, 1989, and 1993, and she believes that during a routine laparoscopy five eggs were removed without her knowledge. Kathleen Linden asserted that eggs were taken without her being aware of it in June 1988; however, she admitted that Asch later informed her he had gathered the eggs to check their quality. She also says that Asch told her that the eggs were unable to induce pregnancy.[42] Pamela Kaoud knew that her eggs were being harvested, but she believed they would be used only for diagnostic purposes to determine the cause of her infertility. Kaoud later discovered, she claims, that the eggs had been sold, fertilized, and implanted in another woman.[43] The university paid her $255,000.

Ashley MacCarthy says that in 1989 Asch persuaded her to donate her fifteen eggs to other women as an act of charity. She was unable to use the eggs, after having invested nearly $20,000 in treatment, because of problems with her husband's sperm and their deepening debt.[44] She now believes that her eggs were sold to other patients. MacCarthy described her experience with Asch: "Every time I came in he would pressure me. Asch would ask: 'What are you going to do with these eggs? There are many women who could use these eggs.' It was persistent and sophisticated manipulation."[45] A couple from Florida filed a lawsuit, although there was no evidence that their eggs or embryos were missing. When they heard the news reports they apparently decided this was the thing to do.[46]

Lila Schmidt, a San Diego fertility specialist and a colleague of the three doctors, sued in February 1997. Schmidt studied, worked, and underwent treatments with Asch during her four-year fellowship. She alleged that twelve of her twenty eggs and her husband's sperm were misused by Asch. Schmidt's attorney explained that the impact on her client was aggravated because of her professional relationship with Asch: "She is so angry, so outraged. She feels unbelievably betrayed. She worked with [Asch], she trusted him, she looked up to him and admired him."[47] When he learned that this suit had been filed, Asch expressed sorrow: "This is the only case and the first case where a person that ever worked with me, in my more than twenty years of professional life, has said anything critical about me. A colleague of mine is accusing me and is criticizing, in a way, my work. It's the first time I've seen it, ever."[48]

Balmaceda remembers performing the transfer for Schmidt—a successful procedure. "She was thirty-nine and had a very bad prognosis," he says. "We thought it was kind of a miracle pregnancy, really. So how could we use the eggs of hers for anything?" Asch surmised that Schmidt, like many of the other patients who had filed lawsuits, was confused, greedy, or manipulated by an attorney. Schmidt withdrew her lawsuit when she discovered that her medical records revealed no wrongdoing.

Two years later, in July 1999, the university had settled 107 of the 113 fertility clinic lawsuits. A university lawyer noted that the "paramount concern is for the patients and families who have been personally affected by this tragedy. We have provided more than $20 million in settlements to these patients, so that these people would not be further victimized by having to wait years to see if the doctors themselves would step up to the plate and make settlements."

The settlements allowed the university to avoid the publicity and uncertainty of jury trials. Such trials also threatened the privacy of the couples and were viewed by attorneys as a risky venture. University officials wanted to avoid discovery proceedings and further unflattering publicity that was sure to result from a trial. Plaintiffs' lawyers were leery because they could not predict how jurors might react to the cases. University counsel John Lundberg offered this explanation for the settlements: "What we are dealing with is emotional injuries for the most part, and we are also dealing with something that is highly personal and private. The couples largely appear whole, and many people, especially men, may be unsympathetic to claims of injury involving the loss of a few eggs."[49] Focus groups conducted by plaintiffs' lawyers agreed that the actions by the doctors were "totally outside the bounds of reasonableness," but they showed little consensus on monetary damages.[50]

The apologies offered by the university as part of the settlements did little to appease many of the former patients. Steve Laverson and his wife, Joanne, who received a $150,000 settlement, said: "All we got was a settlement, but what we wanted was the truth and accountability. We have four embryos that are unaccounted for."[51] Renee Ballou, who received a $460,000 settlement, commented on the university's stance: "I think it's cavalier for them to say the money is paid so everything goes away. They've altered people's lives forever."[52]

Melanie Blum, an attorney who represented at least thirty-five clients, stated: "It was front-page news for years and was damaging all around—to the university and to the patients. It made sense for both sides to come to the bargaining table. For plaintiffs to be able to move on is a huge part of the healing and recovery."[53] This statement seemed somewhat insincere in light of the fact that Blum subsequently decided to seek class-action status in the clinic suits to allow her to make claims on behalf of all potential victims. She expected to file "many more lawsuits in the coming months."[54]

The firm of Blum and Roseman garnered a share of more than $4 million from the settlements. The attorneys also represented a former UCI employee, Linda Martin, who had claimed whistle-blower status.

Martin's case was dismissed after the court ruled that she had failed to exhaust internal remedies. A $325 filing fee offered on Martin's behalf by Blum's firm was accepted by the court, despite the firm's status on a bad check list at the Orange County Superior Court. The check bounced.

Later, in October 2000, Blum would find herself in further hot water when a police and state bar investigation focused on her alleged embezzlement of money awarded her fertility clients as part of the settlement with the university. She claimed that she was so busy with the clinic cases that she had left the day-to-day operations of her law firm to her partner and husband, Mark Roseman. The firm had filed for bankruptcy a year earlier, noting that it owed clinic patients about half a million dollars. Thereafter, Blum and her husband divorced.[55]

In mid-year 2002, a state bar court reviewed the decision that Blum be placed on probation for three years and suspended for nine months. The court noted that she had maintained that she was so deeply involved in what it called "a landmark fertility case" that she was unable to attend to the financial affairs of her office. It also observed that she was commonly working as much as eighteen hours a day and was suffering from migraine headaches, a ruptured disc, and Ménière's disease (an inflamation of the inner ear). It was also pointed out that Blum had fourteen years of discipline-free practice and a bevy of witnesses who testified to her good character. A psychiatrist reported that she was unable to control her husband. Lawrence Sporty, with whom she was in treatment, testified that Blum had suffered from post-traumatic stress disorder and that her husband was abusive, dominating, and controlling.

It was decided that Blum was guilty of moral turpitude but that there was substantial mitigation. The state bar court reduced her sentence to thirty days' suspension and two years' probation.

The reactions of clinic patients to the settlements varied from a sense of relief at having achieved closure in a tragic event to the view that the university had bought its way out from further scrutiny and embarrassment. State Senator Hayden believed that the settlements were not in the best interest of his constituents: "The settlements were a way in which a whole system is spared adverse publicity. . . . There is no trial, no deposition, no face-to-face encounter, no airing of the issue for the benefit of the public."[56]

The three doctors were excluded from negotiations. They discovered from media reports that the cases had been settled. Asch was not pleased:

I think there are three categories of patients. One category of patients [has a] genuine complaint. People in which eggs were misappropriated without their wishes, and for those I can only tell you one thing: I will fight back against everyone, trying to defend myself and clear my name because I know I haven't done anything intentional in those cases. But I'm also going to fight back for them, try to help them to give justice to their lives as well. The second group of patients are only being fueled by opportunistic attorneys, cases in which there is no merit whatsoever. There is a third group of patients in which there is nothing at all in their cases, and they are inventing stories. They are very opportunistic, trying to jump on the bandwagon, trying to get financial benefit from all of this.[57]

Asch was particularly incensed by accusations from persons he said he never had treated: "It is unbelievable to be accused by patients that I have never seen in my life [of which they are many], and to watch on TV patients that I have never taken care of accusing me in front of millions of people." He pointed out that in some cases the procedures were performed when he was not in the United States.

Lawsuits in the fertility cases extended beyond patients. The California Cryobank filed a claim against the university when the company realized that it had been left holding tanks that contained sperm samples and hundreds of frozen embryos from the now-defunct clinic. The cryobank had agreed to store the materials for three months. Four years later they filed suit to force the university to take custody of the tanks. Ownership problems regarding the frozen embryos, however, prompted additional accusations of illicit switches and the court assumed custody in 1999. Couples who were listed on the inventory logs as having stored materials maintained that they were unaware that their embryos were frozen. One woman claimed that her embryos in frozen storage may have been intentionally mixed up before they were sent to the cryobank.

A Cornell University researcher, Santiago Munne, became involved in the legal proceedings after couples discovered that embryos taken without consent had been sent to his research laboratory. In a letter to Asch in 1994, Munne had discussed the thirteen embryos he received from UCI and asked for additional samples. He wrote, "I was wondering if you can send me 10 embryos more" to "round the numbers for publication." A Cornell University lawyer says that Munne was conducting a quality-control test for Asch's lab to determine if the medium used to culture the embryos caused chromosomal abnormalities. Munne claims that the work was done at Asch's request and that it was related to clinical treatment as part of patient care, not to research, despite his memo to Asch. According to court documents, Asch sent as many as twenty embryos from at least six couples to Cornell.

Kimberly DuBont and her husband, Michael, whose embryos went to Munne, settled with UCI for $250,000. The DuBonts had one child after undergoing procedures at the UCI clinic in 1990. They had nine frozen embryos stored at the clinic and three of them were sent to Cornell. Mrs. DuBont says, "They are Mikey to me. Mikey was one of those embryos." DuBont denies giving consent, although she was asked twice if she would donate. Notations on her chart show that she wanted to use her embryos in the future. "They weren't just cells to me. I wanted to give them a chance at life, and I have done that with all of them except the ones they took away." In 1999 she had the remaining six embryos thawed; five survived and were implanted, but no pregnancy resulted.[58]

In September 1997 the fertility scandal appeared to take a further toll on those it had touched when chancellor Wilkening announced her resignation. Wilkening, in her mid-fifties, declared that she planned to work at a "grassroots level" on environmental and women's issues. A glowing UC press release detailed what were said to be her accomplishments. The media were less enthusiastic. One local newspaper noted that she had quit right before the completion of the five-year review of her stewardship—a review that was likely to be less than flattering. Wilkening commented on the fertility clinic scandal and her resignation: "I wish I had grasped the magnitude of the problem [earlier] than I did. I am pleased the cases are being settled. In terms of my timing, I think of it more as coincidence. [The settlements] were a big step to bringing the episode to closure. But that wasn't a defining thing in my decision to resign."[59]

Others are not sure of the accuracy of that last sentence and count Wilkening as another victim of the case.

In July 1999 university officials announced their intention to file a lawsuit against the fertility partnership. Their goal was to recover the $20 million paid out to patients and $1.7 million in unpaid fees that the doctors were said to owe the UCI medical school as part of the compensation plan. James Holst, general counsel for the University of California, commented, "Despite the doctors' predictable claims that they were not aware of the unconsented transfer of eggs, improper billing of insurance companies and the use of a non–federally approved drug, it has become very clear that they knowingly and willfully engaged in a well-orchestrated effort to victimize their patients."

The fertility scandal continued to plague the university into the new millennium. In June 2000 the auditor who had pursued the charges of misconduct at the clinic, Robert Chatwin, filed a lawsuit against the university, which he later withdrew because the amount he might recover made the effort cost-ineffective. He claimed that he was the victim of retaliation for blowing the whistle. Chatwin said that his superiors halted his audit activities and told him "never to set foot on the Medical Center property again."[60] Chatwin had filed whistle-blower complaints in May and June 1998—three years after his report was finished—in which he accused the outside firm that was hired to investigate the clinic of conducting an improper audit. Chatwin also said that in 1997 he discovered that UCI's organ and tissue donor program was misusing human organs and tissues. He claims that his superiors stopped that audit and demanded that he sign a false report. Chatwin agreed to sign only if the university agreed to note that he did so under protest. In October 1998 Chatwin was dismissed. He was told that his position was being eliminated. He first obtained a job at the University of California, Riverside, and currently works for the State Department of Justice investigating Medi-Cal (the state's version of Medicaid) fraud.

The fertility scandal changed the lives of many people. Careers ended, reputations were damaged, and families were forever altered, some for the better, some for the worse. Particularly tarnished were the reputations of three doctors who were tried and convicted by their employer, the public, and the press. It is their individual stories that we turn to in the following chapters.

C H A P T E R **5**

Ricardo Asch, M.D.

■ There is a strong tendency among human beings to fasten upon what seems the most significant aspect of a person and then to select other details that coincide with that overriding identification, be it as a martyr, a saint—or a renowned fertility doctor believed to have transplanted eggs from one woman into another without having obtained the consent of the first women. The public story of Ricardo Asch is replete with these kinds of uninflected portrayals. But Asch is a good deal more than a wayward medical practitioner who allegedly stole eggs and prescribed unapproved drugs. Like most of us, he tries determinedly to put the best light possible on his behavior; but, more significantly, he asks—almost pleads—to be judged not just in terms of allegations against him but in light of his entire life and his career.

Ricardo Asch's glowing reputation as a miracle worker was quickly transformed into that of an evil malefactor who flouted the Hippocratic oath in order to achieve other ends—money, prestige, and power being particularly prominent among them. His flight to Mexico was viewed by most people as an admission of guilt and a somewhat cowardly, albeit sensible, attempt to escape the retribution that he deserved.

Asch is a striking, charismatic man who emanates a sense of confidence and success. He is tall, over six feet, olive-skinned, with wavy black and gray hair. His lean features and stylish manner of dress add to his distinguished look. Asch can be utterly charming; he is quick to smile, and he offers a reassuring touch every once in a while that is familiar but not intrusive. Colleagues and friends often use the word *presence* to describe Asch.

These colleagues and friends found the accusations against Asch troubling and, often, incomprehensible. Ester Polak de Fried, a doctor who worked with Asch to establish a fertility clinic in Buenos Aires, asked rhetorically: "How can a person who has always advocated respect for patients then turn around and do the opposite? That really seems crazy to me."[1] Asch's childhood friend Eduardo Luis Blumenfeld, also a doctor, observes that Asch "didn't need to make a lot of noise for people to notice him. He was not flamboyant. He was not a show-off. He exuded bonhomie, honesty, sincerity, and sensitivity."[2] Such remarks, of course, are becoming increasingly familiar in a violence-plagued country where each successive perpetrator of slaughter in a schoolhouse is seen retrospectively as "a wonderful kid" and "the last person I would have believed would do such a thing." But in regard to Asch these kinds of testimonials carry some weight: they are from people who have known Asch intimately throughout much of his life.

Thirty-five UCI medical students, who viewed Asch as a significant role model, also praised his character. In a written statement they indicated that he had "always demonstrated respect, social responsibility, and integrity." Most of the students had been connected to Asch when he served as assistant dean in the medical school in charge of outreach services for minority students. Their letter to the chancellor offers a strong endorsement of Asch: "Dr. Asch has expected his students to uphold the same high moral and ethical standards in patient care to which he has himself held. In the monitoring of students, Dr. Asch consistently fostered the importance of quality medical care for patients, and the importance of humanistic values in developing effective patient care."[3] The students said that they were "outraged" at what they believed were knee-jerk responses and an assumption of guilt based on inadequate or no evidence.

Former patients formed a support group, Advocates for Asch and Reproductive Health. Their aim was "to disseminate positive information about Asch's accomplishments and integrity."[4] In a letter to RESOLVE, the national referral agency for infertile couples, the Advocates requested that it restore Asch and Balmaceda to their list of recommended treaters: "At this stage, nothing but allegations and unfounded charges are the basis for the media maligning their superlative efforts in the infertility world. Dr. Asch, in particular, struggled on a daily basis deliberating whether a treatment plan was socially, ethically and morally desirable."[5]

The advocacy group, which claimed to represent thousands of patients, friends, and supporters, insisted that Asch was being made a sacrificial lamb in a hysterical vendetta. Many believed that his high status had engendered professional jealousies. "The dark side of greatness is that as soon as one reaches the summit, one becomes a target as sizable as the mountainside just scaled," a rather soaring press release from the group declared.[6] Oddly enough, beyond its first appearance on the scene, the Advocates as a group were seldom heard from again.

Individual patients whom Asch had successfully treated also rushed to his defense. Mary Ann Gentile and her husband remembered having sent Asch a bottle of champagne to celebrate her assisted conception. Frank Gentile said of Asch: "He was very open, very caring. I know for a fact that he held my wife's hand on different occasions while she was going through some tough times."[7] John and Megan McElroy expressed their support in a letter to the *Los Angeles Times*. They indicated that Asch had been realistic about their chances, never offering inflated prospects of success. "We knew a physician who well understood the financial impact the cost of the procedures put on his patients, knew how important having a child was to them and knew that they looked to him to deliver a miracle. The burden weighed heavy on him."[8]

One patient, who asked not to be identified, told us of her relentless pursuit of a child by means of assisted reproduction and of Asch's willingness to go beyond conventional treatment to make that possible. After numerous IVF attempts and one miscarriage, she decided just before her fortieth birthday that she would make a last attempt, the "grand finale," as she put it. She had thirteen frozen embryos—twelve survived thawing. Asch told her that he could implant all the viable embryos, but that he had never put so many into one woman's body. Since this was to be her last try, she told him: "Let's do it." Six embryos were implanted in her fallopian tubes and six were placed in her uterus. She became pregnant and gave birth to a boy. "I am thankful to Ricardo's gutsiness," she says. "I am thankful for his willingness to gamble. I am thankful for his unorthodoxy. I don't think most other fertility doctors would have done what I asked." She offered a general appraisal of her experiences with Asch:

> He was really there for me when I miscarried. People can think of a fertility doctor as a hero if he or she can help you produce that which is part of a lifelong dream. I'm very aware of tendencies to idealize. Where Ricardo came through for me was not only in the pursuit where I chose to play it, but he also came through for me in the sadness in the defeated times. I really felt like there was acknowledgment of how sad it was. How much he was willing to hang in there and do all that could be done before it was time to quit.

Others who had experienced failure also declared that Asch had empathized with their hurt and feelings of emptiness. One put it this way: "You don't forget someone who can be with you when you feel so lost and it looks so dark and you're so vulnerable."

But there is another side to Asch that some say they have encountered and found distasteful. He could be intolerant and quick-tempered, and he was impatient with what he saw as incompetence. His colleagues often viewed him as arrogant: A UCI physician noted that "Ricardo was up in the stratosphere and could barely bring himself to look down on the common people." A former clinic worker, Sharon Gray, is biting in her appraisal of Asch, describing him as "sneaky and conniving."[9] She also believes that "somewhere along the way he quit caring about his patients and began to think of himself as invincible."[10] Asch finds Gray's comments preposterous, particularly since she selected him as her doctor and achieved a successful pregnancy under his care. "Whenever you have people who were responsible for things that occurred in the clinic, what they say must be taken with a grain of salt," he warns.[11]

Reconciling these two perceived faces of Asch is not easy. There seems to be some tendency for his best side to show itself in his relationships with patients and his more forbidding side in relations with colleagues and, particularly, with his subordinates. But this is only partially true: there are many patients who say that they thought him callous, and some colleagues found him considerate. The best assessment we could make is that Ricardo Asch responds to situations and to people in no predictable way: he does not operate within a circumscribed range of behaviors; rather, his actions display the entire emotional spectrum.

During interviews in Mexico City, Asch was generous and accommodating, a gentleman and a gentle man demonstrating great concern for his patients. At the Casa de las Empanadas, the small restaurant where we had lunch, he was warmly greeted by the owner and by other patrons. The man on view in Mexico City was undeniably a person who cares for others. But, given his drive to be the best, to fulfill the dreams of childless couples, or to achieve the perfect life for himself and his family, he may have overstepped the limits of his medical obligations.

Ricardo Hector Asch was born on October 26, 1947, in Buenos Aires, Argentina, into a middle-class family. Asch retains his Argentinean citizenship and, in 2001, became a citizen of Mexico. He was born into the largest Jewish community in Latin America and the fifth largest in the world.[12] Most male Jewish Argentineans are professionals; three of every ten doctors in the country are Jewish.[13] His father, Miguel, a medical practitioner and professor of surgery, had been dismissed from his post when he came into conflict with the tyrannical rule of Juan Domingo Perón. Miguel Asch relocated to St. Vincent's Hospital in Toledo, Ohio, before returning to Argentina after the overthrow of Perón.

Asch's mother, Bertha, was a lawyer and a French professor. She died in the early 1970s from liver cancer. Her husband, then in his mid-sixties, shortly thereafter developed kidney failure and was taken to the university hospital in Buenos Aires, where his son was on duty as a resident. Ricardo was with his father while the staff doctors tried in vain to save him.[14]

Ricardo's brother, Carlos, is eight years older than he. He started to study medicine, but never finished. Asch describes him as an instrumental part of his life. "My brother helped me all my life in everything and was always very supportive," he says. He encouraged Ricardo in his own medical studies despite having abandoned the field himself. Today Carlos is, as Asch words it, a "commercialist," dealing in tin.

Asch graduated from the National College No. 3 Mariano Moreno in

Buenos Aires and received his medical degree from the University of Buenos Aires School of Medicine in 1971. He had worked as a teaching assistant in human reproduction and embryology from his second year of medical school, and had decided almost immediately that this would be his specialty. Colleagues say that he frequently talked of his love for children and his dream to help everyone who wanted a baby but had not yet been able to have one.[15]

He came to the United States in 1975 to do postdoctoral studies in endocrinology at the Medical College of Georgia in Augusta. He worked under Robert Benjamin Greenblatt (1906–1987), a pioneer in the field of ovulation suppression through the use of sequential birth control pills, the development of a new fertility drug, and innovations in estrogen therapy for menopausal women. Greenblatt, his daughter observed recently, thought "very highly of Asch," who "worked very hard." She remembers Asch, who sported a long ponytail, as a frequent visitor to their home. Her father, a man chary of compliments, described Asch as "diligent and committed" and said that he felt as if he were his own son.[16]

Asch edited a festschrift in 1987, *Recent Advances in Human Reproduction*, which included contributions from fellows from around the world who had worked with Greenblatt, honoring their mentor on his eightieth birthday. The group gathered for a gala banquet at the seventeenth annual meeting of the International Society of Reproductive Medicine in Augusta. Asch's tribute was expressed in these words: "For your generosity of heart, for your sharing of yourself, and for your inspiration to us as an example of that which is true and good—a gift that has influenced us, your former postdoctoral fellows, not only as scientists, but also as human beings—we offer our most profound thanks, THERE IS NO GREATER GIFT."[17]

In 1979 Asch received a reproductive biology fellowship in the Department of Obstetrics and Gynecology at the University of Texas Health Sciences Center in San Antonio. He later was named director of the center and began to work with José Balmaceda. Five years later, the two men pioneered the gamete intrafallopian tube transfer procedure. The acronym GIFT was suggested by Asch's oldest daughter, Barbara. GIFT procedures had been carried out with laboratory animals, but Asch and Balmaceda were the first to achieve a successful human pregnancy. The mother was an Englishwoman who was married to an academic from

Lybia. They had sought treatment from doctors all over the world, but Asch came through when others had failed. The couple eventually settled in England and continue to send pictures of the twins to the doctor that helped them achieve their dream.[18]

Unlike in vitro fertilization, which involves incubation of the egg and sperm in a petri dish, GIFT involves uniting a woman's egg with sperm in her fallopian tube. The technique shows a higher success rate than IVF, with birth rates for women under forty estimated to be in the 25 to 35 percent range (the success rate of IVF is 20 percent).[19] The procedure also more closely resembles the normal process of conception. At the same time, as Balmaceda and Asch have noted, "IVF and GIFT are not mutually exclusive and may be complementary in cases where unexpected surgical findings make the transfer of gametes to the fallopian tubes impossible."[20]

GIFT is more expensive and more invasive than IVF procedures. Retrieval of eggs and their replacement are performed in the same operation, but the use of laparoscopy in GIFT requires anesthesia. GIFT also falls short of the ideal because it lacks diagnostic capacity; that is, if the procedure is unsuccessful, the physician will not be able to determine if the sperm failed to fertilize the egg or if the problem resides in the egg's inability to be fertilized.

Asch's outstanding accomplishments in reproductive medicine continued after he joined the University of California medical school faculty in March 1986. His curriculum vitae lists membership in more than thirty scholarly associations. He has been honored by his colleagues with the Abbott Award, the Wyeth Laboratory Award, and the Barbara Eck Manning Award. His research on oocyte donation and GIFT was recognized at the forty-third annual meeting of the American Fertility Society as the prize paper. At UCI Asch received the Lauds and Laurels Professional Achievement Award from the university's Alumni Association in 1994. In 1989 Asch and Balmaceda announced that they had employed a newly developed catheter to implant embryos inside a woman's fallopian tubes, a procedure that eliminated the need for surgery and general anesthesia.

Asch worked hard to provide opportunities for minority students in the UCI medical school. His recruitment of Latinos went hand in hand with efforts to secure scholarship support for many of them. In the class of 1992, there were only three Latinos. Three years after Asch took on the recruitment assignment, that number had risen to thirty.

During 1990 and 1991, Asch lectured in France, Panama, Argentina, Italy, Japan, and Spain; he averaged seven to ten weeks abroad each year, according to the Faculty Absence Calendar, a tabulation that notoriously understates the amount of time that faculty members are away from campus on money-making trips. Asch holds two honorary professorships in Italy and Argentina. He is a first-rate public speaker. A June 1995 address to the Orange County Pediatric Society by Asch dealt with the potential for fraud in reproductive medicine. The lecture was subsequently described by several who heard it as a blueprint of his alleged behavior in his own practice.[21]

Some maintain that Asch's sixty-page vitae, which lists more than three hundred publications, would rule out any likelihood that he might engage in fraud to bolster his reputation. Ronald Brower, Asch's criminal lawyer, says, "You get to that point—his level—you don't have to do unapproved research."[22] But an academic vitae can be misleading if not examined carefully by an insider who understands the rules of the game. Memberships are readily accumulated; a willingness to pay dues is often all that is required. Nor is Asch the first author on most of the publications. Though he is unquestionably a very distinguished scientist, his publication record grew largely because he surrounded himself with competent researchers.

Asch's lifestyle reflected his financial success. He and his wife, Silvia, their four daughters, and their son lived in a five-bedroom, five-bathroom home in upscale Newport Beach. He had a beachfront house in Del Mar, outside San Diego, valued at $2 million before the stunning boom in southern California real estate. His impeccably furnished Newport Beach home featured original sculptures by Salvador Dali and paintings by a protégé of Marc Chagall.[23] He owned five cars, including a BMW and a red Ferrari; one of his cars sported a vanity license plate that identified him as "DR GIFT." He spent much of his free time at the racetrack and owned five thoroughbred horses, including one named, oddly, "Fibs Galore." His most successful horse, Golden Find, is reported to have twenty-three wins and to have earned $156,000.

Asch's interest in sports combined pleasure and business. In 1992 he founded a company, Asch Entertainment, to manage the horses and to manufacture and market sports apparel and videos. Reported sales projections by Dun and Bradstreet were in the half-million-dollar-a-year range. His social circle included the tennis star Andre Agassi. A friend told of a telephone call Asch received from the president of a Central American nation whose wife was experiencing problems becoming pregnant.[24]

Asch's early days in southern California were fruitful, but distorted reports of mishaps and misfortune were made public after the scandal emerged. He was licensed to practice medicine in Argentina and in Texas, but had yet to complete California's Federation Licensing Examination (FLEX). Looking for further fodder for the scandal, the local newspapers inaccurately reported that he had failed the exam.[25] Asch explains that what was in the news, in this and other instances, was distorted. "I have never failed," he notes with confidence. A letter bearing the signatures of Sergio Stone and Philip DiSaia, chief of the medical staff, requested that the state medical board waive this requirement for Asch. Stone denies having signed such a letter. "That's not my signature," he insists. "I don't recall it at all. I never signed M.D. in my life. I never put M.D."[26] Perhaps DiSaia assumed Stone's agreement to what he saw as a routine matter and casually put his name to the letter. The waiver was approved in 1989, and Asch received a license to practice medicine in California.

Difficulties for Asch arose in connection with the training program in reproductive medicine for fellows who were licensed doctors in their own countries, and were in the United States to continue education and training. The usual six or seven program participants were expected to observe procedures and to participate in ongoing research projects. Problems arose when the fellows apparently were allowed by Asch and Balmaceda to conduct IVF procedures, though there had been earlier warnings that they not do so. In one case, a patient complained that a foreign fellow had carried out an unnecessary cervical dilation without her consent.[27] "A ridiculous charge," says Asch.

Asch and Balmaceda were chastised in May 1989 for allowing such things. Thomas J. Garite, chair of the Department of Ob/Gyn, notified the two men that he was "particularly disturbed," since both doctors previously had promised to discontinue this practice. "As both of you know," he wrote, "foreign research fellows sign copies of an agreement clearly stating that participation in patient care activities is forbidden. I am deeply disturbed that individuals whom I hold in such great regard, would so flagrantly violate our agreement."

The visiting research fellow program was discontinued early in 1995 by the American Board of Gynecology and Obstetrics. Dr. Norman Grant, the board's executive director, indicated that the precise reason for the cancellation was a confidential matter, but he observed that the board believed that the fellows were not receiving adequate training.[28] The dean of the UCI medical school, for his part, maintained that the outcome was more of a technical "paperwork problem" than anything more serious. A UCI professor, requesting anonymity, says that the cancellation stemmed from the fact that the fellows were being used almost exclusively to carry out IVF procedures. Asch says that the problem was that the clinic had insufficient surgical cases to satisfy the board's training requirements.

When the allegations of egg misuse became public, Asch was dogged by reporters and his family was plagued by snooping. "I was taking a lot of crap from the media," he says. "I couldn't go to a restaurant because the next day it would be in the *Orange County Register*, or, if I would go to the racetrack. Reporters would jump the fence at my house." After discussing the situation with his attorneys, he decided that it would be wisest for him to leave the United States. He had gone from seeing patients, doing research, and teaching medical students to spending all his time with lawyers. Today, Asch resists the notion that he is a "fugitive," since when he left the country he had not yet been indicted.

In November 1995 the Orange County Superior Court issued an order for Asch to return to the United States to offer a deposition related to pending civil lawsuits. He refused, saying that he feared he would be arrested. He did agree to meet, on his terms, with university attorneys and lawyers representing plaintiffs. The gathering, held in the Grand Hotel in Tijuana, Mexico, deteriorated into a farcical performance. Asch paid each attorney (at least twenty were present) five hundred dollars to cover their expenses. He insisted that he was eager to clear his name and maintained that the deposition would allow him to prove that the egg mishaps were not intentional.

The four days of deposition began on January 19, 1996. Security clearance was required for admittance, and Asch's entourage included several bodyguards. By the second day, a series of bizarre occurrences had created a circuslike atmosphere.[29] At one point, Asch's lawyer threatened to forcibly remove a plaintiff's attorney, Larry Eisenberg, from the room. Then the hotel's front desk received a bomb threat, and the premises had to be evacuated. No bomb was found, but the court reporter was reduced to tears when she discovered that during the confusion her notes had been stolen. Hotel security guards searched the rooms of lawyers and reporters; a plaintiff's attorney was rumored to have taken the notes and passed them along to a reporter, a supposition reinforced when excerpts from the official transcript appeared in the next day's *Register*. At the end of the day, Asch's lawyers announced that the notes had been discovered elsewhere in the hotel in a "wadded-up envelope."[30]

Asch deflected questions related to egg and embryo misuse, repeatedly denying that he had any information on the issue. He turned sarcastic when interrogated about his responsibilities at the clinic, asking whether it was thought that he should be held accountable for cleaning the floors and windows.[31]

University attorneys were unable to have their turn to interrogate Asch because of time constraints. Several weeks later, they requested that the court require him to return to the United States for further deposition hearings. They estimated that these would require at least thirty days.[32] Asch did not appear on the stipulated date—or ever.

In November 1997 an indictment by a federal grand jury was unsealed that charged Asch with ten counts of mail fraud in insurance billing and an equal number of counts of introducing an unapproved drug into interstate commerce. The indictment stated that in 1993 and 1994 Asch sold patients hMG Massone, a fertility drug manufactured in Argentina and not approved for use in the United States. The mail fraud charge included the allegation that Asch intentionally misappropriated human eggs from five women without their consent.

Asch viewed the charges as unjustified. He wrote his lawyer: "After reading the indictment of yesterday, I am not only disappointed and upset, but also with anger because of what I perceive to be a pure and complete case of discrimination against Drs. Balmaceda, Stone and myself." He denied that he and his partners had schemed to defraud insurers, noting that the university and its employees were responsible for billing. He added: "If we wanted to create a scheme to take advantage of

insurance companies, why would we do it only in 35 cases over a number of years, while we performed about 1000 surgical cases a year."

Asch proved to be on shaky ground when it came to defending the
alleged Massone prescriptions, unless the offense is considered an insignificant and harmless technical violation (the drug is now FDA–
approved and regularly prescribed in the United States). Asch had told
university administrators that he dispensed Massone free of charge to
two patients, both indigents who could not afford Pergonal. DiSaia and
Piccione had apprised the California Board of Pharmacy of Asch's action
in an August 4, 1994, letter, noting that Asch has "immediately complied with the request to stop and desist from further use of the drug and
represented that he destroyed the remaining ten vials in his possession."
Perhaps the matter would have ended there had it not been featured in
the whistle-blower complaints. A high-ranking hospital official told us
that he regarded the use of Massone as a minor issue. "If it hadn't been
for the eggs," he said, "the drugs would have been a slap on the hand."

UCI's internal auditor Robert Chatwin, however, later maintained
that Asch had lied to DiSaia. Chatwin located documentation indicating
that the first "indigent" patient had paid for all her medications. The
second so-called indigent, he informed university administrators, "works
full-time, has medical insurance, and the ability to pay."[33] That second
patient was Della Morrison, who had served as a medical assistant in
the clinic. She was responsible for handling patient calls, helping with
ultrasounds and IVFs, preparing patients for surgery, calling in prescriptions to pharmacies, drawing blood, giving injections, and obtaining
consents. Morrison had undergone fertility treatments with Asch and
became pregnant in 1994. She was given Massone at no charge, but
told the university investigators that she decided not to take it because
it was not FDA–approved. She maintained that Asch prescribed the drug
and profited from its sale. Morrison said that Asch directed her to distrib-
ute Massone to specific patients, many of whom were from out of the
country and paid cash for their medication. She did what he ordered
because she feared losing her job otherwise. She eventually spoke with
Jane Frederick about the matter but nothing came of that. When confronted by investigators, Morrison vehemently denied the rumors that
she was getting a cut out of the drug money.[34]

The panel looking into clinic affairs attempted to determine how the
hMG Massone was brought into the country. Asch explained that a pa-

tient had purchased the drug in Argentina and donated it to the clinic. That statement was disputed by Morrison, who said that Asch had admitted to her that he personally obtained the drug in Argentina and imported it into the United States over a period of two years. She said that he had carried two hundred vials of the drug into the country at four or five different times. She also indicated that Asch had asked her to ship the drug via Federal Express to a Florida patient. At that time Morrison complained to Marilyn Killane, who would become the whistle-blower focusing on the inappropriate drug prescriptions.

The Clinical Panel found evidence that 247 ampules of Massone had been sold in the clinic, which they estimated to be four times more than one patient would have been likely to carry into the country. The panel reported that it had thirteen bills that documented the distribution of hMG Massone to at least nine patients from January 1993 to February 1994. When Asch prescribed the drug a clinic employee marked the patient's bill with a circled "A," and in one case the bill noted "Dr. Asch's Meds." The bills indicated that the patients were charged the same amount for Massone as for its FDA–approved counterpart, that the patients paid cash for the drug, and that the money was given to Asch. Asch insisted that he was unaware of the specially marked billings and denied that cash payments were handed over to him.

The Clinical Panel declared that Asch's claim that he believed hMG Massone was approved and marketed in the United States was far-fetched. They found it "difficult to accept that he was unaware that there was only one FDA–approved drug."[35] Morrison had insisted that Asch acknowledged the lack of FDA approval but said that it did not matter. Asch had close connections with Serono Laboratories, the distributor of Pergonal, the approved version of Massone; he had co-authored a patient brochure on assisted reproductive technologies distributed by the company. Asch also had received a research award from Serono and he was involved in a clinical phase-two study of a competitive product—Humegon—for which Serono was seeking FDA approval.

The Clinical Panel concluded that the use of hMG Massone violated FDA regulations, but that it did not compromise patient care. Massone is widely available in many countries, and a research study of six fertility drugs, including Massone and Pergonal, found potentially harmful proteins in all but two brands, proteins that, the authors concluded, "expose patients to contaminating substances which may lead to adverse effects."[36]

Non-approved fertility drugs manufactured in other countries often are used in the United States. An FDA spokesperson said that while this may be a problem in some instances, the agency is concerned primarily with its endorsement of new drugs and with manufacturing processes. It seldom becomes involved in problems associated with clinical practices and believes that "physicians need to be free to use their medical judgment."[37] The agency has a "personal-use policy" that permits individuals to bring small quantities of drugs into the United States from other countries. The amount is limited to a three-month supply because, the agency observes, "imports involving larger quantities lend themselves to commercialization."[38] In early 1995 the FDA had issued a memorandum that permitted patients "working closely with their doctors" to import different forms of hMG because of a shortage of approved fertility drugs.[39]

Fertility drugs are costly for patients. Serono Laboratories asserts that because Pergonal is a natural product—made from the urine of postmenopausal women—it is difficult and expensive to manufacture. At the UCI fertility clinic the estimated cost of medications in 1991 ranged from $1,000 to $4,000 per patient.[40] Pergonal was purchased from Bergen Brunswig for $79 a vial and sold for $110 a vial. Asch reportedly bought hMG Massone directly from Dr. Massone in Argentina at a cost of $10 per ampule and sold the same amount to patients for $100. The university estimates that he could have made half a million dollars from these transactions.[41] Asch simply states, "That is not true."

Some doctors in southern California encourage patients to purchase fertility drugs in Mexico. While Pergonal manufactured by Serono de Mexico does not have FDA approval, most fertility experts and the company maintain that there is little difference between it and the version distributed in the United States. One Orange County fertility center says that if patients cross the border they can save as much as $2,000 on medications. Asch was said to refer patients to a pharmacy in Tijuana where they could buy Pergonal for one-sixth the price charged on the American side of the border.[42] According to the FDA, this practice is legal, but patients should be fully informed of possible risks.

Fertility drugs can have a number of unpleasant side effects, including acute respiratory distress, stroke, abdominal pain, fever, chills, joint pains, nausea, headaches, malaise, vomiting, diarrhea, bloating, rashes, and heart palpitations. The drugs also have been linked to an increase in ovarian tumors, although the research is inconclusive. Some doctors are concerned because the few tumor cases that developed did so with remarkable rapidity.[43]

Hyperstimlation of the ovaries is the most serious problem connected with fertility drugs. Ovarian Hyperstimulation Syndrome (OHSS) involves an enlargement of the ovaries: in severe cases hospitalization is required and extreme cases can result in death. Serono Laboratories describes the syndrome in its informational brochure: "[OHSS] is characterized by enlargement of the ovary and an accumulation of fluid in the abdomen. The fluid can also accumulate around the lungs and may cause breathing difficulties. If the ovary ruptures, blood can also accumulate in the abdominal cavity. The fluid imbalance can affect blood clotting and, in rare cases, could be life-threatening."

The pharmaceutical company reports that OHSS occurs in about 1.3 percent of women treated with Pergonal, but researchers contend that the actual incidence remains unknown because doctors employ varying yardsticks to determine the level of hyperstimulation and the symptoms' severity. Studies show that ovarian enlargement accompanied by abdominal distension or pain (mild OHSS) occurs in approximately 20 percent of patients and severe reactions in an estimated .56 to 6.5 percent.[44]

Debate continues to center around the general use of ovarian stimulation with hormonal drugs. Robert Edwards, a pioneer in reproductive medicine, asserts that he routinely reads manuscripts submitted for publications and hears lectures by physicians that report use of massive dosages of hormonal drugs, despite the risks of hyperstimulation and multiple births. He and several colleagues suggest that the use of such drugs to recover a larger number of eggs is an abuse: "We feel that a laissez-faire attitude to hormone stimulation today, with increasingly powerful agents becoming more freely available, encourages bad practice and shortcuts. This results in various risks to our patients, some known and doubtless others unknown."[45]

Asch was accused of using the drugs to overstimulate women in order to increase the clinic's success rate. Debra Krahel expressed her concern: "What he [Asch] did was represent to the patients that this [Massone] was a more potent form of Pergonal and was better than Pergonal. It was a strong form and this is what I think created the hyperstimulation in so many of the women. If they came in for injections they had no idea if this was Pergonal or if it was hMG Massone."[46]

Toula Batshoun, the disgruntled former office manager, claims that one patient almost died from an overdose of a fertility drug. She maintains that Asch prescribed the dangerously high dosage despite objections from Balmaceda that she overheard.[47] These interpretations and stories regarding the use of Massone are, at best, overblown when examined in the context of treatment procedures. First, Asch points out that Krahel was mistaken, since patients self-inject the drugs and the boxes are clearly labeled. Second, Batshoun's version of events ignores the fact that some patients are hypersensitive to fertility drugs and will have reactions during the normal course of treatment.

Discussions about the improper use of fertility drugs by Asch were connected to the large number of eggs harvested from women treated at CRH. Former patients claim that they were prescribed Pergonal before undergoing diagnostic procedures that did not involve egg retrieval. One commented, "I felt like I was just an egg factory for Dr. Asch."[48] Another patient said that the fertility drugs caused her to swell and within a few days to gain twenty pounds. When she came back to the clinic a nurse jokingly remarked, "Oh, we overbaked you."[49] (Weight gain is a common side-effect of fertility medications.)

No evidence directly links the use of hMG Massone to cases of overstimulation of clinic patients. A UCIMC physician reports that severe OHSS reactions at the fertility clinic occurred in approximately 1 percent of cases—comparable to the rate at other facilities—and notes that Asch's use of the drug was not dangerous and did not cause hyperstimulation.[50]

Others also saw Asch's use of Massone as a minor infraction. A California Medical Board investigator stated: "I guess if the patients were fully informed [about the non-approved drug] we don't have a big heinous crime."[51] Besides, Asch often prescribed the drug for foreign patients who already had been using Massone.

University officials also downplayed the situation after they determined that patients given the drug were not involved in research studies. A year after the complaint about Massone, executive vice chancellor Golub explained the university's position to the National Institutes of Health:

Some of the allegations against one of the physicians concern a matter which may be under the review of the Food and Drug Administration (FDA). Based on what we know at the present time, and after consultation with outside counsel, the university does not believe that it has an obligation to report the matter immediately to the FDA, if indeed, the university has any obligation at all to report to the FDA on any matter within the scope of our investigation.[52]

The most serious accusation against Asch was the unconsented use of eggs and embryos. Many practitioners in reproductive medicine believe that such a scandal was inevitable because professional guidelines lag so far behind rapidly developing technologies and because of increasing competition. A 1994 Maria Shriver interview with Asch dealt with these matters:

SHRIVER: There have been so many advances in the last five years in your field of reproductive work. Are you satisfied that all of them have been useful or are you bothered by some of them?

ASCH: The majority by far are beneficial. However, the technology is growing so fast there should be some kind of, I don't know, whether a group or committee or something appointed by government or the society at large that perhaps should set up some guidelines of what is right and what is wrong, what is good and what is bad. We are in a way creating a new world, a new society. The society at large should decide.

SHRIVER: And what if they don't? What if no one listens to your plea?

ASCH: Then there will be just, absolutely reproductive anarchy.

Asch's words would return to haunt him as accusers employed terms such as genetic rape and reproductive chaos to describe his activities. There was considerable speculation about the motivation behind the presumed misuse of eggs and embryos. Many were convinced that Asch was trying to improve his clinic's success rate in order to attract additional patients. Some clinics report success rates as high as 50 percent while others indicate no live births,[53] but success rates are easily manipulated. The Federal Trade Commission has taken legal action against several fertility clinics charged with having misrepresented pregnancy rates.[54] Numerous variables must be taken into account to interpret the rates sensibly. Do the reporting physicians distinguish among chemical pregnancies, spontaneous abortions, ectopic pregnancies, and viable pregnancies that result in live births? Rates also vary according to the age of the patients and the number of embryos implanted.[55]

Professional groups have made efforts to standardize success criteria. The American Society for Reproductive Medicine and the Society for Assisted Reproductive Technology keep a registry of clinics that voluntarily submit outcome figures. But it would require a very high degree of integrity to commit commercial suicide by reporting a dismal performance record when to do otherwise usually carries no particular risk.

Asch portrays himself as a hard-working physician—an "operator" in the medical sense of the term—whose staff failed to live up to his expectations.[56] He claims that he did nothing wrong and that egg donors were selected by embryologists, nurses, and physicians-in-training. Teri Ord and other clinic personnel, however, say that it was Asch who made the selections. Donors were chosen in terms of their ability to produce at the time when recipients were physiologically prepared to receive eggs. Asch says he never considered whether proper consent had been given and acknowledges that in four or five cases proper agreement mistakenly had not been secured. For their part, clinic workers describe a practice in a constant state of bedlam: what went on with the continuous stream of patients, particularly those in large treatment cohorts, was not tracked with sufficient meticulousness.

Dr. Mary Martin Cadieux, a member of the Clinical Panel, during a hearing regarding Asch's position at the university portrayed consent procedures at the UCI facility as primitive and virtually out of control. She noted that the nursing staff had developed the consent forms and that "apparently" the nurses were responsible for dealing with consent issues. Besides, "In our review of charts we frequently found consents that weren't signed, weren't witnessed, weren't filled out. We found some instances . . . of consents that appeared to be filled out and signed that conflicted with the actual course of treatment without any documentation of discussion that would have changed the consent form."[57]

Asch's own alleged carelessness in patient care came in for criticism as well. Sharon Gray, a clinic worker, claims that Asch could be indifferent to patient welfare, taking calls while patients were under anesthesia, for example, and arriving at the clinic at 9:30 in the morning when he had an 8:30 appointment. She says that he had taken eggs from a woman whose husband had no sperm, and given them to another women. Asch says this happened only when the patient consented to egg donation and declares flatly that these statements are lies and slanders.

However unethical and insensitive, the precise legal status of an act involving the appropriation and use of harvested "extra" eggs without the patient's consent is far from clear. James Griffo, a doctor at the Cornell Medical Center fertility clinic, believes that the "law is very fuzzy regarding non-viable material," though he adds quickly: "But we get consent."[58] In California, the court's decision in *Moore v. Regents of the University of California* established that a doctor intending to do potentially profit-generating research using body materials must so inform the patient and obtain prior consent.[59] A lawyer in the firm that litigated the *Moore* case takes a broad perspective on what was decreed by the California Supreme Court:

> My interpretation of the law is a patient has an absolute right to know all the uses to which his or her body parts are being put, even if they are disposable and of no use to the patient. If it's blood, tissue, ova, what they happen to be. They should have a right to say "I don't care if these parts have any use to me personally." The patient has the right to know the whole truth and nothing but the truth.[60]

Perhaps so, perhaps not. There are significant differences between the *Moore* case and what happened at the fertility clinic. John Moore underwent treatment for hairy-cell leukemia at the UCLA Medical Center. His particular case was unusual and the physician planned to use body materials from Moore for research that might establish what is called a cell-link, a way of keeping alive cells that usually do not survive long outside the human body. Moore's spleen was removed (as it should have been, for medical reasons) and he returned to UCLA several times from Seattle to undergo other procedures linked to the research. Subsequently, the Regents applied for a patent on the cell-link, listing the physician and a UCLA researcher as the inventors. After that, a deal was made with the Genetics Institute and with Sandoz for commercial development of the product.

The California Supreme Court, in a lengthy opinion, ruled against Moore's allegation that the procedures constituted the common-law tort of "conversion," which refers to a plaintiff's loss of goods that the defendant found and did not return but instead converted to his or her own use. The California court noted that it had not located a reported decision that imposed conversion liability for the use of human cells in medical research, and it did not feel moved to break new ground in this regard. But it did determine that a physician seeking a patient's informed consent for a medical procedure "must disclose personal interests unrelated to the patient's health, whether research or economic, that may affect his medical judgment."[61]

The unconsented use of harvested eggs at the fertility clinic differs in ways that might have been viewed differently by a court in terms of the university's tort liability. But there seems little doubt that at the time the unconsented use of embryos and ova did not come under the heading of theft.

Once in Mexico, Asch established a new life, though he went through an initial period of depression. He credits his wife with being a particular source of strength during this transition. He portrays himself as a scapegoat: "I know it's not humble to say this," he declared, "but the person who is heaviest makes the most noise when he falls."[62]

In 1999 Asch's research and medical practice were thriving, but he was still haunted by the debacle. American media harassment continued after Asch moved to Mexico. Undercover reporters posing as infertile couples would come to his office. Asch laughs when he recalls that when he realized that they were pseudo-patients he would order immediate blood tests, hoping to scare them away. In one instance, he arrived at the Mexico City airport to meet his wife and daughter and a camera crew was waiting. Asch's wife wrote an angry letter to the network; she received a written apology from Shriver and an NBC vice president, David Corvo.

In 1995 it was reported that Asch's medical activities had prompted an investigation by the Mexican Ministry of Health. Newspaper stories in the United States maintained that officials were concerned that he might be practicing without proper certification. An official was quoted as saying: "It would be ideal if Asch stops what he is doing immediately because he is endangering the health of our citizenry."[63] The results of an investigation, if any occurred, have not surfaced; Asch continues to practice in Mexico City. Additionally, Asch's efforts to track down the source of the quote found that no such "official" existed.

Asch's civil attorney, Lloyd Charton, said that Asch's reputation remains high: "He is very much in demand. He gives lectures, speaks at conventions, he teaches, and in some countries he does infertility procedures."[64] Two years after the scandal first broke, Asch reported that he had more than fifteen invitations to different countries to talk about his work.[65]

Asch's practice in Mexico originally was with the Grupo de Reproducción y Genética AGN y Associados clinic at the Hospital Angeles in the high-end neighborhood of San Angel. Alfonso Gutiérrez Najar, the director, is considered a premier fertility doctor; the facility is one of the most expensive in Mexico. Asch is now in private practice at the hospital and the director of RAM—Reproducción Assistida de México. Currently, he is opening clinics throughout Mexico, including the cities of Acapulco, Cancún, and Puebla.

Asch's office is piled with papers and files. A statue of Hippocrates and a golden plaque with the oath written in Spanish are prominently displayed. Pictures of Asch's family, including many of his son fishing and playing soccer, adorn the walls. The day that we visited, Asch, his eyes bloodshot, was tending to patients at 5:30 on a Friday evening and had an egg transfer scheduled for early the following morning. He left the office that day with gifts from a patient that included a bottle of Remy Martin and a Mike Tyson T-shirt from Las Vegas; Asch boxes daily at a gym to keep in shape. When we subsequently visited him in 2002, there were a Saturday morning egg retrieval procedure, patient calls on his cell phone, and drop-in visitors to his office. "I give myself to every patient; the moment they want to talk to me, they call," he says.

Asch continues to take pride in his medical prowess. He says that he has a 70 percent success rate on first fertility attempts, while other doctors average 20 percent. He credits his performance to intuition. He shrugs and says that he can no more explain his success rate than John Elway, the Denver Broncos' quarterback, can tell you what goes into completing a pass.

*   *   *

Asch's family is the focal point of his life and he firmly believes that the scandal resulted in strengthening his bonds with his wife and children. He takes great pride in all his children. Two of Asch's four daughters live in the United States and frequently visit Mexico: one works in advertising in New York, and the other is married and lives in Las Vegas. His oldest daughter, who followed in her father's footsteps, is training in genetics in Mexico City, and the youngest is preparing to graduate from high school and apply to college. Asch treasures his adopted son, Max, who is eleven years old. Asch was particularly incensed when attacks from outside parties spotlighted his son.

Asch tells of a confrontation with a plaintiff's attorney, Melanie Blum, regarding his son. Blum said that the egg used for his son's birth had been tracked to a clinic patient, and she accused him of using his sperm and hiring a surrogate to carry the child. Asch's wife was so enraged that she told Blum, according to Asch: "If you pursue this, you will see who I am; not only will I sue you, I'm going to kick your ass. To my husband, Max is the most precious thing in life. He will get a gun and shoot you." Asch notes: "That day I told my wife, let's get out of here. I could live with patients suing me, but I'm not going to live with my family life being destroyed." He felt so pressured by lies about his son that he provided the lawyers with the name and telephone number of the birth mother.

Asch also became the target of other outlandish rumors. One lawyer, ignoring the family's Judaism, implied that because Asch's father was a physician in Argentina there might be a Nazi connection. He also was accused of knowingly transferring an embryo infected with HIV. The case involved Vinny and Roxy Ventola, Los Angeles–based screenwriters, who had been patients before HIV testing became routine. The procedure involved a donor-approved egg transfer, with the oocyte fertilized by Vinny. The implant was successful, but Vinny died in 1990, soon after the baby was born; then the child died of an HIV-related illness. A made-for-television film about the couple, "And Then There Was One," was released in 1994. Toula Batshoun, whose remarks always have to be read cautiously, says that Asch returned from the funeral and told her that he believed he could have prevented the death.[66] But Roxy Ventola told mourners that the most wonderful thing in her husband's life was that Asch gave him a child.

Asch does not believe that the HIV virus was in the embryo when he implanted it: "No one knows whether through an embryo the virus can be transmitted. Still today no one knows. The research I'm doing now is fantastic." Asch has become involved in treating HIV discordant couples (the male partner has the illness, and the woman does not), many of whom are from the United States. His new technique involves washing sperm, obtaining a negative HIV test, freezing the sperm, and then creating an embryo for implantation using intracytoplasmic sperm injection, a procedure we discuss more fully in the concluding chapter. Asch says: "I have now the most important breakthrough in HIV in the field of fertility. In the States no one will touch them." His procedure resulted in the birth of a baby in 1999 testing negative for HIV, though one parent was infected.

Kathryn Wycoff, executive director of the Center for Reproductive Alternatives in San Clemente, California, says that patients seek out Asch in Mexico because of his unorthodox methods. "He'll switch the medicine or try different things, whatever it takes to make her ovaries produce the quality of eggs he needs."[67] Some other fertility specialists remain fans of his work. In the journal *Human Reproduction*, Robert Edwards, the creator of IVF, and Helen Beard defended Asch to his peers: "In the USA, the press treatment of Ricardo Asch and his colleagues over apparent misdemeanors in an IVF clinic has been a combination of condemnation and punishment handed out even before any of them were formally charged. There can seldom have been a more extreme case of judging a man without a trial."[68]

Edwards noted that Asch is "a close and trusted colleague and friend," and in a letter to *Fertility and Sterility* he wrote, "I feared that the outlook seemed to be very dark for Ricardo, and that it would be a desperately sad day for me if a legal judgment went against him."[69] A leading expert in reproductive medicine observes that Asch is well accepted in European circles, but generally is shunned by his colleagues in the United States because they wish to avoid the controversy created by the UCI scandal.[70]

Asch continues to travel extensively, though he checks extradition agreements that each foreign destination has in place with the United States. He is involved in research with colleagues in Barcelona who are trying to perfect Preimplantation Genetic Diagnosis (PGD), a process still considered too risky for general use, which could detect as many as ten chromosomal abnormalities, including Tay-Sachs and Down syndrome.[71] Asch is working as well with a Japanese company on a project that will dramatically change fertility treatment technology and tremendously increase success rates.

Asch depicts the consequences of the fertility clinic scandal in part in terms of money and material assets, though the emotional toll was quite significant: "I had a very good living. I had to sell everything. I had to sell all of my houses, all of my cars. I'm living in a rental house."[72] He is unwilling to discuss specific incidents relating to charges of egg misuse, noting that he does not have access to patient charts. In one case, though, he recalls that the chart indicated that embryos were available for donation, although the consent form had been marked "No." Asch grants that the embryos in that case were used without permission, but points out that they were given to Toula Batshoun's best friend, insinuating that his office worker had intentionally misconstrued instructions.

Asch has little to say about his longtime friend the biologist Teri Ord. He points out that Ord had given him a copy of the jacket of Mary Higgins Clark's book *I'll Be Seeing You.* The plot of this romantic thriller involved the theft of embryos at a prestigious fertility clinic. Ord told Asch she thought the story interesting and that he should read it. "It's very funny that she gave me something like this," he muses. "It's kind of strange." He believes that Norbert Giltner and Ord profited by selling patient charts from the clinic. He says he sought to have Giltner fired in July 1994 for stealing records and making racist comments about Hispanic and African American employees, but the university administration failed to act.

Asch was never viewed by the university, once the investigation picked up speed, as innocent until proven guilty. His mail to the campus was confiscated for two years, until he filed a legal complaint charging theft and vandalism. He was excluded from negotiations over the patient settlements. "I'm not happy with the settlements," he says, "because they don't repair my reputation with the public that was tarnished in the media. My feelings are, number one, I know I didn't do anything wrong; and number two, when a settlement happens, it's all over and there are no innocent or guilty any more."[73] His dismissal from the university in July 2000 was expected, though Asch held some hope that his once-close relationship with Ralph Cicerone, the new chancellor, would gain him a sympathetic hearing. Before the firing, he said of Cicerone: "He's a real man. He's going to do the right thing, if the people in Sacramento will let him. He will do the right thing."[74]

The university faculty Committee on Privilege and Tenure held twelve days of hearings in July 1999 to consider Asch's termination, compiling a transcript of 1,612 pages. Asch himself was present sporadically by video conferencing from Mexico City—but only after the committee chair had ascertained that he was paying the toll himself, approximately six thousand dollars, according to Asch.

Evidence presented during the hearings tilted against Asch, though there was no definitive Perry Mason–style denouement that would lead a neutral observer to conclude categorically that Asch's behavior was so "egregious" and "horrific"—terms often used by those testifying against him—that he unquestionably deserved to be terminated.

Asch accepted responsibility for a few unconsented egg transfers because, he granted, it was he who ran the clinic. But he steadfastly insisted that it was the nurses' delegated obligation to see that proper consent had been obtained, and that he was far too occupied with medical procedures to attend to this chore. He cited two cases in which he claimed that patients had told him personally that they were willing to donate eggs, but when the lure of lawsuit loot surfaced they changed their stories.[75] For Asch this was the pattern running through the case: "Opportunistic patients, hungry lawyers that tried to use the momentum to try to produce some financial contributions for themselves."[76]

Asch's insistence that he was uninvolved in consent issues was forcefully contradicted by Dr. Mary Martin Cadieux, a reproductive medicine specialist from UCLA. She said that she felt "outraged at even the idea that the physician who was supposedly caring for this couple for whom they entrusted their hopes and expectations of starting a family would not feel that it was his primary responsibility to understand their wishes about every aspect of the case . . . and that the delegation of that responsibility to anyone else is simply inconceivable."[77] She also found it "totally implausible" that Asch was unaware of unconsented egg transfers because of the "exquisite coordination required between recipient and donor."[78]

Asch held fast to his story that a patient from Argentina had brought some one hundred vials of hMG Massone with her to the clinic, and had left most of them when her own treatment was concluded. A staff member insisted that Asch had a very large inventory of the drug, and that he directed her to fill prescriptions for various patients, and to have them make out checks payable to him. Asch said he had destroyed what little remained of Massone when told to do so by the medical school—and that, he insisted, was the end of that.

The debate about research done without institutional approval ended with much the same kind of contradictory evidence. Asch granted that perhaps several research probes should have gone through the review board, but he quarreled, article by article, with most of the allegations. He claimed that approval for some of the studies had been obtained at the Garden Grove facility, and that the proper forms could be located if the committee sought them. It tried, without success. Asch also maintained that he assumed that others had gotten approval or that formal approval was not necessary. Regarding two articles, he insisted that he had no idea that the research had been done and the results published with his name listed as an author. He presumed that his signature had been forged on the release forms that many journals require from all authors.

Illustrating the standoffs that marked the hearing was Teri Ord's discussion of what she said was an order from Asch to ship some embryos to Cornell University and his denial that he was involved in the transaction. While Ord's position seems the more persuasive, there was no hard evidence to contradict Asch's claim.

Ord, testifying from Philadelphia by telephone, said that Anna Veiga, a physician based in Barcelona, had come to the clinic saying that she had shipped some embryos from Spain to Cornell for research there. The nitrogen in the shipping tank had evaporated and the embryos had thawed and therefore were of no use to her. Then, according to Ord, "Dr. Asch came to me and said he wanted to help her out and had me get the master list of patients that had frozen embryos that was posted up on one of the cabinets in the laboratory, and he went through that list and wrote off to the side of the patients' name how many embryos he wanted shipped to Cornell."[79]

The embryos were shipped, Ord testified, with an accompanying inventory that included the notation: "To A. Viega [sic] per Asch." The document was not produced at the hearing. Ord said that she and a nurse, Della Morrison, had compassionately eliminated the names of some women who had not yet become pregnant. Asch, for his part, insisted that he had called Ord and told her, "If there is any way that you can help Anna if we have embryos that are going to be discarded because the patients had signed and notarized forms that they didn't want any more of those embryos, please give them to her." Asch's version was backed by a sworn statement from Veiga, who also presented the original transmittal document, which did not have the notation "To A. Viega per Asch." To Asch, this was a story that Ord "obviously did afterward to cover her back."[80] Asch was asked why Ord would have done this on her own. "Just to be nice to the number one biologist [Veiga] in the world," he answered.[81]

Under cross-examination by Asch's attorneys, Ord granted that she had carried away records when she left UCI. She did so, she said, so that the doctors could not jeopardize her future job prospects. At one point in the hearings, Josefina Walker, an Asch attorney, took umbrage when one of the university lawyers, rather than directing his remarks to the chair, as he had been told to do, addressed her. "If he does that once more, I'll carve him a new orifice," threatened Walker. Sidney Golub, representing the university, remained virtually silent throughout the proceedings. At one point, though, he bristled at the intense cross-examination of the Challenders: "I believe there are times when there are things more important than due process," Golub exclaimed. "And I think the reputation of the university, and the pain inflicted on this couple has already exceeded the bounds of propriety. I would urge you to delay this testimony and be done with it."[82]

Asch, fighting a losing battle against a committee that was virtually certain to terminate him, again denied all the accusations in a letter that he submitted to supplement the hearings. He concluded his letter on a religious note:

To end, I am writing this letter in the holiest day of my religion: IOM KIPUR. It is ironic that it is written in the old religious texts that it was in IOM KIPUR that the notion of the SCAPEGOAT was originated to have animals pay for pagan sacrifices of humans, and introduced into the Judeo-Christian culture that we live today. Even though 5760 years have passed the same SCAPEGOAT philosophy has been used to focus all responsibility of what have ever happened at the UCI Center for Reproductive Health on me by the University and the allied media that in the interest of selling news don't stop in distorting the realty.

After observing Yom Kippur three years later, Asch reflected on the aftermath of the scandal: "Before all of this happened to me, I was interested in being recognized by other doctors, universities, newspapers, television, and many people that I did not know. Now, I know what is really important in life: to be recognized only by family, real friends, and my patients. I believe this is one of the great lessons in life that I learned from the UCI ordeal."[83]

While Asch denies any personal scientific or financial motive for his possible involvement with the missing eggs and embryos, he mused hypothetically on the subject during an interview in Mexico City: "I have one justification. If I would have done any of those things they tell me I did, it was to make someone happy. To help a baby be born. To have a family. This was the motive."[84]

Then he added elliptically, responding to the scenario he himself had just scripted: "But it was not the motive. Believe me, it was not." After that, he changed course: "It's not Dr. Kevorkian [the physician who assisted in patient-requested suicides]. I like to help people."

C H A P T E R

José Balmaceda, M.D.

■ Of the three fertility clinic doctors, José Balmaceda's actions and thoughts have been the most difficult to pin down. A considerable element of this elusiveness lies in the role he chose for himself: remote, quiet, geographically removed from the main scene at the UCI Medical Center. Most particularly, Balmaceda did not have a tenured faculty position at UCI; therefore, there was no need for formal proceedings to document wrongdoing to terminate his university appointment. And when Balmaceda left the United States for Chile, he further removed himself from the media and the legal battlefield.

Always in the background was a pattern that Balmaceda had established early in his relationship with Asch. He was the spear carrier, Asch the prima donna. The two physicians, however, were close: they worked side by side, shared meals, and played tennis together. In 1989 Balmaceda had moved his headquarters to Saddleback Memorial Hospital in Laguna Hills and he usually appeared at the Irvine clinic only on those weekends when Asch was not on call. Balmaceda told us that he relocated at Saddleback in part because he was uncomfortable with the hazardous tactics being used by Asch in the partnership's enterprise at Irvine, and that he sought to distance himself from what was going on there. "I thought I solved my problems by creating my own clinic," Balmaceda says.[1] "But it didn't work out."

It is not known whether Balmaceda was complicit in unconsented egg transfers at the Garden Grove facility before he took up his station at Saddleback. The close personal and professional relationship between Asch and Balmaceda and evidence that well over 50 percent of the egg misuse cases occurred at the Garden Grove clinic suggest his possible involvement. Balmaceda grants only that he was well aware of the unconsented egg transfers at the UCI clinic, but that he expected that Asch would transfer his own practice to UC San Diego, nearer to where he kept his horses, and that the potentially explosive issues at UCI would end. As Balmaceda puts the matter today: "I knew we were going to separate and tranquility was going to be much better. Ricardo's move wouldn't be bad for us and would have been appropriate. Moving from school to school is very common. That would have been great. Sergio knew it and we were prepared for it."

For his part, Balmaceda inaugurated an egg donor program at Saddleback, recruiting some thirty or so volunteers a year. Asch was strongly opposed to this method of obtaining eggs. He regarded it as coercive because of the monetary payment involved. Even if it resulted from women's altruistic impulses, it was much less acceptable to him than using excess eggs that had been aspirated from women undergoing fertility procedures. "Ricardo didn't control [the donor program], and if he didn't control something it was not good," Balmaceda says.

Balmaceda indicates that he made efforts to team up with Stone to deal with some of the clinic problems, but he says that Stone was too passive and perhaps intimidated by Asch. "I told him, 'Sergio, I need you. You and me are two. Don't be afraid.'"

When first contacted, Balmaceda expressed surprise that his story would be of interest to us. He maintained that much of what went on at the university fertility clinic, whether it was unconsented egg appropriation or illegal insurance billings, represented the normal course of business in the United States. He said that it is only when someone gets trapped in a situation that cannot be ignored or silently mended that explicit rules, generally ignored, become ropes that will be used to hang transgressors unfortunate enough to have been identified, particularly if the media get hold of the story and the word *lawsuit* is mentioned.

Balmaceda maintains that whatever problems there might have been at the clinic were well known to university administrators, medical school officials, and clinic staff for a considerable period. That they did nothing about them for so long, he believes, can reasonably be interpreted as indicating that they were not bothered by what was happening while the cash continued to flow.

Balmaceda's admissions regarding wrongdoing at the clinic are closely tied to his conviction that primary responsibility fell on Asch's shoulders and that his own work at Saddleback adhered to principles that respected patients' rights and met acceptable standards of practice. Though he was a partner in the operation of the clinic, his position was that of a silent partner who went along with the boss, Ricardo Asch.

José Pedro Balmaceda Riera, referred to as Pepe by friends, is, like Sergio Stone and Ricardo Asch, unusually charming, with graceful Old World manners rarely displayed in the United States today. He has bright green eyes and usually untidy, thick brown hair with just the faintest scattering of gray. He often brushes his hair back with his hand and is soft-spoken. Friends and former patients describe him as having a Hugh Grant look—"cute and gregarious" and as a "teddy bear–type of guy." A professional woman, not disapprovingly, described Balmaceda as "something of a flirt."[2] In conversation, he seems a bit more modest and self-effacing than the usual medical practitioner. He is stocky, slightly overweight, with chubby cheeks, and he dresses conservatively. Balmaceda is articulate, though he struggles with his English at times. He expresses deep concern for the environmental and political problems in Chile, his birthplace and his present home.

Balmaceda was born on August 22, 1948, in Santiago, the son of an industrialist who owned several timber mills. He fondly remembers his father and namesake, José, as an energetic and happy man, even throughout the course of the pancreatic cancer that killed him in 1999. His mother, Juanita, now in her late eighties and living in Santiago, owned a women's boutique when she was younger.

Balmaceda grew up in a family with five sisters, four of them older than he; all still reside in Santiago. At a recent reunion, a photograph of three generations of Balmacedas included eighty-four relatives. Balmaceda's role models were three uncles who worked in the medical field.

Balmaceda first met Sergio Stone, his future partner in the UCI fertility clinic, when both attended San Ignatius, a Jesuit school in Santiago, though Balmaceda is a few years younger than Stone. He graduated from the Catholic University Medical School in 1974 and took up a medical residency at the University of Chile hospital. It was there that his interests moved from internal medicine to obstetrics and gynecology. He believes that the switch might relate to his family situation: he feels at ease with women after having grown up in a largely female household. He also emphasizes that the "incredible experience of delivering a baby" drew him to ob/gyn.

It is an ironic turn of events that the nation from which Balmaceda had been estranged would later become his sanctuary. He was forced into political exile from Chile in 1975, when the country struggled under the totalitarian rule of General Augusto Pinochet. Balmaceda was politically active as a young man, openly supporting the socialist Popular Unity government of President Salvador Allende. When Allende was forced from power in 1973 during Pinochet's brutal coup,[3] Balmaceda, then in his early twenties, already had begun his ob/gyn training.

José and his wife, Veronica Pascal, were targeted by the military police when they learned that the Balmacedas had been hiding political dissidents in their home. One of the men they sheltered had been shot in the leg. Another man for whom the couple provided refuge was the leader of the guerilla leftist revolutionary movement, a nephew of Allende and Veronica's cousin.[4]

Balmaceda says that he was "very lucky" to avoid arrest. When the military police came to the hospital to take him into custody, he asked them to wait while he changed from his scrub outfit. He then escaped through a back door. He hid for two months at an embryology professor's home, and while there he made contact with the Danish embassy. A friend studied the routine of a soldier stationed outside the embassy and learned that he left his post a bit early, before his replacement had arrived, in order to catch a bus. Balmaceda and his wife lifted their two young children over the embassy wall and then climbed over it themselves into the embassy backyard. "I was very frightened," he remembers. "They would shoot you on the spot or subject you to torture." The Balmacedas subsequently were granted political asylum in Denmark, where Balmaceda worked in a research laboratory. He would tell colleagues in later years that his time in Denmark was extremely depressing. The dark, rainy climate and the low status of being a refugee living on government assistance wore on the family's morale. He was recruited in 1976 by the University of Texas medical facility in San Antonio.

He completed an obstetrics and gynecology residency in Texas in 1980 and the following year was awarded a Rockefeller Foundation fellowship in reproductive endocrinology; it was at this time that he began to work closely with Asch. The relatively low salary at Texas was among the reasons that he accepted the offer to work in California in 1987.

Balmaceda, working with Asch, rose rapidly into the higher echelons of physicians practicing and doing research on fertility procedures. He currently belongs to at least seventeen scholarly societies, has co-edited a book with Asch on gamete physiology, and has written more than twenty chapters in books and some fifty journal articles, many of them in collaboration with Asch and other members of the clinic team. He has been a visiting professor at the University of Madrid and the Perugia Medical School in Italy. The list of the sites where he has presented his research findings reads like an around-the-world tour: Kenya, Switzerland, France, Israel, Venezuela, Italy, Indonesia, Korea, Mexico, and England, among other places.

Balmaceda describes his years at UCI as "productive." "The Saddleback Center has helped hundreds of couples realize their dream of parenthood," he says. "Couples came to me not only from Orange County but from around the world."[5] The practice was lucrative. Balmaceda's base salary at the university was $80,300 when he left, but it is estimated that he earned as much as $27,000 a week in his private practice partnership with Asch—considerably more than a million dollars a year. Balmaceda's tax preparer, while properly declining to discuss his client's finances, noted wryly, "He was not the world's greatest bookkeeper and would present me with a shoebox full of records and receipts."[6]

One medical school faculty member who knew Balmaceda and Asch believes that this newfound wealth was intoxicating: "More money than they ever dreamed of possessing, huge amounts, was virtually being thrown at them. It was beyond anything they could have imagined. With the money came a strong feeling of omnipotence. If they were worth so much, they must be doing everything right, must be beyond the bounds created for ordinary people."[7] Balmaceda takes offense at the idea that he went "crazy" over money. "I did not come from a poor background, did not buy a red Ferrari or huge mansions, my lifestyle was absolutely normal," he says.[8] For Balmaceda, the income translated into a Spanish-style million-dollar California house (today worth about two or three times as much) on Poppy Avenue, about two hundred yards from the Pacific Ocean in Corona del Mar. In 1994 the Balmacedas purchased an even more elegant house, valued at $2.5 million at the time, on nearby Bayside Drive. The house, with an eighty-foot dock, sits near the edge of the Newport Harbor and offers a picturesque view of Balboa Island. Balmaceda offers this purchase as evidence that he had no intention at that time of leaving the country.

Balmaceda describes the years of the partnership as tainted by animosity and suffering. Others report loud arguments between Asch and Balmaceda that could be heard in other clinic offices. "I was not intimidated by Ricardo," Balmaceda observes. He believed that the fertility business they were running was deteriorating: "The way patients were being handled, waiting, and abandoned. It was bad for business."

Balmaceda particularly recalls the tension between Asch and Teri Ord, the biologist who came with them from Texas, whom he holds in high esteem. He maintains that Ord had nothing whatsoever to do with the unconsented egg and embryo transfers, and he blames Asch for limiting the procedures that Ord was permitted to perform because she lacked adequate credentials.

At the same time, Balmaceda readily grants that he benefited greatly from his association with Asch, but he also emphasizes that his own talents were not insignificant and that his achievements are highly regarded in the world of fertility medicine. "It never went through my mind to break my relations with Sergio and Ricardo," he claims, but he believes that Asch should have dealt more forcefully with the university in resolving some of the clinic problems, such as inadequate staffing. "It never came to my mind to go to the university authority about the disorganization. Ricardo was always the one that had access to the chairman and the rest of the people." Balmaceda also notes that despite what he regards as Asch's difficult personality, he possessed a panache that advanced their careers:

> The guy is absolutely uncontrollable. He does whatever he wants. He always did. I benefited from that relationship. For ex-

ample: GIFT never would have been what it was . . . if it wasn't for Ricardo. This has to be recognized. Ricardo gave the flair. He made the publicity. He made everything appear to have an importance that it may have had or may not have had. He was a productive guy. A guy with imagination. A guy that knew opportunities, got things together.

He then adds: "Would I have given him my wife to treat? No, no way."

Shortly after the fertility scandal hit the headlines, Balmaceda circulated a letter to the faculty at the UCI College of Medicine that blamed administrators for making him a scapegoat. He pointed out that the clinical panel findings threw him into the cauldron promiscuously, that they failed to take notice of the fact that the three doctors were not equally responsible for everything that was said to have gone on at the facility. "The report which investigated the clinical allegations found no specific instance of wrongdoing by me individually," he wrote, "and all of their findings related to the UCI [clinic], where I rarely practiced."[9] Balmaceda also took exception to what he called "the last straw," "the outrageous press releases issued by the university about the possibility of other [unknown] cases of misdirected eggs or embryos."

Balmaceda's greatest involvement in the scandal occurred in March 1996, when an *Orange County Register* article claimed that he was directly involved in a scheme to buy the silence of Toula Batshoun, the onetime office manager. Batshoun said that Balmaceda and his counsel had suggested a "confidential agreement" to keep her from saying anything about egg thefts. She maintained that Balmaceda had referred to the scandal as the "mess" created by Asch,[10] an observation that, whether he made it or not, accurately reflects Balmaceda's position. Batshoun's testimony about what she labeled a blackmail attempt was largely discounted as a self-serving tactic to place her in line for settlement money.

A colleague from Chile who was visiting Balmaceda during the maelstrom urged him to separate himself from Asch. "Do it now; if not you are stupid. You are going to be burned here." Balmaceda had left the United States in September 1995 to visit his ailing mother in Santiago—and stayed on. That decision, he told us, was dictated primarily by financial and family considerations. "I could not afford to defend myself against the accusations in the States," he says. "Before I left I was spending fifty thousand dollars a month maintaining my defense. I made a conscious decision to leave the country to avoid more humiliation and economic devastation." He insists, much as Asch does, that he "wasn't running," since there were no criminal charges filed against him at the time, nor did he expect any such accusations.

Balmaceda believes that Stone's decision to remain in the United States may have provided the impetus for the accusations against all three of the physicians. "I think he made things worse for everybody by staying there, because I don't think they would have spent the money building up the charges and the whole thing would have fizzled out." He concedes that it was a question of honor for Stone, but he insists that when Stone stayed, "the process had to continue." Balmaceda maintains that the high-profile Stone trial and what he saw as Asch's grandstanding worsened the situation for him. "It was a tactic of Ricardo's, him with his lawyers and doing this thing in Tijuana. This is crazy. For what purpose? Asch was being advised by this crazy lawyer, a very high-profile guy."

Balmaceda has largely avoided the spotlight in Chile, though he has granted interviews to local papers because he feels that they will present both sides of the case, whereas the American press is biased. He remembers his only discussion of his case with a newspaper reporter in the United States. "I didn't have anything to hide," he says. "They knew more than me." The resulting story in the *Orange County Register* irritated him:

> They hang me with this prospective protocol [a reference to a form of research that required but was said not to have received intramural approval] I had done comparing embryo transfers to the tubes versus the uterus. And they said Dr. Balmaceda did unnecessary surgery on the patients, which was not true. The objective of the study was essentially to reduce the surgery. That putting these things [embryos] in the uterus was as effective than doing the surgery which was what we did 100 percent of the time. Not only did 50 percent of the women studied not have surgery in the future; we [thereafter] did uterine transfers.

The study in question, "Embryo Implantation in Oocyte Donation," was published in *Fertility and Sterility;* it involved forty-two patients in the egg donation program who were randomly assigned to one of two experimental conditions: twenty-two underwent uterine transfers and twenty had tubal embryo transfers. The authors concluded that there was no advantage in the more invasive procedure, which involved transferring embryos to the fallopian tubes.[11] The issue in dispute was whether patients had been adequately informed of their role in the research and whether they had consented to be part of it.

"The newspapers played an important role in deforming the reality to the point that we appeared as monsters," Balmaceda believes, using a word—monsters—often employed by his colleagues to describe how they saw themselves portrayed in the media. Balmaceda believes that this research could have been favorably depicted but that his critics portrayed it, and other controversial matters, in a way that invariably made him look bad. "You are living this nightmare," he says about the newspaper stories. In August 2000 he continued to express strong indignation: "My blood pressure goes up and there is no way of defending yourself."

Soon after he arrived in Chile, Balmaceda started working at the private Clinica Las Condes in Santiago, one of the country's most prestigious medical facilities, nestled at the foot of the Andes;[12] his office is on the fourth floor in the first of the clinic's three towers. Colleagues celebrated the return of the "father of Chilean reproductive medicine," and most viewed the UCI events as nothing more than gossip.[13] Dr. Cesar Caffatti Jamarne, a fertility specialist at a competing Chilean clinic, defends Balmaceda: "He is an excellent doctor and a true professional, and until he is proven guilty in a court of law, he should be welcomed to practice medicine in Chile."[14] As early as 1983, Balmaceda had been consulting at the Clinica Las Condes, where he was given a small office by colleagues who had hoped to lure him home. Balmaceda asserts that this opportunity rather than self-protection led him to leave the United States: "I have heard people say that I fled the country because I was guilty and afraid, but I have been involved in the growth of this clinic from the beginning." A representative of the Chilean clinic noted that 180 staff doctors were notified in advance of Balmaceda's possible arrival there and were offered an opportunity to object. None did.

Reproductive technology is largely unregulated by law in Chile, though the Church and conservative politicians are pushing for strict

controls, and some local physicians are concerned that the shadow of
Balmaceda's return might spur a renewed attempt by the legislature to
impose jail sentences for freezing, selling, or destroying embryos.[15] Such
a measure was introduced in 1995 but failed to gain enough support for
enactment.

"Our practice here is a very American type of practice," Balmaceda
says. "Everything is written down. Everything is consented." He com-
pares what goes on today to what was common in the mid-1980s in the
United States:

> We have developed a much more acute sense of the rights of the
> women. They are her eggs and if she wants to throw some in a
> trash can, she can throw them in the trash can. I don't think
> that was clear in 1986. I remember a fight between USC and
> Norfolk about a woman's embryos and the couple moved to Cali-
> fornia and she wanted her embryos. Norfolk said no way, they
> are ours. No, they were the patient's. The whole issue of whose
> gamete is whose and so on now is much developed in the U.S.,
> and other communities are following suit.

Balmaceda was referring to *York v. Jones*.[16] The Howard and George-
anna Jones Institute for Reproductive Medicine in Norfolk, Virginia, had
refused to release Risa Adler-York and Stephen York's frozen embryo
for shipment to Richard Marrs, a physician at the Hospital of the Good
Samaritan in Los Angeles. The Yorks had undergone four unsuccessful
reproductive procedures in Virginia and had one embryo cryopreserved.
The Virginia clinic cited a variety of practical and legal reasons for its
decision: the possibilities of refrigeration failure and theft of the embryo
during shipment, and issues of liability. The plaintiffs relied successfully
on the legal doctrine of detinue, an old common-law principle that
allows persons to recover personal property that is wrongfully held. The
federal district court ruled that the Virginia clinic was merely a temporary custodian of the embryo and had no right to keep it against the
couple's wishes.

Balmaceda indicated in our interview with him that he believes that
careless and callous physician attitudes and an indifference to or ignorance of the importance of genetic materials to their owners were a pri-

mary cause of the troubles that arose at the UCI fertility clinic. "That's why eggs were taken in Irvine," he says. "Nobody cared about taking an egg from a patient who had produced seventy-five eggs, particularly in the late 1980s." But by 1994, he points out, "it was plainly your responsibility and lack of . . ." Balmaceda groped for the proper term, which he could not find.

One Santiago colleague says that Balmaceda, despite his formal acceptance, has been shunned by many doctors in Santiago's medical community, primarily because of stories about the California scandal. Balmaceda has also been the target of a *Newsweek* writer who tried—unsuccessfully—to make a story out of alleged shipments of embryos from the United States to Bolivia. Balmaceda acknowledges that a handful of Latin American patients requested him to arrange for the transfer of their embryos from California to Bolivia, but he finds the notion that he was trafficking in oocytes preposterous. "Who in their right mind would plan to do that, when you could pay two thousand to three thousand dollars for oocytes from a young college student? Why take the time to steal and move embryos?" For the press, in Balmaceda's view, "it's better to do science fiction. Embryos to Bolivia, cocaine, drugs, Latin America."

Balmaceda's life in Chile has been marked by personal tragedy. His wife committed suicide in 1999. The couple was separated at the time. Veronica Pascal was a petite woman with what friends describe as a sweet and animated personality. She was trained as a psychotherapist and was a talented ceramist. Her father was the Chilean ambassador to the Netherlands. Of Veronica, Balmaceda says: "Our marriage had some trouble in California—all the stress." He said that his wife had "a personality disorder that really flourished and ended with this tragedy." He has two adult children, who remain in the United States, and two younger children. His concern today is focused on his two younger children, boys who in 2003 are ten and fifteen and who live with him in Santiago. His daughter, Javiera, worked in Miami at a television station and his son Pedro, who bears a striking resemblance to his father, lived in Los Angeles and has appeared on several television shows, including *Buffy the Vampire Slayer* and *Touched by an Angel*. Both now live in New York City.

Balmaceda lives in Vitacura, a suburb of Santiago, and plays golf in his spare time. He is a "fanatic" about golf, Sergio Stone observes. "He would pantomime his golf swing in the office."[17] In 2001 Balmaceda married a longtime friend, Heather Childress, who had moved to California from Texas in the early 1990s. The couple often is featured on the society pages of Santiago's *El Mercurio* newspaper. Balmaceda points out that his income in Chile is significantly lower than it was in California, but he adds that doctors in Chile receive a great deal more respect than they do in the United States.

Chilean news sources in January 2003 reported that Balmaceda, along with his colleague Emilio Fernandez, was treating the 1987 Miss Universe, Cecilia Bolocco, and her husband, Carlos Menem, who was the president of Argentina from 1989 to 1999, for infertility. Menem, who at seventy-two is twice as old as his wife, had undergone a treatment used for men with low sperm counts so that the doctors could impregnate his wife through an IVF procedure. Bolocco, a South American entertainment celebrity, has been called "Le nueva Evita" (the new Evita), a reference to her husband's forthcoming attempt to regain his country's presidency. In a one-hour Chilean television report on Menem's fertility treatment, Balmaceda and the interviewer exchanged angry words about the Irvine scandal; the interviewer flashed a copy of the FBI's Internet page, which describes him as a fugitive from justice.[18]

When we visited Balmaceda in Santiago, he openly talked about several of the Irvine cases, though he said that he had only a vague memory of many of the patients. He was particularly sympathetic to the situation of Barbara Moore and her husband, Patrick:

> The Moores, they were a nice couple. They had a terrible experience with us. I knew them well because they lived close to Saddleback. They would come to me to do the induction of ovulation, and they would go to the pavilion [at UCI] to have the procedures done with Ricardo. But they were his patients. They went through three cycles and never became pregnant. They came to me before the scandal and told me they appreciated my assistance and I had been very helpful to her, but the whole experience with us was very negative and that they were pregnant now with a minimal correction of a thyroid function after

they spent thousands of dollars. But they didn't sue, didn't make any waves. They are decent, extremely nice people.

Balmaceda adds that his review of the Moore chart showed that her eggs were taken without consent.

Balmaceda grants that there were mishaps with eggs at the fertility clinic, but he dismisses the possibility that there may have been two hundred cases of unconsented transfers, calling it "absolutely ridiculous." "I admit that there were twenty-five to thirty cases at the most involving the transfer of eggs without consent from the donor." Perhaps, he says on reflection, that number might have been as high as fifty. He distributes the blame for what happened among a number of persons:

Asch should have admitted responsibility, he was director the whole time. The funny thing is that everybody in that clinic knew what was going on and nobody cared. I believe it was an issue of laissez-faire management on behalf of the university. Sometimes people just did not check to see if a consent form was signed and it certainly is not the responsibility of the doctor when they arrive on a Saturday morning to perform the procedure to check the necessary forms to make sure that a donor signed the consent form.

He suggests that the clinic employees had good reason to remain silent, and that they "cooperated in every way" in what was going on. There were rewards for keeping quiet. One grateful patient paid the plane fare of some clinic workers to Venezuela so that they could attend her baby's baptism. Staff members were sometimes treated to meals by richer patients. "They were part of the problems," Balmaceda observes of the clinic staff. But when clinic employees were interviewed by the newspapers, he says, they expressed mock surprise and horror about the egg transfers. Balmaceda needs only one word to indicate what he thought of that: "Crap."

Nonetheless, Balmaceda pulls no punches about his own culpability. "I'm not attacking Ricardo. I'm not eluding responsibility, because I was there. I should have been more attentive." He admits that he had "suspicions." "I may have told Toula, get consent from this patient to donate, but nobody bothered to check. This is what happened. I didn't worry about going there [to the clinic] and saying, 'Where is the consent form?' I didn't give it the importance." Balmaceda believes that if Asch had come forward in 1989 or 1990, the outcome might have been very different: "I think Ricardo was too smart for his own good. I think Ricardo at a certain point should have stepped out front and should have said, 'This happened. I'm responsible for it.' And he could have made any explanation. I told him this is what you have to do."

Balmaceda doesn't think much of the way the university handled the fertility clinic matter. "No investigating panel spent much more than an hour with me, despite the list of allegations, testimony of dozens of witnesses, and stacks of documents to ask me about." He had no doubts about the university's complicity in any wrongdoing that came to light:

> The university knew about the accusations four years prior to doing anything about it. The first accusation came from a disgruntled nurse [Norbert Giltner] and was swept under the carpet by the university and when the nurse finally went to the press in 1994, the university realized they had to do something, and what they did was to place all of the blame on the three doctors. It was easy for the university to place the blame on three Latin American doctors and refuse to take any responsibility.

Balmaceda's numerous requests for copies of the final reports of the investigations were ignored. "I was not given one panel report," he says, "after repeated demands, including Public Records Act requests. I never received a completed report and large portions of each report have been redacted without explanations of the reasons for the deletions."

Balmaceda is adamant that nothing that happened at his clinic was done for financial gain or with malicious intent. Early in the clinic's history in California, before cyropreservation was possible, "the issue was not money, not trafficking in embryos; the issue was trash the eggs or give them to another patient." He distinguishes his own work and ethics from those of Asch: "It was better [in Asch's view] to take eggs without permission. Whenever he wanted his patients to be fertilized, it was a good dollar for him. That was Ricardo, that's vintage Ricardo." He adds: "If anyone is naive enough to think we were the exception in the U.S. in those years, they are crazy. I'm not saying this to minimize it, to make it appear less horrible. I think that patients should be protected."

Balmaceda dismisses the alleged failure to pay the medical school assessment, the tax evasion charges, and the allegation of insurance fraud with a single word: "Bullshit." The insurance billing practices at the clinic, he says, were the way things were done in all medical school settings. "I'm guilty. Ninety-nine percent of the professors in the U.S. are. In Texas, I did the same thing." He asked rhetorically: "What's the difference between me signing a chart when I didn't do it [the procedure] and signing as an assistant when the surgery was done by a resident? How do you account for a professor of anesthesiology who charges for nine surgeries that have been done concurrently in the operating room at the university hospital in Orange?" Balmaceda insists that what was done lacked intent: "To me fraud means you're charging for something you didn't do; you're charging for an operation that wasn't done. That goes on in the States a lot."

Since he took up residence in Chile, Balmaceda has limited his traveling to Latin America. He serves as director of the Latin American Assisted Reproductive Network, which includes Chile, Peru, and Bolivia. The group has been focusing on putting together data on success rates for clinics in those countries and standardizing consent forms. Asked about the possibility of extradition to the United States to face the federal court indictments filed against him, Balmaceda responded: "No chance. I don't want to excite anybody to give me a hard time, whereas Ricardo has been traveling everywhere in the world."

Things seemed under control for Balmaceda. He kept a low profile in Chile, adjusted to his smaller income, was raising his young children, and went about his business unobtrusively. But that script altered dramatically when he deplaned in the Ezeiza airport in Buenos Aires on January 17, 2001, and was immediately arrested and held for possible extradition to the United States. The charges were mail fraud and tax evasion. John Hueston, head of the U.S. Attorney's office in Santa Ana, California, heralded the arrest: "Dr. Balmaceda was one of the ringleaders in the fraud that shocked Orange County. Our office is gratified that the long efforts of the FBI and others . . . have paid off."[19]

Orange County newspapers reported that federal authorities had been keeping a close eye on Balmaceda's comings and goings for more than two years. They had received a tip that he planned to travel to Argentina and Panama on business, so they filed arrest warrants seeking his detention if he appeared in either country. To persons acquainted with the extradition process, the government's efforts seemed more like a publicity ploy than a normal enforcement action. Edwin M. Smith at the University of Southern California Law School, an expert in international law, noted: "I have never heard of anyone pursuing extradition for mail fraud. An extradition is usually pursued for some very serious crimes like murder and robbery."[20]

The newspapers, gleefully reviving a moribund story, made it seem as if the FBI's number-one fugitive had been trapped, a man who, in the words of one news story, had "tried to slip into Argentina."[21] They added some spice to the story by writing—incorrectly—that Balmaceda had been attempting to cover his tracks and had traveled extensively in Europe since leaving the United States, and that "his whereabouts have been cloudy since he disappeared in 1995, bound for his native Chile."[22] To the contrary, of course, Balmaceda was settled in Santiago and was as accessible as the nearest e-mail system.

Former clinic patients and workers responded emotionally when they learned of the arrest. Debbie Challender led the charge. "I want you to bring me this news about Asch," she told a reporter. "They got away scot free, and we're left to deal with it all." Debra Krahel commented: "They stole these families' genetic blueprints, and we may never know how much damage was done as a result. But this furthers my faith in the system." Others delighted in the fact that Balmaceda's arrest made it seem more likely that Asch would be returned to the United States as well. "Asch is going to mess up, too. It's just a matter of time," said one former patient. "That makes me feel better that he'll be directly responsible, so he's not in a different country, scot free. He might be able to see some of the pain that he's caused."[23]

Stone, who was visiting his family in Santiago at the time of Balmaceda's arrest, said: "I'm sorry for him, but he needs to be responsible. I believe that he should return and face justice."[24]

The Buenos Aires police jailed Balmaceda as the extradition process got under way. The judge who heard the case, however, released him on ten thousand dollars bail with orders not to leave Argentina. It was said that it might take up to ten months before a decision on the extradition request was rendered. But Balmaceda failed to appear at the scheduled February 9th court hearing in Buenos Aires—and, indeed, Stone by coincidence spotted him about this time browsing in a Santiago shopping mall. The American authorities, who had objected to the bail arrangement, said that they were disappointed with the judge's decision; they had "asked the Argentine authorities to act urgently and to rearrest and detain this notorious fugitive," according to Thom Mrozek, speaking for the U.S. Attorney's office in Los Angeles.[25]

For his part, Asch was ambivalent and yet supportive of Balmaceda's flight to freedom: "I feel that it's a mistake," he said in a telephone interview. "I think he did the wrong thing, but I'm glad that he did it." Asch indicated that he believes that had Balmeceda remained in Argentina he would not have been extradited.[26]

On February 13 a Chilean television news program as well as *El Mercurio*, a Santiago daily, presented interviews with Balmaceda. He maintained that he had fled because it would have been impossible to defend himself satisfactorily in Argentina, though he would be willing to mount a defense in the United States or Chile, a somewhat curious response since the extradition would have forced him to deal with the American charges. "As a Chilean citizen," Balmaceda explained, "I have the right to argue the basis of the charge against me. As for in Argentina, I did not have the right because only the form of the charges could be disputed. I am innocent and the accusations are absolutely artificial."[27] He said of the arrest: "I went to Buenos Aires to negotiate a budget for an educational project and found myself facing an arrest warrant solicited by the U.S. for the 1996 accusations. According to these [accusations] I hadn't declared all of my income sources for 1991 or 1992. The rest are of postal fraud. I plead my total innocence of these two accusations."[28]

Balmaceda defends his decision to flee Argentina to avoid facing the charges:

On the apparent contradiction of saying I would confront the courts in the USA and not stay in Argentina, it would have been like an African American expecting a fair trial in Mississipi in the 1940s. I think what has been uncovered in Argentina in terms of corruption, at the judicial and political levels, demonstrates that I was right in leaving. I reinitiated contacts with the U.S. attorney, but after paying another $16,000 in attorney's fees, I was nowhere . . . so your justice comes at a price that is very

difficult to afford. To ignore the economics of the American justice system is to be naïve or purposely cynical.[29]

At the same time, Balmaceda took this opportunity to try to refute
charges of unconsented egg and embryo transfers:

> I have not been accused of the illegal use of oocytes. It is all
> political and economic pressure on behalf of the administrative
> staff at the university. They are to blame for all that happened.
> These accusations surfaced in 1991 and they exaggerated them.
> Now they need to cover their backs by criminalizing and portray-
> ing doctors as monsters, including my ex-associate Sergio Stone,
> who never even did in vitro fertilization.[30]

The newspaper interview with Balmaceda was headlined "En Chile
Tengo Posibilidad de Defender Mis Derecho"—"In Chile I Have the Possibility to Defend My Rights." Balmaceda labeled the charges against him
a "grotesque fabrication that is insane and ridiculous" and followed this
with a local idiom to characterize the web that had entrapped him and
Sergio Stone: "Hicieron un saco de todos nosotros," which translates as
"They made a single bag of all of us."[31]

C H A P T E R

Sergio Stone, M.D.

■ The story of Dr. Sergio Stone in many important regards stands altogether apart from that of his colleagues, Ricardo Asch and José Balmaceda. Yet Stone's fate became tightly interwoven with theirs because what they were alleged to have done came to be held against him both subtly and in sledgehammer fashion. Stone remained in the United States after Asch and Balmaceda left; by default he emerged as the focus of the university administrators and the federal prosecutors who had no one left to target.

Balmaceda, interviewed in Chile, would seek to explain why he had fled the United States and Stone had remained. "He is an American citizen, his family is there, and he is later in his career. I had more to lose. I have two children in the States and two children here. I have more of my career left in my future and I wanted to continue practicing."[1]

Stone found himself in a nightmare. If certain things he had done were dissected in a criminal proceeding, they could look bad. It did not matter that the things Stone was accused of doing virtually never become the object of judicial process. If they did, the screams of outrage from a horde of powerful physicians would soon put an end to such stuff.

The Stone case offers a look into the virtually unchecked power of a prosecutor, acting within his rights, to bring to his knees a defendant who would not have attracted any attention, except perhaps for a reprimand, for acts that reasonable evidence shows are commonplace. Some may recall that the federal government sent Al Capone to prison for income tax evasion because it could not muster adequate evidence of the much more heinous offenses that he had committed. The Stone case differs in the sense that the defendant had not been engaged in more serious crimes; but it similarly demonstrates how a human being can get caught, like Kafka's insect, in a web spun from threads of others' wrongdoing.

Stone was like a driver exceeding the speed limit who is pulled over by the police while others, going at least as fast, are ignored. Stone was not chosen randomly. He was picked primarily—some would say exclusively—because of what others had done and the glare of publicity that had been focused on the unconsented egg transfers.

In conversation, Stone is polite, soft-spoken, and articulate. He takes pride in having intellectual interests that extend beyond his professional concerns. He is not an easy person to describe; everybody we asked who knew him at least reasonably well was unable to describe his appearance and invariably fell back on portrayals of his personality and character. Stone is about five foot eleven, he tends to wear his brown hair short, his eyes are brown, and he dresses impeccably.

Sergio Cereceda Stone was born in the seaport city of Valparaiso, Chile, on April 16, 1942. His surname is from his English great-grandfather, who had come to Chile to work in shipping. The great-grandfather's fortunes faltered when the completion of the Panama Canal diverted sea traffic from Valparaiso. Stone's grandfather, Robert William Stone, became an admiral in the Chilean navy and died in 1957. Stone's father, also Sergio, never learned English. He practiced law and later served as one of the country's twenty appellate court judges, and so the family moved to the capital city of Santiago. Stone's mother, Luz, was a housewife. Her father was the first chancellor of Santa Maria, a Valparaiso university. Both of his parents, now in their late eighties, live in Chile. A brother, Lionel, who is two years younger than Sergio, practices law there.

Stone attended the Collegio San Ignatius, a Jesuit elementary and high school in Santiago, for ten years. He finished in the upper 10 percent of his class, but says now that he could have done better had he not been distracted from his schoolwork by a passion for reading history and other extracurricular subjects. He adds, as if with a sense of pride, that he did not engage in any school athletics.

Stone was subsequently educated at the University of Chile in a program that combined college and medical school courses. He then completed his residency in ob/gyn at the University of Chile Medical School. He believes that his interest in gynecology was fueled by the example of an uncle, Hernán Cereceda. Cereceda had a practice that occupied an entire floor of a private hospital. He was, Stone observes, "recognized by everybody in Santiago." His parents often told Stone that at the age of five he had been asked what he intended to do when he grew up, and had said that he wanted to be a gynecologist.

In 1969 Stone received a grant from the Ford Foundation to do advanced work in what today is called human reproduction, but then was labeled endocrinology; this was before the development of assisted reproduction techniques. Stone practiced and studied at the University of Southern California in Los Angeles and then accepted a faculty position at the Louisiana State University Medical School in New Orleans, working at Charity Hospital.

He joined the UCI medical school faculty in 1978, and he and his wife, Angelica, bought a house in a posh Villa Park neighborhood, where they raised three children: Sergio, who is a lawyer; Christian, who is a physician; and Angelica, who teaches Spanish literature at the University of Arizona in Tucson. Stone exulted in his job. "I used to tell my wife, I'm doing something I like so much, and then on top of that at the end of the month I get paid." He also adapted to his new homeland. Asked whether he dreams in Spanish or English, he smiles. "English," he says, then adds, "but with a heavy accent."

At the Center for Reproductive Health Stone specialized in uterine surgery and in administering the hormonal treatment needed to induce ovulation. He was involved only in the early aspects of the fertility procedures. He would maintain, and there have been no contradictions of his position, that he was not involved in any of the unconsented egg and embryo procedures. He grants that he probably should have been more alert to what was going on, though, in his words, "The allegations were so ridiculous. How could I believe that eggs were being used without patients' consent?"

Stone became civilly liable for outstanding fertility clinic financial debts and fines because he was one of the three partners legally in charge of the clinic. As the only partner available, he would also become the scapegoat for what had gone wrong. One medical school faculty member has quoted C. P. Snow's observation: "University politics at their worst can be among the most ferocious and duplicitous of any organization." The manner in which Mary Piccione, Herb Spiwak, and Stone were dealt with provides strong evidence of the accuracy of this appraisal.

Stone was arrested on April 25, 1996, and taken to court in hand-cuffs for his arraignment. The federal prosecutors fought the granting of bail, maintaining that Stone was likely to flee the country, as had his two partners. The prosecutors backed their position by noting that he recently had sent about half a million dollars to a Chilean relative. The judge demanded that $475,000 of that amount be returned so that Stone could use it to settle any civil suit judgments that might be entered against him. After Stone had spent twelve days in the Santa Ana deten-tion facility, bail was set at $3 million; the sum was covered by some of his friends who put their houses up as guarantees that he would appear for trial. Stone was placed on house arrest before trial, with an electronic bracelet strapped to his left ankle. The bracelet, about the size of a com-puter mouse, transmitted impulses that could alert federal officials to Stone's movements.

Stone was tried in the federal courthouse in Santa Ana in September 1997, accused of mail fraud in the process of bilking insurance compa-nies and conspiracy to evade income tax payments.[2] The amount origi-nally said to have been gained by the insurance fraud was set at $66,000, but by trial time it had been reduced to $33,000.

Thomas H. Bienert Jr., the lead Assistant U.S. Attorney in the Stone prosecution, is a person you would want to have on your side if ever you were involved in a legal controversy. He is smart, articulate, and forceful. During our two-hour interview with him, first in his office and then in a nearby restaurant, he was quick on the draw, impressively skilled at taking a position, arguable though it might be, and pushing it relentlessly, while intelligently sweeping aside other possible interpretations. He was, throughout, friendly and thoughtful, and very much in command of our conversation.

Bienert, now in private practice with an office overlooking the ocean at Capistrano Beach, says that the U.S. Attorney could hardly ignore the allegations of clinic wrongdoing that were brought out by the media, particularly since medical insurance fraud was a high priority of the Attorney General. The case became a significant showcase endeavor, but only because the media had turned the spotlight so relentlessly on the egg misappropriation. Had a different doctor in the community been charged with a billing fraud, the story likely would have rated a few paragraphs on an inside page at most. Rather than agreeing that Stone, to his misfortune, had been prosecuted because of the egg theft accusations, Bienert insisted that Stone gained some points at trial because he specifically was said not to have been involved in any alleged theft.

Since he now defends persons accused of white-collar crime, we asked Bienert what he would have done had Stone been his client. He would have told Stone, he said, what he believed his chances of winning in a trial were, and would have strongly advised him to consider a plea bargain and thereby avoid the cost and publicity of a trial. Speaking as a prosecutor, he said, "We would have worked this out with the guy because I believe that a low-profile plea with a sentence of probation would have been an appropriate resolution and saved everyone, particularly Dr. Stone, the difficulties of a trial."[3]

The problem here, however, is that the prosecutor was not willing to reduce the charge to a misdemeanor from a felony, and so if Stone had pleaded, he would have been in precisely the same situation that he was in at the end of the trial—and without the on-record exculpating evidence. Stone's lawyer believes that the U.S. Attorney's office might have bargained the charge down had Stone been willing to turn state's evidence, testifying against Asch and Balmaceda. But Stone and his advisors strenuously maintain that he had neither the information nor the records that would have allowed him to do this, even if he had been willing to cooperate with the authorities.

Bienert did not see the Stone case through to its end. He left California to work in Washington with the Kenneth Starr team investigating President Clinton, and was replaced by Debora Rodriqeuz. He was thus not in a position to comment on the jury's verdict or the appellate issues that are discussed later in this chapter.

The outcome of the case had several quirky aspects. On October 30, 1997, the six-man, six-women jury, after deliberating for sixteen hours over four days, unanimously returned a verdict of guilty of mail fraud, but not guilty of income tax evasion.

One of the jurors, Linda Schultz of Santa Ana, sent a note to the judge, late in the panel's deliberations, seeking guidance on whether they could decide for themselves "if the law is being applied justly or unjustly in this case"[4] He replied that they must apply the law as he had instructed them to. Within half an hour those holding out for a not guilty verdict had fallen into line with the majority. Seven months later, when she was part of a protest group demanding that jurors be informed that they can disregard laws that they believe are wrong, Schultz would tell a newspaper reporter that one of the reasons she had gone along with the judge's command was that a male juror had told her that if she did not do so she herself would be put in jail.[5]

Schultz and her fellow jurors, despite the judge's instruction, had the perfect right, without fear of any retaliation, to decide the case in any manner that they thought acceptable. Such an approach, called jury nullification, has a long and honorable tradition. But she and perhaps some of the other jurors felt intimidated. Holdout jurors believed that Stone was not aware that he was doing anything wrong; they said that it was only because the judge maintained that Stone's state of mind was not relevant that they very reluctantly joined in the verdict of guilt on the mail fraud charges.

The most notable early case of jury nullification took place in England in 1670 when William Penn and William Mead were acquitted by a jury of the charge of seditious preaching. The judge fined the jurors for their verdict and imprisoned those who failed to pay the fine. Later Sir John Vaughn ruled that judges cannot punish jurors for their decisions.[6] The nullification doctrine, however, was sidelined by a judiciary determined to retain its control over the legal interpretation of events tried before it. Supreme Court Justice John Harlan in *Sparf v. United States* in 1895 confirmed the reigning doctrine that juries may determine fact but must follow the law as enunciated by the judge.[7] Two exceptions exist, Indiana and Maryland.[8] Had Sergio Stone been tried in

Maryland, the judge would have been obliged to instruct the jury with the following words:

> Members of the Jury, this is a criminal case and under the Constitution and the laws of the state of Maryland in a criminal case the jury are the judges of the law as well as of the facts in the case. So that whatever I tell you about the law while it is intended to be helpful to you in reaching a just and proper verdict in the case, it is not binding upon you as a members of the jury and you may accept or reject it. And you may apply the law as you apprehend it to be in the case.[9]

Except for the final sentence of the instruction, with its seeming aim to negate slightly what was said earlier, Maryland jurors are being told to do what they feel is just. Even Justic Byron White, while carefully avoiding the word "nullification," wrote that "when jurors differ with the result at which the judge would have arrived, it is usually because they are serving some of the very purposes for which they were created and for which they are employed."[10]

Several of the women on the panel came up to Stone in tears after the verdict was delivered, apologized, hugged him, and told him that they had voted for guilt only because they felt that the instructions of the judge had left them no other choice. "Thank you very much," Stone told a sobbing juror. "You don't have to cry." "I've been crying all week, doctor," she answered.[11]

The judge's instruction had stressed that the jurors could not consider university policy but must conclude that Stone committed fraud if he signed incorrect insurance forms that were sent through the mails. Angelita Galvan-Freeman, a nurse who had worked with Stone and attended the entire trial, later wrote a newspaper op-ed piece in which she said that the jurors with whom she spoke did not believe that Stone had committed a crime but felt "hemmed in" by the judge's instructions. One juror told her that he and several other members of the panel had gone to their places of worship "to reflect on their decision . . . because they were so troubled by the weight of the task."[12] The alternative juror told Stone that, had he been on the panel, there never would have been a guilty verdict. But there probably would not have been a not-guilty verdict, either. One juror, Liam Groener, had no doubts of Stone's guilt as charged: "If a good friend gave me the story [Stone] gave on putting down assistant surgeons who were not present, that's fraud."[13]

Judge Taylor sent us an e-mail in which he wrote that in his view Stone had received a fair trial and that the verdict was supported by the evidence. He noted that "jurors are bound by their sworn oath to follow the judge's instructions on the law whether they agree with them or not. A knowing violation of that oath could submit the jurors to various forms of liability."[14] The Lexis-Nexis database produces a directly contrary view, though it is applicable only to the District of Columbia circuit: "[The jury] has an unreviewable and irreversible power to acquit in disregard of the instructions on the law given by the trial judge."[15] More generally, it is difficult to envision a judge publicly holding a juror liable for failing to follow his or her instructions.

What took place in the jury room might reasonably have provided Stone with grounds for a successful appeal, especially since the ninth circuit federal appellate judges, to whom the case would have gone, have the strongest pro-defendant reputation of any bench in the nation. But Stone says that he and his lawyer were told by the prosecutor that, should he choose to appeal, they would put him in prison on the ground that he was an escape risk. Both Asch and Balmaceda had fled the country, and it would be argued that Stone might do the same thing. The judge declared, as Stone recalls, "You belong to a group of people who know how to get papers," a remark that he finds absurd and biased.

Stone also was told by the prosecutor that an appeal would be protracted—that it would take about two years, that it would be extremely costly, and that if he lost the prosecutor would press for imprisonment. If Stone agreed not to appeal, the prosecutor said that he would not request the maximum sixty-three-month sentence. To us, the demand that a defendant surrender his right to appeal in return for an offer of leniency represents an unconscionable exercise of prosecutorial power.

Stone elected to deal. In mid-May of 1998 he was sentenced to a year of home probation, three years regular probation, and a fine of $71,000. Judge Taylor cut to the core of the scapegoating issue when he announced to the packed courtroom, "Without the egg scandal we'd have an empty courtroom." Taylor rejected the prosecutor's demand for a six-month jail sentence. "This sentence in this case," Taylor pronounced, "has nothing to do with the egg scandal. The government has no evidence tying Dr. Stone to the egg scandal." The judge's emphasis here echoed a long line of similar observations, including that of Asch and Balmaceda, who had said that Stone had "zero responsibility" for possible "errors" in egg transfers. As a scapegoat, Stone fit snugly into the definition offered by the ethicist Gregory Mellema:

> What normally is meant when someone is described as a scape-goat is that the person is being blamed for something more than he or she deserves and that some blame could or should in all fairness be directed at others. In the realm of criminal justice, scapegoats are commonly identified as those who have been assigned penalties out of their proportion to their involvement in a crime, where the others involved cannot be prosecuted or are not assigned penalties to the extent that they deserve . . . [though] there usually is some truth to the various claims that a particular person is to blame for some event.[16]

The judge's remarks seem to reflect his awareness and, perhaps, his concern that the case against Stone had been dictated by the egg scandal. This was, of course, beyond the judge's purview: he could deal only with those things presented to him. For his part, Stone expressed satisfaction with the judge's agreement that he was not part of the fertility clinic scandal. After he was sentenced, he declared, "The actions I did, I did not know they were criminal." Ignorance of the law, of course, is rarely an adequate excuse. Courts are wont to consider whether a defendant reasonably should have been aware that what he did was illegal: in a well-known case the U.S. Supreme Court overturned the conviction of Virginia Lambert, an ex-felon, for having driven through Beverly Hills without having registered in Beverly Hills as a once-convicted criminal. Lambert insisted, and the court agreed, that her ignorance of the city ordinance was reasonable and legally excusable.[17]

Throughout Stone's legal battles, the question of who should pay his legal fees was a bone of contention. The university said that the doctors had acted outside the scope of their employment contract. In March 1996 a superior court judge had ordered the university to pay defense costs for Stone and Balmaceda in one case because the patient had been treated only by Asch. But the decision was reversed on appeal because of Stone's alleged "lack of cooperation" with university officials.[18]

The university's unwillingness to pay the litigation costs and its positioning itself in an adversarial role sent waves of concern through the medical school faculty. A memorandum signed by thirty-nine doctors who identified themselves as the "Academic Friends of Sergio Stone" declared that the university's action "should sound an alarm for many medical faculty." The denial of legal assistance to Stone was said to signal that "if it can happen to anyone, it can happen to everyone."

The Friends of Sergio Stone also attempted to line up medical school faculty support for Stone by calling a special faculty meeting on July 6, 1998, in the auditorium of the main medical facility, with a television hookup to faculty working in the nearby Orange County Medical Center. The atmosphere of the meeting can best be described as nasty. The chair, Gerald Weinstein, a dermatologist, had voting senate members take front seats and peremptorily and roughly challenged several Stone supporters' right to be present, finally ordering them from the room. (We were both present, though apparently unnoticed.)

The proceedings were singularly and alarmingly one-sided. A long-retired medical school dean, perhaps the faculty member most conversant with rules of procedure, alleged that the university had paid little attention to its own bylaws in dealing with Stone. Thereafter, a university attorney, whose performance in the handling of the fertility clinic case could at best be regarded as controversial, scornfully opposed the proposal that the assembled faculty vote to support Stone. Among other things, he incorrectly tied Stone to the egg issues. The medical school dean, generally regarded as a preeminently decent man, argued that the school would look bad in the eyes of national funding agencies if it did not take action against Stone, that it would appear to be condoning wrongdoing. Several faculty members noted that an internal auditor had reported that Stone's billing practices were the norm for the medical school, a position vehemently denied by the head of the department of obstetrics and gynecology. Finally, Sidney Golub, now back on the medical school faculty after having been replaced as executive vice chancellor by the new chancellor, Ralph J. Cicerone, a fifty-four-year-old geophysicist, argued forcefully against support for Stone. Inasmuch as Golub had played a leading role in structuring and moving forward with the case, it might have been more appropriate for him to sit out this debate. When Golub had resigned his administrative post, a newspaper story had observed that "critics said that he sometimes delivered contradictory information" about the clinic scandal.[19]

In the end, the faculty vote, by a considerable majority, was to table the motion to support Stone.

Several weeks later, a group of forty-one faculty members, almost entirely medical school professors, circulated a memorandum to the medical school faculty. It noted that they were "greatly distressed" by what had gone on during the faculty meeting. It pointed out that before their motion was even seconded, the chair had permitted "over an hour long de facto filibuster by the Administration and its lawyer that recited many previously made unverified, or already proven incorrect charges against a professor." These presentations, the memorandum maintained, "were minimally if at all pertinent to the Resolutions and resulted in an atmosphere that precluded rational discussions and decisions." It observed that all this occurred without Stone, "the accused," being present. The signatories hoped for "a more even-handed atmosphere" in which their position might be considered by the faculty.[20]

Later, in a January 4, 1999, memorandum, the Friends of Sergio Stone pointed out that the final report of a five-doctor medical school inquiry board that had examined Stone's case for more than a year concluded that nothing that he had done justified removing him from full staff privileges at the hospital or modifying his status there. The school bylaws required that the accused receive a copy of the findings, but the medical school's executive board labeled it an "interim report," on the ground that new material had surfaced since it was completed. As an interim report, its contents were not disclosed to Stone, and he was thus prevented from using it in his defense.

The Friends of Sergio Stone not only offered professional support, but often expressed strong personal sentiments regarding Stone's character and integrity. But these attitudes were not universally shared. For many persons, Stone's most memorable trait was a quick and explosive temper. One medical school staffer, then new on the job, cannot forget an incident when Stone tripped on an uneven section in the clinic's entryway. He yelled mightily, she recalls, and within a few hours the flooring was repaired. The lesson she learned, she says, was that that's the way you get things done around here. She also remembers the common anguished cry uttered by Stone when things went awry: "I am surrounded by incompetence" (though she has difficulty duplicating his accent, which, she says, made the remark so memorable). A friend and colleague of Stone used other words to summarize the same issue: "Sergio," he says with a hint of a wry smile, "could be a bit of a terror." Another medical colleague emphasizes that Stone calmed down quickly and never held a grudge. She calls Stone a perfectionist and remembers with amusement his usual remark to those around him when he was absorbed in microscopic surgery: "Don't move, don't breathe, and don't help me!"[21]

There are some vitriolic contributions scattered among the strongly supportive messages from persons who made their feelings known on Stone's Web page. There is, for instance, this bitter, unsigned comment: "Now you know what it feels like to be backed into a corner with nobody. It feels just like your patients felt when you herded us like cattle into a room for 2 hours with full bellies for an ultrasound and gave us nothing but your self-serving God complex. May you rot in jail."

Apparently uncertain that the whole message had been conveyed through cyberspace, the writer resent the final sentence, with an addition: "May you rot in jail for the rest of your life."

Stone responded:

I am sure you are disappointed that I will not "rot in jail." I feel sorry for all the anger and frustration that your messages reveal. Without the grace of the Lord, that allows us to understand the sorrows of our lives, we are always bitter, without hope and unhappy. I pray that you can see life in a different light, enjoying the wonders that God gives us every day, in his mercy and love for us.

Stone received no response.

Others offered Stone their best wishes and support. "My prayers are with you," one friend wrote. "My respect for you has never been stronger," wrote a stranger. A couple noted they had Stone to thank for their "two beautiful daughters" and that their "prayers go out to you and your family." Jeff Deutsch pitched in with the statement that he had worked at UCIMC for several years and that he believed "Dr. Stone's character to be beyond reproach." He wished him well. One medical doctor offered a comment in accord with our own judgment of the Stone criminal case: "Greetings from an old friend. There is not a doctor, clinic or hospital in this country that could not be put in the same position as yours. Anytime a federal prosecutor wants to get one of us he can. My brother is a federal prosecutor so I know this to be true."

There is some truth in what Deutsch said. In 1988, for instance, Congress passed the Citizens Protection Act, which decreed that federal prosecutors must adhere to state rules and those of the local federal court in which they work. The measure was spearheaded by Congressman Joseph McDade. McDade had been indicted in 1988 by a grand jury on five counts of bribery-related offenses involving campaign contributions. He claimed that federal investigators had harassed and hounded him and "had turned his life into a living nightmare." McDade testified to a congressional committee that he had firsthand experience with the "overzealousness and excessiveness of federal prosecutors," and that "the power of prosecutors is tremendous and the problem of misconduct is serious."[22]

Stone's felony conviction automatically led the state licensing board to review his case and, in the end, it chose a relatively light punishment. Stone's license to practice medicine was revoked, but the revocation was stayed for three years, during which time Stone would be on probationary status. Conditions imposed by the board were that Stone take a course in ethics and reimburse the State for the seven thousand dollars that its investigation had cost. The state medical board, in its ruling, felt compelled to take a sideswipe at the university. Stone's conduct, it noted, "did not take place in a vacuum. Rather it took place in an academic milieu in which a practice developed to obtain reimbursement for services performed by residents and interns." The medical authorities thought that Stone had thoroughly learned his lesson and that he "would prepare future operating reports accurately regardless of medical center practice or policy."[23]

This action was in line with common licensing board practice, in which a strong distinction typically is drawn between fiscal waywardness and medical ineptitude. Medical boards across the nation generally assume that when the work is sound, revoking the license of healers, with their long and expensive training, has no social benefit. Fiscal waywardness can be dealt with by monetary and symbolic kinds of punishments. For Stone, the victory was Pyrrhic. Besides what he said was his tortured mental state, he found that his felony conviction kept him from obtaining malpractice insurance, without which he could not work. He did some volunteer work at a free clinic, but was nervous that his clients, often poor women who had no previous prenatal diagnoses or care, and who in some cases had long histories of drug use, would file a suit against him if they had a stillbirth or other difficulties that they were, statistically, more susceptible to than other expectant mothers.

Meanwhile, some five years after the original allegations against the fertility clinic physicians had surfaced, Stone remained on the UCI payroll, receiving his basic faculty salary, which at $88,000 annually constituted a small fraction of the $450,000 that he was said to earn ordinarily.[24] All told, Stone had received more than $350,000 while on leave, including the periods when he was in jail and under house arrest.

This situation undoubtedly prompted the university to terminate Stone on March 15, 2000, though a tenured professor had never been fired during the institution's thirty-five years of existence. The 44,000-member American Association of University Professors notes that on average no more than a dozen tenured professors are terminated nationally in any given year.

Very early, Stone had been barred from appearing on university property, a ruling that kept him from attending his son's graduation from the medical school. Chancellor Wilkening sent a petition to the UCI Committee on Privilege and Tenure (CPT) on September 22, 1995, seeking Stone's dismissal. That committee, made up of a dozen members of the Academic Senate who were elected by the faculty for three-year terms, conducts hearings on charges of faculty misconduct. The charges leveled against Stone were: (1) failure to cooperate with the investigation; (2) noncompliance with the Clinical Compensation plan; (3) retaliation against an employee; and (4) research misconduct.

Four months later, on the basis of a subcommittee inquiry, the CPT decreed that there appeared to be "probable cause" to proceed to a full-scale adjudication—but on only one of the charges: research misconduct. The CPT pointed out that the internal auditors had described Stone as extremely cooperative and forthcoming; that while Asch was unwilling to turn over records, Stone did not have possession of much of the information being sought: the records were Asch's patients'. The committee also found insufficient evidence to support the administration's claim that Stone had failed to meet his obligations to the clinical compensation program, and it concluded that it was unclear whether he had any financial control at the Center for Reproductive Health.

Details of the charge of Jane Frederick's prescribing hMG Massone indicate the sometimes careless and high-handed manner in which allegations were made. Asch, it turned out, was apparently the only doctor at the clinic who had prescribed the drug. Executive Vice Chancellor Golub also had charged Stone with illegally prescribing hMG Massone because two patient charts were marked hMG and signed by Stone. After the CPT found that there was no probable cause to proceed with that charge, Golub wrote to the committee that he found its conclusion "troubling" and complained that the committee "once again appears to have applied a standard much higher than probable cause." The committee was annoyed; its chair, who had legal training, wrote back that it could find "no merit" in Golub's stand, and he added that the members were "perplexed" by his reference to their "once again" having used an incorrect standard: they had not done so now, they responded, and were unaware of any previous instance in which they might have done so. Nonetheless, the committee decided, on reflection, to add all the charges leveled by the chancellor against Stone—not only the one pertaining to research misconduct.

The case languished for three years after the administration failed to proceed on the 1995 allegations because its investigation had not yet been completed. Finally, in October and November 1998, a four-member Hearing Board of the CPT opened what turned out to be thirteen days of consideration of the Stone case. It listened to twenty-six witnesses and collected some two thousand pages of documents, including briefs from some of the parties involved. The hearings were chaired by William Thompson of the Department of Criminology, Law and Society. Thompson had been one of the twelve members of the legal defense team in the O. J. Simpson trial. (He once invited O. J. Simpson to speak in one of his classes.)

The hearing board of the university Committee on Privilege and Tenure included Richard Friedenberg, a retired radiology professor from the medical school, Terence Parsons, a philosopher, and Kenneth Pomeranz from the history department. This is what the hearing board concluded in regard to each of the four allegations against Stone.

(1) The Felony Conviction

The code of conduct at the University of California, Irvine, calls for the dismissal of any person involved in the "commission of a criminal act which has led to a conviction in a court of law and which clearly demonstrates unfitness to continue as a member of the faculty." One presumes convictions on most misdemeanors would not meet this standard; nor would, probably, felony drunk driving and, at least in calm political times, acts such as picketing illegally at an abortion clinic or refusing an order to disperse during a rally against trade relations with China. In short, the criminal conviction itself only flags the possibility of a punitive university response.

Stone had been convicted on the basis of nine postoperative notes that he dictated in which he listed Asch, Balmaceda, or Frederick as the assisting surgeon. Thereafter, bills based on these notes were submitted to insurance companies. Nurses' records, however, indicated that the assisting surgeons were not in the room throughout the operations, if they were there at all, and that in three instances they were not even in California.

Stone's defense was twofold. First, he denied any criminal intent (that is, mens rea). What he did, he maintained, was common practice at the medical school as he understood it. Second, he pointed out that the nine surgeries were complicated laparoscopic procedures (incisions into the abdominal wall that require a pair of surgeons to operate the scope). Stone's assistance came from fourth-year medical residents. Stone insisted that the residents were supervised by senior staff members who either came into the surgery room to check on whether all was going well or who were available nearby should their expertise be required. Stone's testimony was backed by Joe Gallegos, a scrub nurse. The faculty hearing board said that it found Gallegos's testimony "credible."

Stone denied that any foreign residents took part in the surgeries; their presence was merely as observers. He also claimed that the cases in which the stipulated senior doctors could not have been present in any capacity were the product of his faulty memory or his tendency to write in the name of the physician who usually supervised a particular resident. He said that in his mind this was not an important matter because it was a group practice.

The faculty hearing board report pointed out that the criminal conviction had been based on the judge's instruction that all that the government was required to prove was that the insurance companies had been misled, not that Stone had intended to mislead them or that he had known that what he was doing was illegal, though it was necessary that he had been aware that the statements on the insurance forms were false. Under the judge's instructions, an innocent but mistaken belief that the practice was entitled to the payments, when coupled with a deceptive act to obtain payments, was sufficient for a felony conviction. This then had a considerable element of strict liability, a type of offense often disparaged by law professors because it does not require proof of wrongful intent.[25] The board's conclusion on this point favored Stone:

> While it may appear to be splitting hairs, these subtle distinctions are vital to appreciating the scope and gravity of Professor Stone's crimes. In particular, it is important to understand that the jury could have convicted Professor Stone of a felony without necessarily finding that he intended to break the law. Indeed, the judge specifically instructed the jury that the government was not required to prove that Professor Stone knew that his actions were unlawful.[26]

Stone's conviction, it was emphasized, could have occurred even if the jurors believed that Stone held "an honest but mistaken" belief that the clinic was entitled to the payments for the assistant surgeons. Faculty members who testified before the university hearing board took contradictory positions regarding the propriety of billing for attending physicians not physically present throughout the procedure, but it was noted that the nation's medical schools as a group had recently gone to court to seek a ruling that the Medicare position disallowing the practice was unreasonable.

The board concluded on this first point that Stone's misconduct was not of the magnitude or seriousness that one typically associates with a felony: "We find it more plausible that Professor Stone was simply careless and cavalier about billing than that he intended to perpetrate a fraudulent criminal scheme. We do not believe that his crime was the product of an evil or malevolent character. It was more akin to an error in administrative judgment. In our view it should be treated as such."

There was a further observation that the committee members were convinced that Professor Stone had learned his lesson; there was no likelihood that such things would happen again.

(2) Failure to Comply with Compensation Plan
   The hearing board focused a good deal of its attention on the charge that Stone and his clinic partners were implicated in a scheme to defraud the university of earnings that it was entitled to share, in accord with a stipulated formula. The hearing board came down very hard on this issue—but largely on Stone's side. It all but directly accused medical school personnel of gross negligence in failing to inform the state auditor of the details of the financial arrangements that had been made with Stone and his colleagues, which thereby triggered recurringly inaccurate estimates by the auditors of what was owed.
   The medical school's financial dealings with private practices that come under its wing, such as the Center for Reproductive Health, often are arcane. The fertility clinic partners from 1991 to 1994 had been exempted from following the standard compensation program. The exemption was based, the dean noted, on the unique nature of the CRH practice, its importance for the teaching mission of the school, and the substantial revenues it generated for the hospital. The CRH nonetheless was required to adhere to certain accounting arrangements and to contribute a portion of the doctors' income to the so-called Dean's Tax, to the Department Assessment fund, and to the Practice Development Assessment.
   In the wake of the egg scandals and Asch's and Balmaceda's flights from the country, a medical school committee had issued a report that found the clinic not to have complied with the compensation program. Both the dean and the chancellor endorsed the report. Two years later, in May 1998, the California State Auditor issued a damning report charging that the partners had falsely listed revenues and, as a consequence, had underpaid assessments. The state audit concluded that from 1992 through 1994 the three doctors had failed to report revenues of $7,830,000, which led them to underpay their assessment by $1,470,000. It also said that the university had not received $216,379, the fee on 1993 revenues that had been reported. The auditor added that these failures constituted criminal behavior and maintained that her findings "highlight the rather lax administration that existed at UCI with respect to its agreements with physicians who work at the univer-

sity, so lax that millions of dollars are owed to the university by just these three physicians." These allegations, the CPT committee believed, were "the most dramatic and disturbing" of the charges against Stone and his partners.

But there was a great deal more than initially appeared in these claims. The faculty hearing board noted that the partnership arrangement at CRH provided Asch and Balmaceda with 40 percent of the clinic earnings, though other income of the group was to be split into three equal portions. The hearing board, saying that there was no evidence to support Stone's contention that $112,884 of the $216,379 amount due from 1993 earnings already had been paid, recommended that he pay his usual share of that amount before he would be allowed to resume his faculty duties.

Thereafter, the hearing board pulled few punches in its castigation of the other elements of the auditor's report, though it emphasized that the fault lay not with her but with those who had not provided her with accurate information: "The Hearing Board," its report stated, "concluded that the State Auditor's report was based on incorrect information and should be disregarded." The report was labeled "highly misleading" because the auditor did not understand how UCI calculated gross professional income in its arrangement with the fertility clinic.

Testimony from UCI administrators, the board stated, had established "beyond any doubt" that the state auditor had failed to take account of the fiscal rules pertaining to CRH. "The agreement should have been reported to the state auditor, but was not." The hearing board, its irritation growing, noted that there were any number of meetings in which the auditors could have been told truthfully of the financial arrangements between the parties. "The reasons for this critical and unfortunate communication are not readily apparent to the Hearing Board," the report stated, "and [are] beyond the scope of our inquiry. But the chancellor might well wish to investigate this issue."

Not only did the chancellor apparently not wish to look into the issue, but the fiscal fiasco continued unmended. On becoming aware of misconceptions that underlay the initial report, the state auditor tried again, and this time determined that the so-called underreporting amounted to $4.9 million, not $7.8 million. But the hearing board pronounced this new calculation flawed as well because it did not take into account the billing-based system for determining gross professional income that the university had agreed to let the clinic use. The auditor, when she had done the follow-up report, was still in the dark about this and so produced "a fatal flaw" in the revised calculation. What an accurate appraisal might find, taking the specifics of the arrangement into account, could not be determined by the faculty committee because the U.S. Attorney's Office had seized all the relevant papers and apparently was not willing to part with them.

The hearing board therefore determined that the second charge against Stone was unfounded, and noted that it might have been deliberately misleading. It concluded:

> The administration's claim that there was underreporting of income in 1992–1994 has not been proven to the satisfaction of the Hearing Board. . . . [It] finds both sets of calculations to be speculative and therefore unreliable. It is by no means clear whether a careful review of the 1992–1994 billing records would show any underreporting. However, the burden of proof in this matter rests on the administration. That burden has not been met.

The matter did not end there. The university continued to publicize the auditor's reports that, at least where the hearing board was concerned, had been found to be faulty. Thompson had specifically called the matter to the attention of the counsel for the University of California system, who responded by saying that he would bring it to the attention of his clients, the university administrators.

Nothing happened. "We are unaware what steps, if any, [the university counsel] took to bring the problems of the State Auditor's report to the attention of relevant university officials," the CPT group noted. In mid-July 1999, the university issued a press release announcing plans to sue the CRH doctors. The press release stated that the amount owed was $1.7 million, a statement that the hearing board found irresponsible in view of its own uncontested conclusions. The hearing board notified those UCI officials named in the news story about their error and recommended that the chancellor "consider carefully whether additional actions are necessary to correct any unwarranted damage done to Professor Stone's reputation by the State Auditor's report and by the university's press release about it."[27]

The recommendation went unheeded.

Finally, well after Stone's hearing was over, the California State Auditor's office granted that indeed it had twice miscalculated the fertility physicians' financial situation. "Unfortunately," the auditor observed, "we have since learned that the methodology we used to come to our conclusion was flawed."[28] The audit office now admitted that the term "gross professional fee income" possessed "a meaning that we did not fully understand."[29] The true meaning allowed the fertility clinic physicians, just as Stone had claimed, to deduct from their revenues their costs for medications, laboratory fees, and an undefined "technical component."

The auditor observed that Stone had maintained that the physicians had paid all that they owed. Then the new report concluded, gracelessly: "Because federal investigators seized the physicians' financial records, neither the physicians nor the university presented proof of the claims. For this reason, neither we nor the [faculty] committee can determine how much the physicians *understated* their income [emphasis added]."[30]

(3) Failure to Obtain Institutional Research Approval

Faculty doing research that might put human subjects at risk are required to obtain approval beforehand from an Institutional Review Board (IRB). This nationwide requirement was an outgrowth of, among other things, the controversial work of the psychologist Stanley Milgram, then at Yale University. Milgram had volunteers administer what they believed were extremely painful shocks to a hidden person, who actually was a confederate of the experimenter. The experiment demonstrated the disregard that people can show for the suffering of others when they believe they are adhering to the commands of an authority figure.[31] Milgram's work is considered a classic demonstration of the pathology that underlay events in Hitler's Germany. Today, it is extraordinarily unlikely that experiments such as Milgram's, in which volunteers were exposed to the risk of discovering their own potential for evil, would get the approval of a campus review committee.

Such committees (IRBs) generally comprise a combination of faculty and outside members, with religious leaders often involved. No scholar seriously doubts the necessity of external examination of a research plan that has the potential to harm participants. But IRB procedures can be irksome and time-consuming. A committee may meet so infrequently that initial decisions are delayed and follow-up submissions may not be considered for weeks or more. A considerable portion of the research community regards IRBs as a bureaucratic irritant with a tendency to exercise undue caution and, at times, to reach conclusions that extend beyond their stated mission.

This last point can be illustrated by the notably difficult time the first author of this book underwent to obtain IRB approval when she began to look into affairs at the fertility clinic. Objections to the research were never transmitted in writing but were conveyed orally by an IRB staff member. As best it could be understood, committee members were concerned that persons interviewed about clinic business might say something that could get them into trouble. We suggested that these were adults who presumably were well aware of the possible consequences of what they said and that they were under no compulsion whatsoever to talk with us. Did the committee want us to use a Miranda warning and get a signed release from persons who had agreed to discuss things either anonymously or with voluntary disclosure of their identity? Did the committee not appreciate that the media were perfectly free to talk with any of these people?

Ultimately, perhaps out of weariness, IRB gave permission for the research without any stipulations. But we strongly suspect that it was not the persons who would be interviewed whom it sought to "protect," but rather the university and some of its leaders.

In Stone's case, a special medical school committee had scrutinized ninety-six of the publications that listed one or more of the CRH partners as authors that came out between 1989 and 1995. The committee determined that Stone was a co-author of nine of the twenty-six articles that were lacking IRB approval. The CPT hearing board devoted a good portion of its report to a reexamination of these papers. Members noted that it had further input from Stone and from co-authors (none of whom were subjected to the same type of scrutiny) of the disputed reports, information not considered by the medical school group.

Stone was only peripherally involved in many of the papers in question. Research publications often include a string of authors; those listed at the end have contributed marginally, at best, to the work. A senior scholar in whose laboratory research is conducted often will be listed as one of the authors on the resulting work; so too might someone who supplied equipment or an idea or two, but had no real involvement in the work. Listed as the fourth of four authors on one of the controversial articles, for instance, Stone said that he had "provided minor technical advice [to the first author] regarding artificial insemination procedures" and that he had not expected to be listed as an author, but thought that he would be acknowledged in a footnote. Such arrangements work quite nicely for academics whose status and career advancement are tied to the quantity of their publications. But we see the downside when fraudulent research results are discovered and the senior scholar listed at the end of a line of co-authors has to admit that he or she has not read the material and has only a passing knowledge, if any, of the research.

In Stone's case several of the controversial papers had as their first author persons affiliated with institutions other than UCI who, it was presumed, had obtained proper authorization at their home base. Stone nonetheless should have obtained UCI permission as well, though his failure to do so may well be more the rule in regard to such work rather than an exception to it.

The hearing board concluded that five of the nine articles in question appeared to be retrospective studies that did not require IRB review. In three of the others, Stone's involvement was limited to a write-up and analysis of material collected by others and his failure to obtain IRB approval was seen as a "relatively minor ethical lapse." In regard to one case, however, in which Stone was the lead author, the committee came down hard on his failure to secure approval. But it concluded that such misconduct was not egregious enough to warrant dismissal from the faculty, though "it does warrant a significant punishment."

Two things might be noted about this last conclusion. First, of course, the matter never would have been in dispute had the charges of unauthorized egg and embryo usage not triggered the casting of a wide net. Second, were the same scrutiny to be made of the entire roster of research by medical school and other university faculty it is possible that few researchers working closely with living subjects would emerge with altogether clean hands. The hearing board in the instance of this single Stone article scrupulously followed the letter of the rules without attending to the full context in which the conduct was embedded.

(4) Failure to Cooperate

The hearing board found the failure to adhere to a contractual obligation to supply income tax information to the university was "a clear and serious case of failure to cooperate." But the committee also found mitigating circumstances. Stone was under university suspension and under criminal investigation by federal authorities, and "four different attorneys advised him not to turn over any records to anyone at all—including the university administration."

On the charge that Stone had failed to provide patient records, the hearing board reached the following conclusions:

1. For the most part, specific patient records that were sought from Dr. Stone were produced, although some were missing. Stone alleged that these had been taken by the whistle-blowers.

2. Many of the documents that the university sought were not in Stone's possession.

3. A substantial number of records that were sought were not produced by Stone on the advice of counsel. His lawyers insisted that the documents referring to patient care were protected by California's privacy laws. At one point the university had advanced its position in civil court, and lost, though it had been encouraged to try again with a more detailed pleading. It chose not to do so. Given these circumstances, the hearing board concluded: "We ultimately decided that if it was difficult for us to determine for ourselves what the law requires, and if competent lawyers on both sides of the case disagree, and if the issue remains unresolved in the courts, then we could not fault Dr. Stone for following the advice of his attorney and not turning over the records." In a conflict between university research and patient privacy, the Board declared, "One expects a University doctor to have a heightened respect for patient privacy."

The university subsequently would aid in the passage of a law that mandated that medical records be made available to it by its physician employees upon request. Among other reactions was that of Dr. Luis de Maza, a pathology professor who lambasted the measure as "unprecedented in the history of medicine" and insisted that patients would be wary of UCI physicians if they knew that their records could be seen by nonmedical persons.[32]

One final charge regarding Stone's alleged failure to cooperate with the university was melodramatically phrased: "On April 25, 1995 a dramatic event occurred," its brief read. "Without warning, Dr. Stone and his colleagues removed frozen embryos, laboratory equipment, laboratory records, computers and other university equipment" from the clinic. But what the university failed to point out was that two weeks earlier authorities had ordered Asch and his colleagues to be out of the facility by 5 P.M. on April 28. The biologist's log, which particularly interested the university, went with everything else because it was a working log and was required for the ongoing treatment that the doctors were giving their patients. Stone noted that the log was never in his personal possession and his own work was not closely related to it.

Finally, the university charged that Stone had known of wrongdoing by his colleagues and had failed to inform university officials of their misconduct. On this point, the hearing board concluded that Stone had no evidence that was not already known to the university. More basically, it concluded that "the burden of proof is on the university to show wrongdoing [on Stone's part] and they have failed to do so on this matter."

Overall, however, the board scolded Stone for failing to cooperate amiably and fully with the university's inquiries. If we examine the record as a whole and look at the outcome, we might decide that Stone cooperated *too* much.

The hearing board report concluded that although Stone had engaged in misconduct, the penalty should not be dismissal but reduction in rank from the third step to the first step on the professor scale. Typically, full professors like Stone advance one step in rank every three years, with commensurate salary increases.

"This is not the conclusion we expected to reach," the hearing board wrote. "Although we approached the hearing with open minds we fully expected based on what we had heard about the CRH scandal that we would end up recommending dismissal." They summarized the reasons they had changed their minds: "Although the case against Professor Stone appeared formidable at the outset we were surprised to find that it partially unravelled under close scrutiny." Were it not for his association with Asch and Balmaceda, the committee observed, "it seems highly unlikely that he would have faced criminal prosecution."[33] The panel concluded: "Professor Stone's crime seems more akin to an error in administrative judgment than to a truly evil or malevolent act and, in our view, should be treated as such."

Stone called the CPT report "fair," but he regretted that the board had felt compelled to lay out in such detail the negative allegations in order to rebut them. This would make it easier, he believed, for the chancellor to ignore favorable interpretations and to treat the allegations, accurate or not, as grounds for termination.

The hearing board had one further chance to sway the administration. The chancellor had, as required, sent them the statement he planned to dispatch to the head of the university system. It called for Stone's dismissal. The committee in respectful prose tried to persuade the chancellor to alter his position. The board's chagrin and distress—and, at times, barely concealed scorn—was clear. First, the board sought to establish the spirit with which the case should be viewed:

> We think it is important to the character of the university that we exercise great care in evaluating faculty misconduct, and that we avoid making individuals into scapegoats as we respond to public outcry over a scandal. Particularly in a case such as this one, where the scandal arose from misconduct of several faculty members, it is important to make individual determinations of culpability and to avoid assuming guilt by association.

This paragraph ended with a finger pointing at what the hearing board obviously had concluded lay beneath the action being recommended in regard to Stone: "We must," they wrote, "gauge the punishment by the seriousness of the individual misconduct rather than by our desire to disassociate the university from the underlying scandal."

The committee's memorandum to the chancellor indicated that it intended to point out "issues on which you have misunderstood the facts or have ignored important information." If this wasn't clear enough, they added, "We are concerned that you have accepted propositions for which no evidence was presented"; additionally, "It is unfair to judge [Stone] on the basis of unproved allegations, mistaken assumptions, or questionable inferences."

On the billing issues, the committee noted that its claim that the state auditor had, at best, been innocently misled had been ignored by the chancellor; therefore, some of his "factual conclusions are so clearly contradicted by the evidence in this case as to be indisputably wrong." The committee could not see "how a reasonable person who reviewed the evidence could be persuaded to adopt another interpretation." The chancellor had repeated conclusions on billing issues "that are not only wrong but unsustainable."

The committee went on to review matters connected to Stone's charged failure to obtain proper approval for his research and his alleged failure to cooperate with the university; they reached essentially the same conclusions: that the chancellor's reasoning was flawed or, if not flawed, unsuitably one-sided. They reiterated their earlier position that they did not find Stone an "evil person" and then stressed their hope that the chancellor would take a higher road than the one he was traveling. The rules governing his verdict, they noted, required that he find "serious and compelling reasons" to overrule the hearing board. They did not believe he had come near to finding such reasons:

> As you consider whether such reasons exist, we urge you to resist the temptation to find a scapegoat for a damaging scandal and to focus solely on Professor Stone's culpability as an individual. We also urge you to take care that your assessment is based on a correct understanding of the facts and that you rely solely on facts that have been developed in a manner that respects Professor Stone's right to due process. While the values of the university require that misconduct be punished, they also require care and fairness in assigning punishment.

Some skirmishing had taken place before the final round of the Stone case. Melvin Beal, the deputy university counsel, had requested that the Privilege and Tenure panel members remove from their report any statements that attributed partial responsibility for any clinic problem to university officials. Thompson, the committee chair, declined to specify for us the specific issues or persons discussed. Beal argued that it violated the due process rights of the individuals if they were not allowed the right to hear and respond to the charges. Thompson thought this argument was "clever but misleading." The hearing panel concluded that since the administrators had not been charged with anything, there was no violation of due process for it to allege that their incompetence or neglect had contributed to the scandal.[34]

In addition, a senior medical school faculty member met with the chancellor to plead the merits of Stone's case for retention on the faculty. He was told that he was naïve, that dismissal was a political imperative. The faculty member has chosen to have nothing to do with the chancellor since that meeting.[35]

The University of California Regents at their March 2000 meeting in San Francisco seconded the recommendation of the president of the system, Richard Atkinson, to terminate Stone. This was only the fourth time since the 1950s—the red-baiting McCarthy period—that a tenured faculty member at a University of California campus had been fired. This was a fairly dramatic action for the Regents, a group of political appointees who typically vote unanimously on personnel matters, about which they know only what they have seen in the carefully packaged materials sent beforehand.

The UCI chancellor had presented his case not in terms of wrongfulness but in terms of fallout. If Stone was not dismissed, the Regents were told, the university's reputation, financial security, capacity to attract students, and ability to ensure academic freedom would be threatened.[36] None of these supposed outcomes, on reflection, seems particularly likely. The medical school enrollment and the quality of students it attracted would hardly suffer if Stone was not fired, nor would his retention jeopardize the university's financial security or undermine academic freedom. It might more sensibly be argued, as the Committee on Privilege and Tenure had, that the heavy hand laid upon Stone was much more of a threat to academic freedom than was anything he had done.

The UCI chancellor's review of the case for the Regents attended to the four charges that the board had inquired into.

On the felony conviction, Cicerone argued that no evidence heard by the hearing board had established that Stone's practice of billing for doctors who were not present was "common or acceptable." Cicerone found these to be "acts of deception and dishonesty" and to "concern matters that are substantially related to the qualifications and duties of a physician and a teacher."

The chancellor's position on concealed income, like his other statements, did not examine the evidence and rebut it, but set out categoric conclusions that flew in the face of the documentation and findings of the hearing board. "I am persuaded," he wrote "that the state auditor was aware of the issue of deduction, but chose not to consider it." This took the university employees who were alleged not to have informed the state auditor of these arrangements off the hook, but it makes strange reading. In essence, he is saying that the auditor knew the figures were incorrect—had been told so—but had decided to use them anyway.

In regard to Stone's failure to get proper approval for a number of research inquiries, Cicerone paid no heed to the mitigating factors, such as Stone's peripheral association with most of the work in question. He concluded: "The evidence clearly demonstrates Professor Stone's unwillingness to understand and comply with long-established laws, regulations, policies, and procedures on human subjects research. Such unwillingness is unacceptable because it not only puts patients at risk but it also puts the entire academic research enterprise in jeopardy."[37]

On the issue of cooperation, the chancellor decided that Stone's "admitted refusal was deliberate and his excuses are not legitimate." He paid no heed to the legal advice that Stone had been given.

The conclusion inevitably flowed from the analysis. "Professor Stone did not live up to the standards of the faculty" and his were "not actions that inspire the confidence of students, patients, and the university community or the public in general." Professor Stone's behavior, said the chancellor's document in what was its least controversial statement, had proven to be "an embarrassment."

The grounds for the chancellor's conclusion are oddly framed: He asked himself, he wrote, "Could the university meet its responsibilities and sustain itself if every faculty member behaved as Professor Stone had?" In regard to each of the four charges, he used this rhetorical question to come to his conclusion. For example, to take the first category of charged wrongdoing: "If every faculty member of a given academic department were convicted of felonies, that department would not survive because our students, staff members in the department and faculty members from other departments could not respect it, nor would the public trust it." After a similar query in regard to the other issues, Cicerone concluded, "In other words, if every faculty member behaved as Professor Stone did, we would not be able to fulfill our missions of teaching, research and service."

Stone thought that the chancellor's review was the product of the lawyers, whom many saw as acting ruthlessly in the case because they believed it was their duty to protect the university at all costs. A *Los*

Angeles Times columnist thought that Cicerone was trying to respond to negative publicity that the medical school had received about not only the fertility clinic scandal but also several other cases, including the sale of body parts by a contractor who had been supplied with corpses by the medical school hospital. The columnist was also puzzled that Cicerone would reject the conclusions of both the faculty committee and the administrative law judge who had heard the case for the licensing board.[38]

For his part, Cicerone told the press that the faculty committee had viewed the charges against Stone individually rather than seeing them as a constellation of unacceptable actions, which would make them, in their numbers, much more damning.[39] "I consider each of these as a serious breach of our standards of behavior," he noted. "Yet, these are not just isolated incidents of misbehavior. Rather they reflect a pattern of deception, dishonesty and callous disregard of the rules that guide our behavior."[40] But this, of course, is not very good science, as Cicerone, a first-rate scientist whose research focuses on global warming, surely knew. Four pieces of inconsequential and incorrect evidence added together are no more persuasive than any of them individually.

In a March 15, 2000, e-mail to all UCI employees, Cicerone offered a brief summary of why he had determined to fire Stone: "If the university is to uphold the significance of tenure and the essential values it protects, we must be diligent in our review of serious violations of the Faculty Code of Conduct. This diligence is rarely easy or unanimous, but whatever its outcome, it reaffirms the core of the university's principles."[41]

William Parker, a longtime high-level administrator at UCI, put his spin on the rupture between the faculty committee and the chancellor: "There is no disagreement about the facts," he told a reporter. "It is a question of whether the actions were severe enough to warrant removal of tenure, and people will disagree about that."[42] This soothing judgment is, at best, only partially true: there was considerable dispute about some of the "facts" underlying the charges that led to Stone's dismissal.

The chancellor indicated that he was unwilling to discuss the Stone case with us for two reasons: first, because he did not desire to publicize academic personnel issues, and second, because lawsuits were still pending.[43]

A demonstration of no-nonsense power and a keen attention to the dictates of popular opinion seem to have played a significant part in

Cicerone's decision to fire Stone. Writing as far back as 1918, Thorstein Veblen put his finger on how such things work:

[The chief of the university] will have certain officially recognized advisers—the various deans, advisory committees, Academic Council, University Senate, and the like,—with whom he shares responsibility, particularly for measures of doubtful popularity, and whose advice he formally takes *coram publico* [publicly]; but he cannot well share discretion with these, except on administrative matters of inconsequential detail. For reasons of practical efficiency, discretion must be undivided in any competitive enterprise. There is much fine-spun strategy to be taken care of under cover of night and cloud.[44]

Large research universities tend to be made up of fragmented fiefdoms that render it difficult to determine what the faculty might think about any particular matter beyond its own borders. For many, the chancellor's sentiments stood as no more than pious pronouncements to undergird a political decision. First-rate university faculties generally are made up of intelligent people with a healthy skepticism mixed with a dose of cynicism. For many UCI professors, the chancellor's remarks were but another example of an overpaid administrator protecting himself and his colleagues.

Stone had taken the unusual step of asking that he be allowed to present his side of the case to the Regents in an open session before they reached a decision. Most speakers on other subjects were given three minutes; Stone recalls that they often took five. Graciously, the Regents offered him ten minutes to make his plea, so he took twenty. Among other things, he insisted that the jury that had found him guilty had been "confused." But he felt that the Regents were inattentive to what he had to say, as they talked among themselves and stirred restlessly. Stone stressed that he had become embroiled in this situation because of the malefic acts of others: "They refused to treat me individually," he told the Regents. "They continue to try to punish me for the sins of others."[45]

When the closed-door discussion was held and the vote taken, two of the eighteen members present voted for him; he wonders today how many, if any, abstained.

After the Regents' decision, Stone told newspaper reporters that he had not yet decided to pursue his case through the courts. "It's been five years," he said. "I'm exhausted and destroyed. I am not the despicable person described by the administration. If it were true I would have left the university long ago. They continue to try to punish me for the sins and crimes of others."[46]

Stone notes that, as human beings, we are "defined by our virtues." In answer to a question from us, he describes himself as "an honest and useful individual with strong ethical and moral standards. My life as I lived it does not exist any more. And my future. I cannot find my future any more. I don't know what to do and where to direct my life. My life is nowadays a waste. I was always useful. I could now disappear and nobody would care." Asked whether, had he known how his situation would turn out, he would have left the United States as Asch and Balmaceda had done, Stone has no hesitation: "No, I would not leave." But his view on what happened to him is stated forcefully and without equivocation. It uses essentially the same words that we had heard from Mary Piccione, though the two were only superficially acquainted with each other.

"The U.S. legal system cannot deliver justice," Stone declares flatly. "It can only play a game."[47]

C H A P T E R

Conclusion

■ Looking back, it is easy to see that the combustible ingredients that led to disaster were firmly in place well before the Great Fertility Scandal erupted. There was a medical school confronted with severe financial problems, and there were two newly recruited superstar fertility physicians with the potential to contribute a considerable chunk of cash to help bail the school out. The doctors were deeply dedicated to their work and viewed the production of children as their superordinate mission. At the same time, they knew that their professional reputations and incomes were closely related to the compilation of a sterling record of satisfactory treatment outcomes.

The physicians also knew that many women voluntarily undergo abortions during their lifetime, a matter which may be taken to indicate that their emotional investment in offspring has limits. The doctors had abundant experience with clients who produced "excess" eggs, and had their extra embryos frozen, and then forgot all about them. In early 2001, well after Asch and Balmaceda had fled the scene, there were more than four thousand embryos from clinic patients still in storage at diverse sites in Orange and Los Angeles counties. The storage banks had sought to inform the owners of the location of their property, but could find only about a third of them, and, of these, only half responded to the information. At first, the university disclaimed any responsibility, but it later agreed to bear the storage costs. Some of the embryos were said to belong to Debbie Challender, but she was doubtful about using them. "We've lost a good deal of faith in physicians and in the system in general," her husband said.[1]

The fertility clinic doctors were well aware that they were required by the rules of medical ethics to obtain prior consent from patients whose supposedly supernumerary eggs and embryos were implanted in other patients. California law states that there is an absence of consent when patients can show that if they had been informed of all the pertinent information, they would have declined to consent to the procedure.[2] If the doctors could not have obtained a satisfactory number of donations, there were numerous women willing to supply their own eggs for implantation in other women as an altruistic gesture, no strings attached. But at the UCI clinic such tactics apparently seemed bothersome and beside the point. Perhaps this was in part because they were men, and men and women generally have very different ideas about the importance of their procreative products.

There also was speculation that Asch's and Balmaceda's South American experiences had given them ideas about the practice of medicine that were not in line with standards in the United States. Helene Wright, an American mother whose son was severely brain-injured while working in Bolivia, notes that the doctor who treated him, born in Bolivia and trained in Kentucky, told her: "In this country [Bolivia], we don't have to worry so much about malpractice insurance, bureaucratic policymakers, and on and on. We are not hemmed in by all of that."[3] A lawyer points out that in Argentina today "rumors of trade in fetuses are quite common" and that, though there has been some expression of legislative concern, assisted reproductive procedures, carried out in fifteen clinics, remain unregulated.[4]

For one of the doctors, himself the parent of an adopted child, the idea that genetic material plays much of a role in human success or failure seemed fallacious. While not widely shared, this view has some support in the scientific community. "We cannot think of any significant human social behavior that is built into our genes in such a way that it cannot be modified and shaped by social conditions," Richard Lewontin and his colleagues have written.[5] Besides, the involuntary egg and embryo donors were very likely to remain blissfully unaware of their contributions and those who received the gifts and then conceived and gave birth were thrilled by their good fortune.

The case of Julia Thornton of San Juan Capistrano illustrates the psychological impact of assisted reproductive procedures: "It's a horrible thing being infertile," she says. "You have to give so many samples and do so many tests that it almost became callous. You don't want to see pregnant people. You don't want to go to baby showers. You get so hopeful only to be let down again and again. It's heartbreaking. But you're so driven, you want this child so bad, and you just want to keep going."[6]

Thornton went through five attempts at artificial insemination with her husband's sperm. A sixth try using in vitro fertilization under Asch's supervision succeeded. "It is worth every second of the pain, every penny. He's brought us a lot of happiness," she says.[7]

There is a very strong tendency for such patients to idolize the doctor who has produced a "miracle," and there is a concomitant tendency on the part of those idolized to accept the glowing praise heaped upon them. Physicians represent one of the most highly respected professional groups in our country.[8] As wits point out, How many other total strangers are most of us willing to undress for? "Any profession which so monopolizes some socially important body of knowledge is likely to be considered potentially dangerous," the sociologist Howard S. Becker observes. "It might use its monopoly to enrich itself or enlarge its power rather than in the best interest of its clients."[9] It became easy—almost reflexively unquestioned—to see expediency as an acceptable means to a desired and desirable end.

The business-as-usual regimen of unconsented egg and embryo transfers began to crumble when new employees at the fertility clinic, often hired by the university and apparently only casually vetted by the doctors, found themselves in an awkward position. It is arguable whether that awkwardness was primarily engendered by their fear that they might lose their jobs because of their own lackluster performance or whether it was caused by moral outrage at what was going on about them.

The three whistle-blowers in the fertility clinic case fell well outside the norm for persons who allege wrongdoing and protect themselves from retaliation by formally obtaining whistle-blower status. Most whistle-blowers by far are men, most are longtime employees, most have more positive reactions to their work than their fellows, most have been recently recognized for good performance, and most are employed by organizations perceived by others to be responsive to complaints.[10] None of these conditions was applicable to the whistle-blowers in the fertility clinic scandal. They were nudged into their status by an internal auditor who perhaps sensed that they might be more forthcoming if they believed they were better protected. Later, the auditor himself would be demoted from his supervisory job, allegedly on grounds unrelated to his investigation of clinic business.

The whistle-blowers ultimately settled for monetary awards that together totaled nearly one million dollars. Before that, they took one step that proved vital to the demise of the clinic and to the $20 million in payouts to some of its patients and $3.6 million in litigation costs: they contacted the local newspaper, the *Orange County Register*, which launched a probe characterized by all the glory of investigative journalism and all the unprettiness of a self-righteous and sometimes unreflective crusade. It may well be that the newspaper was the major winner—perhaps the only winner—in the scandal: it garnered highly prestigious awards for its intrepid performance. But there are unhappy memories among those who felt they were subjected to ill-mannered verbal assaults by at least one of the star reporters, who loudly claimed that her priorities were the only priorities.

The award-winning newspaper tried very hard to provide depth and interpretation in its reportage. Many of its stories, however, were merely a rehash of earlier ones, with new names attached. "Seventieth Couple Sues UCI," a headline might proclaim, and there would be a recital of this most recent court filing, with the names and ages and addresses of the new complainants and perhaps a capsule summary of their experience. The newspaper report would then repeat the chronicle of events, before this one went to the top of the heap. There was little effort to dig deeply for what might be uncomfortable findings (say, for example, that a couple had stored their embryos for five years but never paid the small annual storage fee). There was no inquiry into the previous employment history of the whistle-blowers or a study of the claimants and the tactics of their lawyers.

The prizewinning newspaper clearly viewed the university as a foe that waffled and withheld important information. In a revealing editorial titled "Egg-Gate," the *Register* documented some of its disdain for what it regarded as stonewalling by university officials. It pointed out that it had reported that more than sixty women might have been victimized in the fertility clinic case. The university had denied that, setting the figure at about half that number, and that only after one of its attorneys suddenly discovered information he'd earlier overlooked. "If there hadn't been a history of half- and three-quarter answers to questions about the fertility-clinic affair," the editorial writer observed, "this explanation might invite no skepticism, but if top UCI officials have demonstrated one thing through this sad saga, it is that candor and a rigorous sense of accountability do not come reflexively to them."[11]

The writer added that information had to be "pried" from the university spokespersons or disinterred by avid investigative reporting. "It has not been offered freely by public officials mindful that they are stewards of public trust."[12] Evidence on this point was supplied by Chancellor Wilkening during a deposition by Jane Frederick's lawyer, Joseph Hartley. The dialogue went like this:

HARTLEY: Do you usually take notes when you're reviewing academic discipline matters?
WILKENING: I did not.
HARTLEY: And that's your policy?
WILKENING: That's my policy.
HARTLEY: Is there any particular reason you don't take notes?
WILKENING: My experience is that it is not very helpful.
HARTLEY: In terms of refreshing your memory?
WILKENING: Well, the problem with anything written is that it's subject to the California Public Records Act.
HARTLEY: Ah.
WILKENING: And so it's generally—my experience that it's not helpful is that it's not helpful for one's notes to appear in the newspaper.[13]

Faced with deadlines and the need for a saleable product, the newspapers created a story line and tended to accommodate ensuing events into that viewpoint. Diane Vaughan, a sensitive and sensible sociologist, noted that later examinations of what was breaking news require our being careful about newspaper sources:

> We tend to see the media as our colleagues, for in keeping with our critical stance toward the power elite, journalists tantalize us with exposés that attack the powerful. In our enthusiasm for the bounty of information that the sensational case produces, we must remind ourselves of what we know about the manufacture of news and the social construction of knowledge for public consumption.[14]

A review of what was reported in the media about the fertility debacle suggests that the case involved dark and sinister deeds committed by a triad of wealthy foreign doctors. The scandal provided fodder for dramatic, satirical, and creative media endeavors, but, as we have tried to demonstrate, the process—not only what went on during the scandal, but how it was handled—was a matter that usually was beyond the reach of the media.

The university chancellor sent by e-mail a rather world-weary lament to the "UCI Community" that reflected her irritation with the local newspaper. "All of us hope to put the problem of the Center for Reproductive Health behind us and resume, full time, the business of building a better UCI," she began; she then noted, "I suspect that we may now have to endure a continuing media inquiry into many aspects of UCI life." Wilkening praised the national media for its "very responsible" coverage of the case, but inveighed against those (obviously referring primarily to the *Register*), who, though "the story is largely told, will continue to rake over its embers and try to bring it back into flame." Such coverage had included, she lamented, "third-hand accounts of what I said, and stories concentrating on minor or imagined inconsistencies in statements by UCI or other officials. . . . We cannot predict what issues will be raised and who may find them embarrassing."[15]

The chancellor's e-mail had at least one solid foundation: a not inconsiderable part of the *Register*'s zeal was fueled by its long-standing circulation war with the Orange County edition of the *Los Angeles Times*. The *Register* generally came out on top in that battle, but it had to be ever-vigilant. Kim Christensen, one of the major figures in the *Register*'s coverage of the clinic, has noted: "It's a really dog eat dog newspaper war here in Orange County. So virtually any story that's of any interest really takes on a life of its own because of the competitive thing. Nobody wants to get beat by the other. Sometimes I think both papers are beating a dead horse. I mean things take on too much of a life of their own."[16]

For the newspaper, the patients were the heroes and the doctors the villains. Patients' stories tended toward bathos. As Arthur Caplan, the prominent ethics expert, put it, there is "a media audience which can't wait for the next sad or pathetic tale."[17] Stories about the doctors, on the other hand, were portraits of Machiavellian manipulations. There were, no doubt, too many reporters covering the clinic case; none of them focused on the intricacies of the issues at hand.

Our initial reading of the *Register*'s tilt later was confirmed by Susan Kelleher, a key reporter on the fertility clinic scandal, who now works for the *Seattle Times*. When Kelleher appeared on a panel at a session for newspaper reporters, she said, "Yeah, I did get too close to those people [patients]. I got very angry with the doctors." She added: "I also felt a little too close to the whistle-blowers."[18] These sentiments are evident in the stories that her paper ran under her byline.

Kelleher also told the audience that she had discovered a way to acquire information that avoided the possibility of being compromised by a court that wanted to determine her source. She would tell those she interviewed that she would be obligated to identify them if she was the object of a legal proceeding. But then she would add, slyly, that she drove a Toyota Tercel with cowhide-covered car seats, ate lunch at a specific Sizzler restaurant, and always left her trunk open. She would also point out that anything she received through the mail that had no return address could not possibly be identified by its source in court.

Besides drawing the attention of the local newspaper to the fertility clinic issues, one of the whistle-blowers alerted the federal government about wrongdoing in clinic procedures. The government responded promptly, but its involvement signified little. The government had the potential to cut off research funding for the medical school if it documented wrongdoing. But the government never plunged deeply into the issues; rather, it breezed in and out, put on a fierce face, and then departed the scene, leaving vital questions unanswered. It was fairly obvious that no penalty would be forthcoming if university officials jumped through a few hoops.

Even more fleeting was the involvement of Tom Hayden and his state senate oversight committee. The committee served an important purpose in unleashing the whistle-blowers from their coerced (or, perhaps, *bribed* is the better word) pledge of silence, but the committee's work was largely a hit-and-run operation, much like the performance of the federal authorities. Hayden played to the gallery and fulminated against the doctors and the university. Perhaps the best testament to the relative impotence of his committee's inquiry was his churlish and childish gesture of making Asch remain at the committee hearing much longer than was necessary, to demonstrate—what?

Several bills were enacted by the legislature in the wake of the committee hearings. Hayden's measure, though unlikely ever to be prosecuted, created the felony of transplanting eggs without the donor's consent. Violations carry a possible five-year prison term, a $50,000 fine, or both for knowingly using sperm, ova, or embryos in assisted reproduction without the written consent of the donor and recipient, except in the case of sperm donated to a licensed collection organization.[19]

A companion measure was sponsored by Assemblywoman Jacqueline Speier, who was exasperated by the stance taken by the academic officers during the state senate hearings in which she was invited to participate. "There have been enough scandals within the University of California over the years," Speier told a newspaper reporter, "to suggest that it is on auto-pilot most of the time." The bill Speier shepherded through the legislature requires a physician who removes sperm or ova from a patient to obtain the patient's written consent prior to using the material for purposes other than reimplantation in the same patient or implantation in the patient's spouse. Violations are defined as "unprofessional conduct" and are subject to a civil penalty payable to the person whose required consent was not obtained. The fine ranges from $1,000 to $5,000, with court costs assessed for the second offense.[20]

Both laws, predictably, met with opposition from the California Medical Association and the California Attorneys for Criminal Justice, the latter a defense-oriented group. The best judgment of the importance of the enacted legislation was likely that expressed by Arthur Caplan, the bioethicist. To Caplan, the measures seemed "closer to a Band-Aid on a serious, deep wound than truly something that will be appropriate therapy for what is wrong."[21]

A law review writer has mistakenly maintained that the absence of the subsequent Hayden-sponsored proscription was what pushed federal prosecutors to resort to mail fraud charges against Sergio Stone, but Stone was uninvolved in the illicit egg transfers.[22] Had the Hayden measure been on the statute books, it very well might have deterred the transfers, though the doctors must have been aware of the dire consequences that awaited them if what they were doing was revealed publicly. The civil penalties in the Speier measure seem inconsequential, given the amounts that had to be paid to settle the Irvine clinic civil suits.

Beyond these enactments, nothing really significant marked the legislative hearings. There was no serious attempt to pin down responsibility, though Hayden thought he saw wrongdoing by others than the physicians. Predictably and understandably, given the nature of the process, other matters soon shoved the clinic off the legislature's radar screen.

By settling the numerous actions filed against it, the university was able to forestall the courts' scrutinizing the field of reproductive medicine and determining whether common-law doctrines such as conversion might be applicable to the unconsented use of reproductive materials[23]—and determining as well the legal implications of other novel considerations that marked the case. On the other hand, as Janet Dolgin has noted, "Courts, uncertain about how to react [to the new reproductive techniques], have as a group behaved with confusion and ambivalence."[24]

The university attorneys involved in the fertility clinic case do not present a very pretty picture. They generally used the law as a weapon to shield their clients from close scrutiny and to intimidate those they saw as threatening their clients with disclosure or disrepute. In a deposition, Andrew Yeilding was asked whether he recalled the counsel to the university chancellor saying that the "university was not going to cover up for Dr. Asch again." Yeilding testified that he could recall the attorney making a statement "something like that," but he could not remember the specific wording. Nor were the plaintiff lawyers as a group likely to add to the much-disparaged reputation of their profession. But contingency-fee work has never enjoyed particularly high repute.

The criminal trial of Stone and the dismissal of Piccione and Spiwak seem to have occurred not in the name of justice but as an exercise of power and expedience. Should this judgment appear overstated and intemperate, we point to a recent instance in which a trial judge ruled that outside counsel hired by the University of California, Irvine, would not be allowed to present a defense of his client because of the attorney's deceitful behavior.

The plaintiff, thirty-four-year-old Denise deSoto, was comatose at the UCI Medical Center after an operation to correct complications from previous hand surgery. Her car had rolled over in an accident, and she had to have two fingers amputated and two others reattached. In a follow-up operation, a blocked breathing tube had caused cardiac arrest. Her lawyer claimed that the attorneys hired by UCI had lied, had kept a key witness in hiding, and had withheld significant paperwork, including the information that the anesthesiologist had only five months' experience. Dr. J. A. Makena Marangu, who worked at the medical center, filed a statement saying that she had been told by a university-hired attorney "that if I didn't go along with the defense story that Mrs. DeSoto's injuries were a freak, unavoidable accident, I could face huge personal liability from an adverse judgment and costs of defense."[25]

The university had billed Mrs. DeSoto for $200,000, the amount not covered by her insurance. In court, she was awarded $18.3 million. Judge C. Robert Jamieson said that the behavior of the university's outside attorney was "intentional, despicable, and unprofessional" and that the attorney had "stonewalled this thing from the get-go." Mrs. DeSoto's attorney declared: "This [the behavior of the university's lawyer] constitutes a virtual handbook on how to wage an effective total assault . . . on the rights of both the plaintiff and the co-defendant." Governor Gray Davis observed, "I am outraged over the seemingly unending hemorrhage of millions of dollars of public funds to clean up and compensate for misconduct by university officials."[26]

We began our examination of the fertility scandal intending to write something like a detective story, a whodunit. The questions we presumed that we would address concerned whether the eggs had been "stolen," who had done it, and why. We expected that answers to the last question might well lie in the personalities of the alleged perpetrators, with perhaps some of the explanation residing in the structure and the ethos of the university and, more particularly, the medical school that housed the fertility clinic, as well as the clinic itself.

These considerations became less important as the story unfolded. Our attention was drawn again and again to the way the clinic scandal was being handled by the diverse players: the whistle-blowers, the claimants, their lawyers, and the various investigatory committees. Most particularly, we became intrigued with the actions that the university took as the drama unfolded.

The University of California at Irvine may well have had a number of skeletons in its academic closet that it much preferred to keep there. It pursued a vigorous campaign to distance itself from the doctors involved in the fertility clinic scandal. It threw the hospital manager and her assistant to the wolves without a decent hearing and a full explanation. It refused to pay for Stone's legal counsel or to use its very considerable power to strike a much more palatable deal with the justice system, one that Stone deserved. In the end it fired Stone, despite a sophisticated report by an official faculty committee that recommended that it not do so. Later, Stone's defamation suit against the university was thrown out of court because the one-year statute of limitations had passed; it was refiled largely on the basis of allegations made by the university attorney at the medical school faculty meeting. The suit also sought damages for attorney's fees, for interference with Stone's earning his living, and the violation of his civil rights (this last was based on his allegation that he had first been fired and only then granted a hearing). When we asked for an interview with the university attorney Diane Geocaris to get her side of the story, she declined on the ground that, as a person being sued in the Stone case, she could not ethically discuss the fertility clinic affair. "Well, what is at issue?" we inquired. "What do you think?" she asked, and then answered, "He wants his job back."[27]

The university responded to Stone by filing a SLAPP (Strategic Litigation Against Public Participation) suit against him, a tactic for claiming triple damages on the ground that the plaintiff is filing a frivolous suit. The tactic had first been taken by business forces trying to prevent "tree-huggers" from seeking court redress for what they regarded as environmental abuses.[28]

SLAPP suits have been bitterly criticized as conferring harassment power on well-heeled organizations. Typical critical newspaper stories carry headlines such as "Lawsuits Aim to Silence Public"[29] and "SLAPP

Suits Called a Threat to Democracy."[30] In a move to de-claw such actions, Rhode Island's legislature recently modified its law by requiring that such a suit would prevail only if the party's claim was "a mere sham" and "objectively baseless."[31]

Most of the many persons knowledgeable about the fertility case to whom we have talked—both insiders and individuals in the surrounding community—are convinced that Stone was meanly scapegoated. The allegations of misbehavior filed against him were reviewed very thoroughly by a faculty committee that had expected to readily come back with a recommendation for discharge; but when they carefully examined the allegations, they found they tended to evaporate or assume a much less ominous form. But strict liability principles carried the day when Stone was prosecuted in a federal court. It did not matter that what Stone had done—charging insurance providers for operating assistants who did not qualify for reimbursement—was a common practice. Nor did it matter whether he actually intended to defraud or whether he understood that what he was doing was unacceptable.

The chancellor, after he reviewed the faculty committee's report, indicated that there was no evidence to support the allegation that Stone's method of billing was a common practice at the university and in many teaching hospitals throughout the country. Yet not long afterward, the University of California system paid out $22.5 million to Medicare as a result of a multiyear federal probe of billing "errors" at the system's five teaching hospitals. A major issue, the report noted, was "whether medical faculty inappropriately billed the government for care actually provided by residents or doctors in training, persons who are not eligible to bill Medicare."[32]

The suit against the university had been initiated by Debra Krahel through the offices of the law firm of Phillips and Cohen in Washington, D.C., who filed a qui tam action on her behalf. Such lawsuits come under the federal False Claims Act, with the phrase itself derived from the ancient doctrine of *qui tam pro domino rege quam pro sic ipso in hoc parte sequitur*, which translates as "he who sues on behalf of the king as well as himself." The provision allows a citizen of the United States to file a suit against an agent or agency that uses government funds in a fraudulent manner. The whistle-blower's complaint is assigned to a government lawyer. If the government prosecutes successfully or reaches a settlement, the whistle-blower is entitled to at least 15 percent and no more than 25 percent of the amount recovered. In Krahel's case, however, the fact that the entity sued was a government agency precluded her sharing in the $22.5 million settlement.[33]

The government argued successfully before a federal district court that a previous decision—*Stevens*—precluded Krahel from collecting a portion of the settlement.[34] The unpublished district court ruling further noted that because the individuals in the government's suit were themselves not entitled to file their claims against the Regents, they also were not entitled to claim any share of the settlement proceeds. Krahel's lawyers have taken the case to the ninth circuit court of appeals, claiming that the considerable cooperation given by Krahel to the authorities, and, most particularly, what they believe to be the district court's misinterpretation of *Stevens*, demands that she receive a part of the settlement sum. "The government simply wants to keep all of the money," her attorneys observe.[35] They also point out that in a notably similar case the government paid out a portion of a $140,000 settlement without quarrel.[36] "According to the government's argument," Krahel's attorneys note sarcastically, "*Stevens* means one thing when only a few thousand dollars are at stake, but it means something else entirely when millions of dollars are at stake."[37]

University of California officials noted that they had agreed to the settlement, without admitting guilt, in order to avoid further audit and litigation expenses, which they said had by then amounted to $15 million. John Lundberg, who had been deeply involved in the fertility clinic case, thought that the settlement was "relatively nominal" but questioned whether the federal government's effort to recover the money "is an appropriate public policy and whether federal dollars are being spent inappropriately." It was a thought that he obviously had not entertained when the university was in the role in the fertility clinic case that the Department of Justice occupied in this case. UCI's share of the settlement amount came to $4.1 million. No individual offender was named and, of course, no one was charged in criminal court for the alleged wrongdoing.

The University of California probe was but one of thirty throughout the nation. The University of Pennsylvania had already settled for $30 million and, subsequently, eight other hospitals coughed up a total of $17.3 million for allegedly bilking Medicare. A considerable number of medical schools went to court in 2000 to challenge the rule that assisting physicians must be physically present at the procedure. They did so to try to avoid the potential liability that might result from PATH (Physicians at Teaching Hospitals) audits, though the court ruled that the case was premature, since the investigations had not been completed.[38] Sergio Stone obviously had a good deal of company in the billing practices that led to his felony conviction.

In another case, four specialists at St. Joseph's Cardiac Surgery Associates in Syracuse, New York, were discovered by the Federal Bureau of Investigation to have filed false claims over seven years for work allegedly performed by assistant surgeons. The doctors had realized at least half a million dollars from the practice each year. They pleaded guilty to a misdemeanor charge, were fined $1.2 million, and went off to set up a new corporate group to continue doing open-heart surgery. In that field, they stood at or near the top of the state's list for the lowest death rates among patients.[39] Had Sergio Stone been allowed to cop a plea on a misdemeanor charge, the downward trajectory of his professional career might well not have been so steep.

Somewhat surprisingly, Debra Krahel, the most controversial and by far the most visible of the whistle-blowers, targeted the university rather than the physicians for most of her wrath. In an interview she declared: "They have a corrupt administration and I think that needs to be dealt with. I feel like no one is taking on the task of exposing these individuals because they are so insulated under the corporate veil. They use that to shroud their incompetency and their ability to get out of any accountability, to get out of this whole thing."[40]

In August 2002 Krahel's anguish and anger seemed not to have lessened a whit. "One thing I've learned," she told us, "is that there's no way to win going up against the establishment."[41] Since her initial whistle-blowing report, she has gone through a divorce, she says that she suffers from "tremendous emotional scars," and her career has come to a standstill. She continues to believe that the University of California system has failed to attend to its problems and that the fertility clinic scandal only taught the university how to be more clever in covering up wrongdoing.

A similar observation, one that we often heard from others as well, was made by Yossi Neev, a laser physicist, born in Jerusalem and now president of an Orange County technology firm. "My opinion is that it's the university's fault," Neev told us. "They never had the guts to confront the doctors."

Neev, who wrote a number of scientific articles with Asch and Balmaceda, research in which they had minimal participation, notes that to him Asch "seemed always to have a tragic face and looked like a don of a Mafia group, like he was suffering through a necessary chore. He rarely smiled, but he was a handsome man. He seemed to be carrying the burden of life." Neev remembers that when he was talking Asch held his hands near his face, around his nose, as if in prayer. But then Neev reverts to his recurring theme: "He's human," he says of Asch. "It's the system that screwed up." He says that only when Asch began to fall did the university "join the pack."[42]

Neev's wife, Debra, also a physicist, had undergone four treatment cycles at the clinic, none of them successful, at a cost of $55,000. The Neevs ultimately tried their luck at the Cornell Medical Center in New York City, where they sought the services of Jacques Cohen, an embryologist who had been a member of the British team responsible for the world's first IVF birth, and a man who does not have a medical degree. Cohen carried out a successful IVF procedure and the couple had twin boys on their first try at Cornell.[43]

The *Orange County Register*, in one of its best bits of reportage, pinpointed what it saw as the subterfuge practiced routinely by the university. The three reporters who wrote the story—Kim Christensen, David Parrish, and Ernie Slone—noted that the chancellor had made no public statement until six weeks after the revelations about clinic activities came out. Then the reporters offered a roster of similar defaults:

1. Executive Vice Chancellor Golub in a tape-recorded interview told reporters that the university officials had not talked with persons believed to have been victimized by egg and embryo misuse. Golub's exact words were: "We didn't go see anybody. I don't know what you're talking about." But the Challenders had met with university officials more than a week before this statement. When confronted with the discrepancy, Golub said that his comment was made out of concern for the patients. "We are not liars," he insisted. "We have told the truth as we see it. Truth is an evolving thing in this."

2. The recollection of dates by university administrators often

altered when new disclosures arose. Chancellor Wilkening first maintained that she had initially learned of the egg and embryo misuse allegations in the summer of 1994. Hayden's committee discovered that she had been informed in April 1994. The chancellor described the specified times as "consistent" in one interview, "inconsistent" in another.

3. The university failed to comply with a state law that mandates that documents sought under the Freedom of Information Act be delivered within ten days. The newspaper reporters learned that an employee with fourteen years' experience at the university had resigned her position as the medical school's communications director because of the manner in which officials handled the release of information. She was told to delay the release of information to the public for as long as legally permissible.

4. Paul Najar, assistant to the chancellor's counsel, told reporters that he had been unable to locate copies of the settlements with the whistle-blowers. Yet eight days earlier they had been provided by a university lawyer to the attorney representing one the doctors. From that attorney's viewpoint, the university was engaging in "an orchestrated campaign of misinformation, the selective revealing of some information, the withholding of other information, and taking other information out of context."[44]

Why did the university administrators and lawyers act as they did? Nobody in university circles who might know has been willing to answer this question for us in any detailed and straightforward manner. The university said that its highest goal was to protect the privacy of the patients; but few patients, it turned out, preferred privacy to payoffs. It claimed that the doctors were rogue actors who sneakily had engaged in awful behavior that was almost incomprehensible in an institution built upon trust and integrity. It said, almost always only after it became necessary to say something, that the university authorities had taken proper actions once they had been informed of wrongdoing.

These claims are but partial truths, and apparently only a minor part. It seems that the university's focal concern was to erect a firewall between itself and what had gone on at the clinic in order to reduce liability, or worse—and also to keep the details of its own shortcomings from scrutiny. Had the university wanted—as it should have—a comprehensive, unprejudiced review of the fertility issue, it could have—and should have—hired a highly regarded outsider (Warren Christopher, among others, comes to mind) to determine who was truly responsible for what and how to prevent a repetition of what had happened.

The possible culpability of campus administrators at earlier stages hovers in the background as one of the matters that the university may have sought to obscure. The settlements with claimants precluded David Swanberg's fully telling his story of reported egg theft as given in his 1992 notes until 2000. At that time, an outside counsel for the university petitioned the court to excuse Swanberg from being deposed in regard to Sergio Stone's claims against the university because, the attorney claimed, Swanberg was suffering from Parkinson's disease. Superior Court Judge Robert E. Thomas slapped a $1,800 sanction on the attorney on the ground that his representation was hearsay and that "he had no personal knowledge of the matters to which he testified." Stone's lawyer, Karen Taillon, thought she knew what was going on: "His [Swanberg's] testimony, and that of the other internal auditors, is critical to the ongoing effort to ferret out the truth in these cases that the university was involved in a cover-up from the get-go, and when they got caught they tried to cover-up the cover-up, and when they couldn't do that they slung crap at my client."[45]

Taillon's observation brings to mind the Watergate scandal, probably the most horrific tale of uncovered cover-up in our nation's history. "If you cover up, you're going to get caught," Richard Nixon is heard telling John Ehrlichman, an aide, on the tapes. "And if you lie you are going to be guilty of perjury. It is not the issue that will harm you, it's the *cover-up* [Nixon's emphasis]."[46]

Stephanie Ander, who dealt with the handling of oocytes during 1991, was said by Krahel in her testimony before the clinical review panel to have implicated Peltason, Lundberg, and others. Peltason, the university chancellor in 1991, has denied that he was aware of wrongdoing: "It was all brand new to me," he said when the scandal first made headlines.[47]

There is no evidence that Peltason knew what was going on at the clinic, but it is likely that either he or somebody else in the upper administrative echelons was aware and should have taken some remedial action. One lower-level administrator remembers being told in 1991 by Chang-Lin Tien, then Irvine's executive vice chancellor, that Tien had heard rumors of irregularities at the fertility clinic, but after some time passed and nothing more came to his attention, he presumed that the matter had been attended to or the rumor was unfounded. Tien shortly thereafter left Irvine to become chancellor at Berkeley.

The fact that the suit of Patricia and Edward Haynes in 1993 alleging egg mismanagement did not alert the administrative and legal echelons of the university is another puzzler. Two irreconcilable stories emerge: Swanberg insists that he told the university system's lawyer in charge of health care about his suspicions. The medical school maintains that it forwarded the Hayneses' complaint to the university system's lawyer in charge of health care. John Lundberg, the lawyer in question, denies that he ever saw the Hayneses' material and intimates that Swanberg's story is less than accurate. As for the Hayneses, who now live near Las Vegas, they have abandoned the idea of having children, saying that they have lost faith in fertility doctors and the legal system. "What the university did," Edward Haynes says, "was to allow this to continue, and to capitalize on something that could break a person's heart."[48]

The triumvirate of doctors caught up in the scandal must be disaggregated, an approach that the university and the media seemed incapable or unwilling to do with any consistency. Asch almost surely replanted eggs taken from patients into other patients without the consent of the original owners. He certainly used a non-approved drug in his treatments. How much money, if any, he siphoned off that rightfully belonged to the university remains undetermined. That he could be cavalier and arrogant goes with the medical territory.

Balmaceda may have also resorted to unconsented egg transfers at the Garden Grove facility—or he may not. He knew what Asch was doing, and he was aware that it had the potential to be a devastatingly dangerous situation if it came to light. He probably thought the odds that it would become public knowledge were low. Besides, Balmaceda thought—or at least he told us that he thought—that Asch likely would accept a position at the University of California, San Diego, medical school, where he would be nearer the racetrack, and that such a move would see the end of jeopardy at Irvine. It is also possible that Balmaceda separated himself geographically from the Irvine clinic to avoid the possibility of being complicit in later unconsented egg usage.

The outcome for Mary Piccione and Herb Spiwak and Sergio Stone was, in our eyes, the most indefensible element of the fertility clinic drama. Looked at cold-bloodedly (which is how their antagonists viewed the situation) each of them was vulnerable and rather helpless. Piccione and Spiwak had no employment contracts, so they could be fired at will. The report of the external lawyers, the Wiggins-Snyder report, was not an adequate basis for terminating them, as even those who wrote it viewed the firings. The university used the report to support an insupportable discharge, intending to place blame on two handy targets. There was no formal hearing, no opportunity to cross-examine, no judicial redress.

What we also find disturbing about the Wiggins-Snyder report is that it is riddled with assumptions and conclusions that are not supported by evidence. It is at least arguable that Krahel was disciplined because of the "mere fact" that she had criticized clinic operations. Krahel, as we noted earlier, had expressed doubts about the competence of Killane, another whistle-blower, and specific examples were offered by hospital administrators and doctors to suggest that she might not have been doing her job satisfactorily.

It would be unjust to declare that Krahel sought to save her skin by gathering up documents to support her claim that the fertility clinic employed unacceptable practices. But it would be equally unjust to conclude the opposite, as did the Wiggins-Snyder report in its high-handed way.

Meanwhile, fertility procedures continue to improve. Asch's GIFT procedure has largely fallen into disuse because of the development of less invasive measures, though GIFT enjoys the advantage of being the only "artificial" fertilization procedure that has received Vatican approval.[49]

The newer approaches include intracytoplasmic sperm injection (ICSI), which involves the injection of a single sperm into an egg, itself no larger than a pencil point, using a micropipette one fourteenth the diameter of a human hair. The sperm is immobilized by crushing its tail. The resulting embryos are transferred to the uterus forty-eight hours after the egg collection.

The ICSI approach has overcome the previous assumption that men with low sperm counts, who typically are older, cannot produce children. In Belgium, where the process was originated in 1992,[50] about 60 percent of IVF cycles involve ICSI, and increasingly the procedure is being used for problems in the female such as tubal malfunction and "unexplained infertility," as well as for instances in which standard IVF has failed.[51] A subsequent reanalysis of the Belgian data by an Australian team, however, indicated that the number of birth defects from the process was higher than reported, in part because the original investigators had used "an unusually narrow definition" of defects. The Australians found that ICSI children were twice as likely as other IVF-produced children to show major birth defects.[52]

In another new technique, assisted hatching (AH), a laser or an acidic solution is employed to create a small opening in the outer coating of a six- to eight-cell embryo to allow it to break away and to hatch. (The egg and sperm are brought together first in a petri dish.) This procedure allows the implantation of better-quality embryos and has reduced the percentage of multiple births from an average of 38 to less than 3 percent.[53]

Infertility, Gina Kolata recently noted, has become a big, fiercely competitive business, with a billion dollars in revenues annually and with more and more doctors fighting for a limited number of patients.[54] The commercialism of the fertility business is epitomized by programs that offer to return the patient's money if the process does not work. About one in five of the country's fertility clinics now has adopted this approach. Instead of touting money-back guarantees, most prefer to use more comfortable terms, such as "shared risk" or "warranty." One can only presume that such clinics will shun couples who have less than a very good chance of bearing a child. Inveighing against the tactic, one doctor notes, "The most obvious and immediate concern is that physicians will have powerful financial incentives to ensure that the specified goal is met," and will increase risks to patients by using higher dosages of fertility drugs and more invasive egg retrieval techniques, and by implanting more embryos. The American Medical Association has declared that the refund practice is unethical because a physician's fee should not be contingent on the successful outcome of treatment.

There also is lack of full disclosure in the approach: First get the couple into your clinic because of their interest in the financial arrangement, and only later inform them that there will be a considerable fiscal outlay that is not covered by the agreement, including items such as drug costs, the initial work-up, and non-obstetrical expenses.[55]

Typical is Pacific Fertility Medical Center in Los Angeles, which allows three money-back tries. But the cost is $7,725 per try under the regular plan and $16,500 under the money-back program. About eight of ten of Pacific's clients opt for the refund program. Pacific's advertisements employ the seductive words "guaranteed," "full refund," and the clincher, "baby."[56]

The fertility clinic scandal at the University of California, Irvine, can be explained from any number of perspectives. Like most such complex situations, its occurrence required the combination of a variety of circumstances. Without these particular doctors, or with them in a different setting at a different time, matters might have gone otherwise. The nature of the fertility business shaped developments in a way that would not have happened in, say, a kidney dialysis unit. Nor would there probably have been a scandal if different employees had been engaged to work at the clinic or if early warning signs had been heeded.

We have focused on what we see as the university's self-protective actions, the behavior of bureaucrats seeking to keep things under wraps with as little cost to themselves as possible. These actions often were dictated by the advice of a cadre of attorneys who, in the tradition of the profession, saw their job as aiding their clients, the truth or a sense of public responsibility be damned—unless it paid off. Presumably, opposing attorneys would balance matters out as they worked in the best interests of their clients. As so often happens in big cases, adversarial justice did not work the way it is supposed to: the tricks and the power on opposing sides did not balance out.

We took particular care to try to talk with as many members of the university community involved in the scandal as we could. Most often we were stonewalled, sometimes on the ground of pending litigation. Calls were not returned; letters went unanswered. This response was in contrast to that of those accused: they generally were willing to take considerable time and effort to talk with us; many claimed that what they had to say had never been given satisfactory attention. We recall the observation of Diane Vaughan:

Documentation of misconduct within an organization prior to an enforcement action or public investigation is and always has been difficult for researchers to obtain. After a violation has become public knowledge, an offending organization is understandably reluctant to have a sociologist loosed in its midst, and evidence documenting internal activities that is obtained by social control agents is not always admissible in judicial proceedings, let alone open to perusal by social scientists.[57]

The atmosphere of the medical school was a vital contributing factor to what took place in the fertility clinic. Medical school physicians have to deal with research pressures as well as patient care and teaching demands. Medical schools traditionally are aberrant features of major universities. Samuel McCulloch, UCI's official historian, offers a vignette that speaks to this point: "[There was] a chancellor who died and went 'down under.' The devil showed him a marvelous university and told him that he could be in charge of it. When the chancellor asked what the catch was the devil replied, "'This university has not one but two medical schools.'"[58]

One UCI medical school professor, who understandably preferred anonymity, labeled his working life "an insane situation" and the medical school atmosphere "a recipe for disaster." He added that the money shuffle at UCI medical facilities is "so radical it's a scandal itself." The same doctor suggested that the periodic threats to close the Medical Center promoted a "get it while you can" attitude among the physicians. He noted that the business face of medicine has been accentuated with the takeover of health care by corporate interests,[59] and that this new mood inevitably infiltrated clinic operations.

The Clinical Panel that investigated alleged wrongdoing at CRH believed that, despite the labyrinthine arrangements of responsibility in the medical school, oversight of the center clearly fell within the province of the university: "We . . . believe that UCIMC and the Department of Obstetrics and Gynecology had both the authority and responsibility to oversee CRH to ensure good medical practice because it was a private practice on university grounds and staffed by university employees."[60]

This was a view the university did not share. Its attempt to place responsibility anywhere it could, no matter how many lives and careers were affected, can only be seen as indefensible.

Notes

1. Phat X. Chiem, *Orange County Register [OCR]*, 13 October 1995.

2. *Corona, California: Economic Development Project* (Corona, Calif.: Team Corona, 1995).

3. On the press conference and its immediate fallout see Michelle Nicolosi, *OCR*, 8 June 1985; Lisa Richardson, *Los Angeles Times [LAT]*, 9 June 1985; Douglas E. Beeman, *Riverside Press Enterprise*, 9 June 1995.

4. Anne Ready, telephone interview, 21 September 2000.

5. Letter to the Editor, *LAT*, 30 July 1995.

6. Ibid.

7. Ibid.

8. Julie Marquis and Tracy Weber, *LAT*, 24 July 1995.

9. Kelly O'Donnell, *NBC Nightly News*, 7 March 1996 (transcript).

10. Ricardo Asch, interview, Mexico City, 11 February 1999.

11. Peter J. Neumann, Soheyla D. Gharib, and Milton C. Weinstein, "The Cost of a Successful Delivery with In Vitro Fertilization," *New England Journal of Medicine*, 331 (1994):239–244.

12. *Bragdon v. Abbott*, 524 U.S. 624, at 639, 1988; Thomas D. Flanagan, "Assisted Reproduction Technologies and Insurance under the Americans with Disabilities Act," *University of Louisville Brandeis Law Journal*, 38 (2000):777–816; Kimberly Horvath, "Does *Bragdon v. Abbott* Provide the Missing Link for Infertile Couples Seeking Protection under the ADA?" *De Paul Journal of Health Care Law*, 2 (1999):819–841.

13. Julie Appleby, *USA Today*, 19 December 2001.

14. Jane Gross, *New York Times [NYT]*, 7 December 1998; Peter K. Rydel, "Redefining the Right to Reproduce: Assisting Infertility as a Disability under the Americans with Disabilities Act," *Albany Law Review*, 63 (1999):593–636; Lisa M. Kerr, "Can Money Buy Happiness? An Examination of the Coverage of Infertility Services under HMO Contracts," *Case Western Law Review*, 49 (1999):599–643.

15. Tarun Jain, Bernard L. Harlow, and Mark D. Hornstein, "Insurance Coverage and Outcome of In Vitro Fertilization," *New England Journal of Medicine*, 347 (29 August 2002); see also David Guzick, "Should Insurance Coverage for In Vitro Fertilization Be Mandated?" ibid.

16. *California Statutes*, 1989, p. 2428; Note, "In Vitro Fertilization, Insurance Coverage, and Consumer Protection," *Harvard Law Review*, 109 (1996):2092–2109.

17. Michelle Nicolosi, *OCR*, 9 June 1995.

18. David G. Whittingham, "Fertilization In Vitro and Development to Term of Unfer-

tilized Mouse Oocytes Previously Stored at –196 Degrees Centigrade," *Journal of Reproductive Fertility*, 49 (1977):80.

19. Julie Marquis, *LAT*, 2 November 1995.

20. See, generally, Rebecca S. Snyder, "Reproductive Technology and Stolen Ova: Who Is the Mother?" *Law and Inequality Journal*, 16 (1998):289–334; Alice M. Noble-Allgire, "Switched at the Fertility Clinic: Determining Maternal Rights When a Child Is Born from Stolen or Misdelivered Genetic Material," *Missouri Law Review*, 64 (1999):517–594.

21. Michelle Nicolosi and Laura Saari, *OCR*, 7 July 1998.

22. Michelle Nicolosi and Laura Saari, *OCR*, 8 July 1995.

23. Julie Marquis, *LAT*, 6 August 1995.

24. *CBS This Morning*, 7 July 1995 (transcript).

25. Ibid.

26. Lawrence Von Gelder, *NYT*, 9 March 1996.

27. Stan Brin, *Orange County Jewish Heritage Weekly*, 14 July 1995; Marilyn Kalfus, *OCR*, 7 July 1995.

28. Brin, *Orange County Jewish Heritage*, 14 July 1995; Chally Povarsky, "Regulating Advanced Reproductive Technologies: A Comparative Analysis of Jewish and American Law," *University of Toledo Law Review*, 29 (1998):409–483; Elliott Dorff, "A Jewish Approach to Assisted Reproductive Technologies," *Whittier Law Review*, 21 (1999):391–399.

29. Robert Snowden, "Psychological Discontinuities Introduced by New Reproductive Technologies," *Journal of Community & Applied Psychology*, 5 (1998):352–355.

30. Joseph F. Fletcher, *Morals and Medicine* (London: Victor Gollancz, 1955).

31. Susan Kelleher and Ernie Slone, *OCR*, 1 March 1996.

32. Asch interview.

33. Michael Granberry and Rebecca Trounson, *LAT*, 26 May 1995.

34. Michelle Nicolosi and Laura Saari, *OCR*, 7 July 1995.

35. Ibid.

36. Kim Christensen and Michelle Nicolosi, *OCR*, 16 August 1997.

37. Jean Veevers, "Voluntary Childlessness: A Review of Issues and Evidence," *Marriage and Family Review*, 2 (1970):3.

38. Robert J. Edelmann and Kevin J. Connolly, "Psychological State and Psychological Strain in Relation to Infertility," *Journal of Community & Applied Social Psychology*, 8 (1998):310.

39. Robert J. Edelmann, Kevin J. Connolly, and Helen Bartlett, "Coping Strategies and Psychological Adjustment of Couples Presenting for IVF," *Journal of Psychosomatic Research*, 38 (1994):355–364.

40. Linda Forrest and Mary S. Gilbert, "Infertility: An Unanticipated and Prolonged Life Crisis," *Journal of Mental Health Counseling*, 14 (1992):42–58; Barbara Eck Menning, "The Infertile Couple: A Plea for Advocacy," *Child Welfare*, 54 (1975):454–460; James H. Monach, *Childless: No Choice* (London: Routledge, 1993).

41. Charlene E. Miall, "The Stigma of Involuntary Childlessness," *Social Problems*, 33 (1986):268–282; see also Arthur L. Greil, *Not Yet Pregnant: Infertile Couples in American Society* (New Brunswick, N.J.: Rutgers University Press, 1991).

42. Paul Lauritzen, *Pursuing Parenthood: Ethical Issues in Assisted Reproduction* (Bloomington: Indiana University Press, 1993).

43. Ellen W. Freeman, Celso-Ramon Garcia, and Karl Rickels, "Behavioral and Emotional Factors: Comparisons of Anovulatory Infertile Women with Fertile and Other Infertile Women," *Fertility and Sterility*, 40 (1983):201.

44. Amir H. Ansari, "Indications and Screening of IVF Patients," pp. 163–169 in *Foundations of In Vitro Fertilization*, ed. Christopher M. Fredericks, John D. Paulson, and Alan H. DeCherney (Washington, D.C.: Hemisphere, 1987).

45. Lorraine Dennerstein and Carol Morse, "A Review of Psychological and Social Aspects of In Vitro Fertilization," *Journal of Psychosomatic Obstetrics and Gynecology*, 9 (1988):159.

46. Erin McLam, *OCR*, 8 February 2002.

47. Patrick C. Steptoe and Robert G. Edwards, "Birth after Reimplantation of the Human Embryo," *Lancet*, 2 (1978):336; Robert G. Edwards and Patrick C. Steptoe, *A Matter of Life: The Story of a Medical Breakthrough* (New York: Morrow, 1980).

48. Carey Goldberg, *NYT*, 27 October 1999.

49. Amy Dockser Marcus, *Wall Street Journal*, 17 April 2002; Lori B. Andrews and John L. Hendricks, "Legal and Moral Status of IVF/ET," p. 339 in *Foundations of In Vitro Fertilization*, ed. Fredericks et al.

50. Sheryl Gay Stolberg, *NYT*, 25 February 2001.

51. Peter L. Lutjen, Alan Trounson, John L. Leeton, Jock Findlay, Carl Wood, and Peter Renou, "The Establishment and Maintenance of Pregnancy Using In Vitro Fertilization and Embryo Donation in a Patient with Primary Ovarian Failure," *Nature*, 307 (1984):174–175.

52. Ricardo Asch, José Balmaceda, Teri Ord, Claudia Borrero, Eleanor Cefalu, Carlo Gastaldi, and Francisco Royas, "Oocyte Donation and Gamete Intrafallopian Transfer in Premature Ovarian Failure," *Fertility and Sterility*, 49 (1988):264.

53. Roberta Lessor, Nancyann Cervantes, Nadine O'Connor, José Balmaceda, and Richard H. Asch, "An Analysis of Social and Psychological Characteristics of Women Volunteering to Become Oocyte Donors," *Fertility and Sterility*, 59 (1993):65–71.

54. Jan Hoffman, *NYT*, 5 January 1996.

55. Mary Power, Rod Baber, Hossam Abdalla, Angela Kirkland, Terry Leonard, and John W. Studd, "A Comparison of the Attitudes of Volunteer Donors and Infertile Patient Donors on an Ovum Donation Programme," *Human Reproduction*, 5 (1993):352–355.

56. Aaron Zitner, *LAT*, 22 March 2002.

57. Kari L. Karsjens, "Boutique Egg Donations: A New Form of Racism and Patriarchy," *DePaul Journal of Health Care Law*, 5 (2002):57–89; Tony Saavedra, *OCR*, 19 December 1996.

58. Gina Kolata, *NYT*, 8 March 1998.

59. MacHelle M. Seibel and Susan L. Crockin, *Family Building through Egg and Sperm Donation: Medical, Legal, and Ethical Issues* (Boston: Jones and Bartlett, 1996).

60. Harvey Cushing, *The Life of Sir William Osler* (London: Oxford University Press, 1940), pp. 447, 177.

61. Dorothy Fielding, Sarah Handley, Lindsay Duqueno, Sue Weaver, and Steve Lui, "Motivation, Attitudes and Experiences of Donation: A Follow-up of Women Donating Eggs in Assisted Conception Treatment," *Journal of Community & Applied Social Psychology*, 8 (1998):273–287.

CHAPTER 2

1. See, generally, Linda R. Cohen, "Soft Money, Hard Choices: Research Universities and University Hospitals," pp. 147–169 in *Challenges to Research Universities*, ed. Roger G. Noll (Washington, D.C.: Brookings Institution Press, 1998).

2. Thomas Cesario, interview, Irvine, 4 December 1996.

3. California Legislature, Senate Select Committee on Higher Education, "A Hearing to Investigate UC Irvine's Fertility Clinic," 14 June 1995 (hereafter cited as Calif. Senate).

4. Carol Masciola, Agustin Gurza, Peter Larsen, and Katie Hickox, *Orange County Register [OCR]*, 21 May 1995.

5. Judith F. Daar, "Regulating Reproductive Technology: Panacea or Paper Tiger?" *Houston Law Review*, 34 (1997):610.

6. *Frederick v. Golub*, Case No. 779687, Orange County Superior Court, Golub deposition, 19 February 1998, pp. 87–88.

7. UCIMC physician interview, 21 July 1997; Julie Marquis, *Los Angeles Times [LAT]*, 21 March 1996.

8. Susan Kelleher, *OCR*, 22 October 1995.

9. Susan Kelleher and Kim Christensen, *OCR*, 16 December 1995.

10. *Batshoun v. University of California Board of Regents*, Case No. 757130, Orange County Superior Court, 15 December 1995.

11. Ibid.

12. Ricardo Asch, interview, Mexico City, 11 February 1999.

13. UCI Internal Investigation Document, "General Notes," undated.

14. Calif. Senate, testimony of Norbert Giltner, 14 June 1995.

15. Calif. Senate, Statement of Tom Hayden, 14 June 1995.

16. Personal communication with UCI administrator, 18 December 1996.

17. "Review of Center for Reproductive Health Conference Notes," 3 December 1992.

18. "UCIMC—Investigation General Notes," undated internal audit notes.

19. Michael Jonathan Grinfeld, "Embryo Imbroglio," *California Lawyer*, 29 (1 October 2000):46–49, 89–90.

20. Ibid.

21. Debra Krahel, interview, Orange County, Calif., 28 March 1996.

22. Ibid.

23. Wiggins-Snyder Report, 6 April 1995.

24. Anonymous patient interview, 22 January 1996.

25. Calif. Senate, testimony of Marilyn Killane.

26. Krahel interview.

27. Ibid.

28. Debra Krahel, letter to Robert Chatwin, 18 July 1994.

29. Herb Spiwak, interview, Laguana Beach, Calif., 14 July 2000.

30. Carol Chatham, interview, Orange County, Calif., 5 June 1996.

31. Ibid.

32. Wiggins-Snyder Report.

33. Marilyn Killane, letter to Chris Taylor, 15 March 1994.

34. Tracy Weber, Nancy Wride, and Julie Marquis, *LAT*, 2 July 1995.

35. Reporting of Government Activities Act, California Govt. Code, sect. 8547.

36. Written senate testimony of Golub, 14 June 1995, p. 4.

37. Carol McGraw and Bruce Strong, *OCR*, 13 August 1995.

38. UCI Internal Investigation Document, "UCI Medical Center Meeting with Internal Auditors," 6 December 1994.

39. Tracy Weber and Michael G. Wagner, *LAT*, 19 July 1995.

40. UCI I/A Review, Diane Geocaris interview, 12 July 1995; Tracy Weber and Michael G. Wagner, *LAT*, 19 July 1995.

41. Ricardo Asch interview.

42. Krahel interview.

43. Personal interview with attorney, 14 September 1996.

44. Chatham interview.

45. Ibid.

46. Michael Granberry, *LAT*, 12 August 1995.

47. Tracy Weber and Michael Wagner, *LAT*, 19 July 1995.

48. Report of Improper Governmental Activities at UCI Medical Center, 10 September 1994 (whistle-blower complaint).

49. Clinical Panel physician interview, 21 June 1996.

50. Stanley Korenman, letter to Tom Hayden, 12 June 1995.

51. Gary Ellis, telephone interview, 23 January 1996.

CHAPTER 3

1. Gary Ellis, telephone interview, 23 January 1996.

2. Debra Krahel, interview, 28 March 1996.

3. UCI Electronic ZOT Mail, 11 August 1995.

4. Thomas Cesario, interview, Irvine, Calif., 4 December 1996.

5. Allen C. Snyder, interview, San Diego, 18 April 2001.

6. Wiggins-Snyder Report, 6 April 1995, p. 19.

7. Ibid., p. 55.

8. Ibid., p. 56.

9. Ibid., pp. 57–58.

10. Snyder interview. (Wiggins did not participate in our interview. He commutes to San Diego from Portland, Oregon, to meet his classes. He jokingly notes that he thereby "avoids the traffic.")

11. Allen Snyder to Gilbert Geis, e-mail, 20 April 2001.

12. Michael Granberry, *Los Angeles Times [LAT]*, 25 June 1995.

13. UCI Settlement Agreement and General Release with Debra Krahel, 8 May 1995.

14. Ibid.

15. Krahel interview.

16. *Regents U.C. v. Asch, et al.*, Superior Court, Case 747155, Orange County, Calif.

17. Calif. Senate, testimony of Maureen Bocian, 14 June 1995.

18. Krahel interview.

19. Ricardo Asch, letter to Philip DiSaia, 19 May 1995.

20. See, generally, Terry Morehead Dworkin and Elletta Sangley Callahan, "Buying Silence," *American Business Law Journal*, 36 (1998):151–190.

21. Michael Granberry, *LAT*, 13 June 1995.

22. Julie Marquis, Tracy Weber, and Martin Miller, *LAT*, 23 June 1995.

23. Ibid.

24. UCI press release, 14 June 1995.

25. Marcia Dodson and Bill Billiter, *LAT*, 3 June 1985.

26. Michelle Nicolosi and Peter Larsen, *Orange County Register [OCR]*, 24 June 1995.

27. UCI press release, 14 June 1995.

28. Ibid.

29. Peter Larsen and Michelle Nicolosi, *OCR*, 1 July 1995.

30. Julie Marquis, *LAT*, 17 June 1995.

31. Thorstein Veblen, *The Higher Learning in America: A Memorandum of the Conduct of Universities by Business Men* (New York: B. W. Huebsch, 1918), p. 260.

32. Scott D. Sagan, *The Limits of Safety: Organizations, Accidents, and Nuclear Weapons* (Princeton: Princeton University Press, 1993); but see also Diane Vaughan, *The Challenger Launch Decision: Risky Technology, Culture, and Deviance at NASA* (Chicago: University of Chicago Press, 1996).

33. Mary Piccione, interview, Beverly Hills, 20 May 2000.

34. Herb Spiwak, interview, Laguna Beach, 14 July 2000.

35. Diane Seo, *LAT*, 23 June 1995.

36. Ibid.

37. Julie Marquis and Michael Granberry, *LAT*, 1 July 1995.

38. Anonymous interview, 8 May 1997.

CHAPTER 4

1. Susan Kelleher and Jim Mulvaney, *Orange County Register [OCR]*, 28 March 1996.

2. Julie Margola and Leslie Berkman, *Los Angeles Times [LAT]*, 31 May 1995.

3. Ibid.

4. Alan DeCherney, "General Overview of the Current Status of the Field of Assisted Reproductive Technology (ART)," paper presented at the UCI Ethics of Reproductive Medicine Conference, Irvine, Calif., 11 April 1996.

5. Christine Overall, *Ethics and Human Reproduction: A Feminist Analysis* (Boston: Allen & Unwin, 1987).

6. Gena Corea, *The Mother Machine: Reproductive Technologies from Artificial Insemination to Artificial Wombs* (New York: Harper & Row, 1985).

7. Janice G. Raymond, "Reproductive Gifts and Gift Giving: The Altruistic Woman," *Hastings Center Report*, 20 (1990):7–11.

8. Michael Soules, "Now That We Have Painted Ourselves in a Corner," *Fertility and Sterility*, 66 (1996):693–969.

9. Tracy Weber and Julie Marquis, *LAT*, 4 June 1995.

10. David Lodge, *Small World: An Academic Romance* (New York: Macmillan, 1984).

11. Title 18, U.S. Code §1341, 2.

12. "Fertility Doctor Arrested," *UCI News*, 1 May 1996.

13. Davin Maharaj, *LAT*, 27 April 1996.

14. Susan Kelleher and Kim Christensen, *OCR*, 26 April 1996.

15. Susan Kelleher, *OCR*, 1 May 1996.

16. Mimi Meyers, Ronny Diamond, David Kezur, Constance Scharf, Margot Weinshel, and Douglas S. Rait, "An Infertility Primer for Family Therapists: Medical, Social, and Psychological Dimensions," *Family Process*, 34 (1995):219–229.

17. Susan Kelleher, Kim Christensen, David Parrish, and Michelle Nicolosi, *OCR*, 4 November 1995.

18. Michael Granberry, *LAT*, 6 September 1995.

19. Julie Marquis and Michael Granberry, *LAT*, 8 August 1995.

20. David Parrish, *OCR*, 4 November 1995.

21. Attorney interview, Orange County, 26 February 1996.

22. Lauren Wilkening to UCI Community, 21 July 1997.

23. Kim Christensen and Michelle Nicolosi, *OCR*, 16 August 1997.

24. "Anonymous Letter Alleges Eggs Used without Consent," *OCR*, 19 May 1995.

25. Ibid.

26. "An Unfolding Drama," *OCR*, 25 May 1995.

27. Diane Porter, testimony during administrative proceedings against Professor Ricardo Asch, Committee on Privilege and Tenure, Academic Senate, Irvine Division, 12 July 1995, vol. 3, p. 24.

28. Susan Kelleher, *OCR*, 14 July 1995.

29. Porter, testimony, vol. 3, p. 7.

30. Susan Kelleher, *OCR*, 14 July 1995.

31. Porter, testimony, vol. 3, p. 15.

32. Ibid., p. 70.

33. *OCR*, 14 July 1995.

34. Ibid., p. 11.

35. Asch, testimony during administrative proceedings, vol. 11, p. 67.

36. Michelle Nicolosi, *OCR*, 19 July 1997.

37. Ibid.

38. Ibid.

39. Susan Kelleher and Kim Christensen, *OCR*, 18 February 1996.

40. Diane Seo, *LAT*, 12 February 1996.

41. John A. Robertson, "The Case of the Switched Embryos," *Hastings Center Report*, 25 (1995):13–19.

42. Ernie Slone, *OCR*, 29 January 1996.

43. Susan Kelleher, *OCR*, 13 January 1996.

44. Susan Kelleher, Kim Christensen, David Parrish, and Michelle Nicolosi, *OCR*, 4 November 1995.

45. Ibid.

46. *OCR*, 13 March 1996.
47. Geoff Boucher, *LAT*, 20 February 1997.
48. Susan Kelleher, *OCR*, 1 March 1997.
49. Peter Warren, *LAT*, 13 June 1999.
50. Ibid.
51. Ibid.
52. Susan Kelleher, *OCR*, 23 June 1999.
53. Ibid.
54. Peter Warren, *LAT*, 13 June 1999.
55. Mayrav Saav, *OCR*, 7 October 2000.
56. Nick Anderson and Esther Schrader, *LAT*, 19 July 1997.
57. Ivan Sciupac, *New University*, 8 April 1996.
58. Peter Warren, *LAT*, 12 July 1999.
59. *LAT*, 4 September 1997.
60. Michael Jonathan Grinfeld, *Los Angeles Daily Journal*, 1 June 2000.

CHAPTER 5

1. Carol Masciola, Agustin Gurza, Peter Larsen, and Katie Hickox, *Orange County Register [OCR]*, 21 May 1995.
2. Ibid.
3. College of Medicine students, letter to Laurel Wilkening, 12 June 1996.
4. Advocates for Asch and Reproductive Health, 1 August 1995.
5. Andrea S. Feiner, letter to Diane D. Aronson, 6 July 1995.
6. Ibid.
7. Masciola et al., *OCR*, 21 May 1995.
8. John and Megan McElroy, letter to *Los Angeles Times [LAT]*, 19 June 1995.
9. KPMG Peat Marwick—confidential investigation notes; Sharon Gray, interview, undated.
10. KPMG Peat Marwick—confidential investigation notes.
11. Ricardo Asch, interview, Mexico City, 14 September 2002.
12. David William Foster, Melissa Fitch Lockhart, and Darrel B. Lockhart, *Culture and Customs of Argentina* (Westport, Conn.: Greenwood Press, 1998).
13. Robert Weisbrot, *The Jews of Argentina: From the Inquisition to Perón* (Philadelphia: Jewish Publication Society of America, 1979).
14. Masciola et al., *OCR*, 21 May 1995.
15. Former CRH patient interview, 22 January 1996.
16. Deborah Karpis Neese, telephone interview, 6 May 1998.
17. Ricardo H. Asch, ed., *Recent Advances in Human Reproduction* (Rome: Fondazione per Gli Studi sulla Riproduzione Umana, 1987), p. 11.
18. Asch interview.
19. Geoffrey Sher, Virginia M. Davis, and Jean Stoess, *In Vitro Fertilization: The A.R.T. Method of Making Babies* (New York: Facts on File, 1995).
20. José P. Balmaceda and Ricardo H. Asch, "Gamete Intrafallopian Transfer," p.

155 in *Foundations of In Vitro Fertilization*, ed. Christoper M. Fredericks, John D. Paulson, and Alan H. deCherney (Washington, D.C.: Hemisphere, 1987).

21. Panel investigator interview, 24 September 1996.

22. Ronald Brower, interview, 5 February 1995.

23. Masciola et al., *OCR*, 21 May 1995.

24. Ibid.

25. Michelle Nicolosi, *OCR*, 15 June 1995.

26. California Senate, testimony of Sergio Stone, 14 June 1995.

27. Michelle Nicolosi, *OCR*, 30 November 1995.

28. Kim Christensen and Susan Kelleher, *OCR*, 16 May 1995.

29. Susan Kelleher, *OCR*, 21 January 1996.

30. Julie Marquis, *LAT*, 21 January 1996; Jim Mulvaney and Susan Kelleher, *OCR*, 21 January 1996.

31. Plaintiff attorney interview, November 1996.

32. Susan Kelleher, *OCR*, 2 February 1996.

33. Robert Chatwin, Internal Audit Report, 19 July 1994.

34. Internal investigation document, 21 February 1995.

35. Clinical Panel report, 17 March 1995, p. 7.

36. Eleonora Guidice, Carmelina Cresci, Aliza Eshkol, and Ruben Papoian, "Composition of Commercial Gonadotrophin Preparations Extracted from Human Postmenopausal Urine: Characterization of Non-gonadotrophin Proteins," *Human Reproduction*, 9 (1994): 2298.

37. FDA official interview, 1 May 1997; Agustin Gurza, *OCR*, 5 June 1995.

38. Food and Drug Administration, Press Office Release, 9 January 1991.

39. Agustin Gurza, *OCR*, 5 June 1995.

40. Mary Partridge-Brown, *In Vitro Fertilization Clinics: A North American Directory of Programs and Services* (Jefferson, N.C.: MacFarland, 1993).

41. UCIMC physician interview, 21 July 1997; Kim Christensen, *OCR*, 9 March 1996.

42. Gurza, *OCR*, 5 June 1995.

43. Marian E. Carter and David N. Joyce, "Ovarian Carcinoma in a Patient Hyperstimulated by Gonadotropin Therapy for In Vitro Fertilization," *Journal of In Vitro Fertilization and Embryo Transfer*, 4 (1997):126–128.

44. Sheila M. Pride, Christopher St. J. James, and Basil Ho Yuen, "The Ovarian Hyperstimulation Syndrome," *Seminars in Reproductive Endocrinology*, 8 (1900):247–260.

45. Robert G. Edwards, Rogerio A. Lobo, and Philippe Bouchard, "Why Delay the Obvious Need for Milder Forms of Ovarian Stimulation," Letter to the Editor, *Human Reproduction*, 12 (1997):400.

46. Debra Krahel, interview, 28 March 1996.

47. Julie Marquis, *LAT*, 20 March 1995.

48. Kim Christensen, *OCR*, 11 November 1995.

49. Michael G. Wagner, *LAT*, 19 July 1995.

50. Clinical Panel investigator interview, 21 June 1996.

51. Gurza, *OCR*, 5 June 1995.

52. Sidney Golub, letter to William Dommel, 13 February 1995.

53. Shannon Brownless, "Regulation of Reproductive Technologies," pp. 150–157 in *Reproductive Technologies*, ed. Carol Wekesser (San Diego: Greenhaven Press, 1996).

54. Michael A. Katz, "Federal Trade Commission Staff Concerns with Assisted Reproductive Technology Accounting," *Fertility and Sterility*, 64 (1995):10–12.

55. Lori B. Andrews, *New Conceptions: A Consumer's Guide to the Newest Infertility Treatments* (New York: Ballantine Books, 1985).

56. Kim Christensen and Jim Mulvaney, *OCR*, 20 February 1996.

57. Mary Martin Cadieux, testimony during administrative proceedings against Professor Ricardo Asch, Committee on Privilege and Tenure, Academic Senate, Irvine Division, 12 July 1999, 1:105–106.

58. Susan Kelleher and Laura Saari, *OCR*, 7 June 1995.

59. *Moore v. Regents of the University of California*, 272 Cal. Rpt. 146, 51 Cal. 3d 120, 793 P.2d 479, 1990.

60. Kelleher and Saari, *OCR*, 7 June 1995.

61. *Moore*, at pp. 131–132.

62. Kim Christensen, *OCR*, 15 November 1996.

63. Garcia, *OCR*, 16 November 1995.

64. Christensen, *OCR*, 15 November 1995.

65. Susan Kelleher, *OCR*, 1 March 1997.

66. Julie Marquis, *LAT*, 20 March 1996; Susan Kelleher, *OCR*, 20 March 1996.

67. Susan Kelleher, *OCR*, 1 March 1997.

68. Robert G. Edwards and Helen K. Beard, "Destruction of Cryopreserved Embryos," *Human Reproduction*, 12 (1997):4.

69. Robert G. Edwards, "High-Resolution Map for Assisted Reproductive Technology," letter to the editor, *Fertility and Sterility*, 65 (1996):679.

70. Fertility specialist, phone conversation, 20 December 1996.

71. Mayrav Saar, *OCR*, 18 February 2001.

72. Ivan Sciupac, *New University* (UCI campus paper), 1 April 1996.

73. Kelleher, *OCR*, 1 March 1997.

74. Ricardo Asch, interview, Mexico City, 11 February 1999.

75. Administrative proceedings against Asch, 11:145.

76. Ibid., pp. 60–61.

77. Ibid., 2:36.

78. Ibid., p. 75.

79. Ibid., 10:44.

80. Ibid., 3:122–125.

81. Ibid., 11:127.

82. Ibid., 4:88.

83. Ricardo Asch, e-mail, 17 September 2002.

84. Ricardo Asch, interview, 1999.

CHAPTER 6

1. José Balmaceda, interview, Santiago, Chile, 16 August 2000 (subsequent quotes are from the same interview).

2. Karen Taillon, interview, Orange County, Calif., 12 July 2001.

3. Genaro Arriagada, *Pinochet: The Politics of Power* (Boulder, Colo.: Westview, 1991).

4. Lee Romney, *Los Angeles Times [LAT]*, 30 November 1995.

5. California Senate, testimony of José Balmaceda, 14 June 1995.

6. Ed Benoe, telephone interview, 10 July 2001.

7. Anonymous interview, 8 August 2000.

8. José Balmaceda, e-mail to Mary Dodge, 6 August 2002.

9. Peter Larsen, *Orange Country Register [OCR]*, 7 July 1995.

10. David Parrish, Susan Kelleher, and Kim Christensen, *OCR*, 22 March 1996.

11. José P. Balmaceda, Teri Ord, Veronica Alan, Kellie Snell, Daniel Roszjtein, and Ricardo Asch, "Embryo Implantation Rates in Oocyte Donation: A Prospective Comparison of Tubal versus Uterine Transfers," *Fertility and Sterility*, 57 (1992):362–365.

12. Calvin Sims, *New York Times [NYT]*, 20 April 1996.

13. Romney, *LAT*, 30 November 1995.

14. Calvin Sims, *NYT*, 26 April 1996.

15. Ibid.

16. 717 F. Supp. 421 (E.D. Va. 1989). See generally John A. Robertson, *Children of Choice: Freedom and the New Reproductive Technologies* (Princeton: Princeton University Press, 1994); Janice G. Raymond, *Women as Wombs: Reproductive Technologies and the Battle over Women's Freedom* (San Francisco: HarperCollins, 1993).

17. Sergio Stone, interview, Orange County, Calif., 16 July 2001.

18. Rio Negro Online, "Menem y Cecilia Bolocco Siguen un Tratamiento de Fertinidad Asistida," www.rionegro.com (20 January 2003).

19. Jack Leonard and Stuart Pfeifer, *LAT*, 20 January 2001.

20. Julie Marquis and David Mararaj, *LAT*, 15 Novemer 1996.

21. Leonard and Pfeifer, *LAT*, 20 January 2001.

22. William Heisel and Mayrav Saar, *OCR*, 20 January 2001.

23. Ibid.

24. Leonard and Pfeifer, *LAT*, 20 January 2001.

25. Richard Marosi, *LAT*, 15 February 2001.

26. Ricardo Asch, telephone interview, 14 June 2001.

27. "Médico Chileno Acusado de Fraude en EE.UU huye a Chile," *La Tercera*, February 2001.

28. Carlos Vergara, "Soy Absolutemente Inocente," *Las Últimas Noticias* (Santiago, Chile), 13 February 2001.

29. José Balmaceda, e-mail to Mary Dodge, 6 August 2002.

30. Ibid.

31. Fernando Paulsen, "Médico Acusado en EE.UU Denuncía Presiones," *La Tercera*, 21 November 1997.

CHAPTER 7

1. José Balmaceda, interview, Santiago, Chile, August 2001.

2. *United States v. Stone*, Case No. SA CR 96–55 (U.S. Dist. Ct., Cent. Dist. Calif., 1997).

3. Thomas Bienert, interview, San Juan Capistrano, Calif., 10 August 2002.

4. John McDonald, *Orange County Register [OCR]*, 31 October 1997.

5. John McDonald, *OCR*, 13 January 1998.

6. William Penn, *The Tryal of William Penn and William Mead for Causing a Tumult* (Boston: Marshall Jones, 1919); *Bushel's Case*, 124 Eng. Rep. 1006 (King's Bench, 1670).

7. 156 U.S. Code, §51.

8. Indiana: Constitution, art. I, §19; Maryland Constitution, art. XXIII. See generally Clay Conrad, *Jury Nullification: The Evolution of a Doctrine* (Durham, N.C.: Carolina Academic Press, 1998).

9. *Wyley v. Warden, Maryland Penitentiary*, 372 F.2d. 742 (4th Circuit 1967) (upholding constitutionality of the provision). R. Alex Morgan, "Jury Nullification Should Be Made a Routine Part of the Criminal Justice System, but It Won't Be," *Arizona State Law Journal* 29 (1997):1137.

10. *Duncan v. Louisiana*, 391 U.S. 145 157 (1968).

11. Susan Kelleher and Kim Christensen, *OCR*, 31 October 1997.

12. *OCR*, 22 March 1999, Commentary, p. 4.

13. John McDonald, *OCR*, 31 October 1997.

14. Judge Gary Taylor, e-mail to Gilbert Geis, 13 August 2002.

15. *United States v. Dougherty*, 1972 (D.C. Circ. Ct. of Appeals), 154 U.S. App., 473 F2d. 1113, 1132.

16. Gregory Mellema, "Scapegoats," *Criminal Justice Ethics*, 19 (Winter–Spring 2000):3, 5.

17. *Lambert v. California*, 355 U.S. 227 (1957).

18. *OCR*, 18 December 1999.

19. Kimberly Kindy, *OCR*, 27 June 1999.

20. Letter, Academic Friends of Sergio Stone to Members of the Representative Assembly, College of Medicine, 29 July 1998.

21. Interviews with physicians who prefer to remain anonymous, 8 November 1995 and 21 June 2001.

22. Fred C. Zacharias and Bruce A. Green, "The Uniqueness of Federal Prosecutors," *Georgetown Law Journal* 88 (2000):209, 214.

23. *LAT*, 25 February 1999.

24. *LAT*, 21 March 2000.

25. Jerome Hall, *General Principles of Criminal Law*, 2d ed. (Indianapolis: Bobbs-Merrill), 1960.

26. Richard Friedenberg, Terence Parsons, Kenneth Pomeranz, and William Thompson, "Report on the Formal Hearing before the Committee on Privilege and Tenure, Irvine Division, on Disciplinary Charges Against Professor Sergio Stone," 16 September 1999.

27. Confidential Report to Chancellor Ralph J. Cicerone from Formal Hearing Board of the Committee on Privilege and Tenure, 4 January 2000.

28. California State Auditor, Investigation of Improper Activities by State Employees: July through December 1999, chapter 46: Update on Previously Reported Issues, 11 April 2000, p. 43.

29. Ibid.

30. Ibid.

31. Stanley Milgram, "Behavioral Study of Obedience," *Journal of Abnormal and Social Psychology*, 69 (1963):137–143; Stanley Milgram, *Obedience to Authority* (New York: Harper & Row, 1974).

32. Sarah Klein and Michael Granberry, *LAT*, 7 July 1995.

33. Friedenberg et al., "Report," p. 31.

34. William C. Thompson, e-mail to Gilbert Geis, 16 July 2002.

35. Phone interview with anonymous faculty member, 8 August 2002.

36. *OCR*, 16 March 2000, News, p. 16.

37. Ralph Cicerone, letter to William C. Thompson, 10 November 1999.

38. Dana Parsons, *LAT*, 20 March 2000.

39. Kenneth Weiss, *LAT*, 16 March 2000.

40. Ibid.

41. Ralph J. Cicerone, e-mail to all employees, 15 March 2000.

42. Weiss, *LAT*, 16 March 2000.

43. Ralph Cicerone, e-mail to Gilbert Geis, 14 August 2002.

44. Thorstein Veblen, *The Higher Learning in America: A Memorandum on the Conduct of Universities by Business Men* (New York: B. W. Huebsch, 1918), p. 91.

45. Weiss, *LAT*, 16 March 2000.

46. Ibid.

47. For a particularly forceful endorsement of this view, see William T. Pizzi, *Trials without Truth: Why Our System of Criminal Justice Has Become an Expensive Failure and What We Need to Do to Rebuild It* (New York: New York University Press, 1999).

CHAPTER 8

1. William Heisel, *Orange County Register [OCR]*, 18 February 2001.

2. *Moore v. Regents of the University of California*, 793 P.2d 479 (1990) (Mosk, J., dissenting).

3. Helene Wright, *Somebody Stole Yesterday* (Franklin, Tenn.: Providence House, 2000), p. 17.

4. Claudia Lima Marques, "Assisted Reproductive Technology (ART) in South America and the Effect on Abortion," *Texas International Law Journal*, 35 (2000):65–91.

5. Richard C. Lewontin, Steven Rose, and Leon J. Kamin, *Not in Our Genes: Biology, Ideology, and Human Nature* (New York: Pantheon, 1984), p. 267; see also Ruth Hubbard and Elija Ward, *Exploding the Gene Myth: How Genetic Information Is Produced and Manipulated by Scientists, Physicians, Employers, Insurance Companies, Educators, and Law Enforcers* (Boston: Beacon Press, 1999).

6. Carol Masciola, Agustin Gurza, Peter Larsen, and Katie Hickox, *OCR*, 21 May 1995.

7. Ibid.

8. Pamela H. Bucy, "Fraud by Fright: White Collar Crime by Health Care Providers," *North Carolina Law Review*, 67 (1989):855–937.

9. Howard S. Becker, "The Nature of a Profession," pp. 27–46 in *Education for the Professions*, ed. Nelson B. Henry (Chicago: University of Chicago Press, 1962), p. 36.

10. Marcia P. Micelli and Janet P. Near, "Individual and Situational Correlates of Whistle Blowing," *Personnel Psychology*, 41 (1988):267–281.

11. Editorial, *OCR*, 12 November 1995.

12. Ibid.

13. *Frederick v. Golub*, Case No. 779687, Orange County Superior Court, Wilkening deposition, 26 February 1998, pp. 62–63.

14. Diane Vaughan, "Sensational Cases and Flawed Theories: Lessons from the *Challenger* Case," paper presented at the annual meeting of the American Society of Criminology, November 1995.

15. Wilkening, e-mail to UCI community, 26 July 1995.

16. Brent Dale Johnson, "The Fertility Clinic Controversy at the University of California, Irvine: A Case Study in the Social Ramification of Reproductive Science" (Master's thesis, California State University, Fullerton, 1997), p. 70.

17. Julie Marquis and Tracy Weber, *Los Angeles Times [LAT]*, 24 July 1995.

18. Susan Kelleher, "How Fertility Clinic Misuse of Eggs Was Exposed" (Second Watchdog Conference Panel), http://www.nieman.harvard.edu/events/conferences/watchdog2/4th_panel_nonprof.html (16 July 2002).

19. California Penal Code, §367g.

20. Martin Miller and Julie Marquis, *LAT*, 24 June 1995; California Business and Professional Code, §2260.

21. Kim Christensen, *OCR*, 30 August 1996.

22. Meena Lal, "The Role of the Federal Government in Assisted Reproductive Technologies," *Santa Clara Computer and High Technology Law Journal*, 13 (1997):517–543.

23. *Moore v. Regents*; see also Judith D. Fischer, "Misappropriation of Human Eggs and Embryos and the Tort of Conversion: A Relational View," *Loyola of Los Angeles Law Review*, 32 (1999):381–430.

24. Janet L. Dolgin, *Defending the Family: Law, Technology, and Reproduction in an Uneasy Age* (New York: New York University Press, 1997), p. 32.

25. Susan Kelleher, *OCR*, 23 April 1997; Kimberly Sanchez, *LAT*, 23 April 1997.

26. Kimberly Sanchez, *LAT*, 23 April 1997.

27. Diane Geocaris, telephone interview, 14 June 2001.

28. George Pring and Penelope Canan, *SLAPP: Getting Sued for Speaking Out* (Philadelphia: Temple University Press, 1995); Joseph J. Brecher, "The Public Interest and Intimidation Suits: A New Approach," *Santa Clara Law Review*, 28 (1988):105–141.

29. James Coates, *Chicago Tribune*, 24 March 1991.

30. Daniel Boorenstein, *Contra Costa Times*, 11 March 1991.

31. Carlotta E. McCarthy, "Citizens Cannot Be 'SLAPPED' for Exercising First Amendment Right to Petition the Government—*Homestead Properties, Inc. v. Fleming*," 680 Atl. 2d 56 (R.I. 1996), *Suffolk University Law Review*, 31 (1998):759–770.

32. Lisa Rapaport, *Sacramento Bee*, 3 February 2001.

33. Pamela H. Bucy, "Growing Pains: Using the False Claims to Combat Health Care Fraud," *Alabama Law Review*, 51 (1999):57–103; John T. Boese, *Civil False Claims and Qui Tam Actions*, 2d ed. (Gaithersburg, Md.: Aspen Law & Business 2000).

34. *Vermont Agency of Natural Resources v. United States ex rel. Stevens*, 529 U.S. 765 (2000).

35. *United States ex rel. Krahel v. Regents of the University of California,* Plaintiff's reply brief, C.A. No. 01–27039, 2002, p. 33.

36. *United States ex rel. Haas v. South Carolina State University,* No. 3:98–1568–17 D.S.C.

37. *U.S. v. Regents,* Plaintiff's reply brief, p. 34.

38. *Association of American Medical Colleges et al. v. United States,* 217 F.2d 770 (9th Cir. 2000).

39. John O'Brien, *Syracuse Post-Standard,* 29 April 2001.

40. Debra Krahel, telephone interview, 16 August 2002.

41. Ibid.

42. Yossi Neev, interview, Laguna Beach, Calif., 1 May 1998.

43. Regarding Cohen, see Trip Gabriel, *NYT,* 8 January 1996.

44. Kim Christensen, David Parrish, and Ernie Slone, *OCR,* 21 July 1995.

45. Michael Jonathan Grinfeld, "Judge Fines Attorney in Fertility Clinic Case," *Los Angeles Daily Journal,* 25 October 2000.

46. Stanley L. Kutler, ed., *Abuse of Power: The New Nixon Tapes* (New York: Free Press, 1997), p. 93.

47. Julie Marquis, Michael Granberry, and Tracy Weber, *OCR,* 17 June 1995.

48. Michael Jonathan Grinfeld, "Embryo Imbroglio," *California Lawyer,* 29 (1 October 2000):46–49, 89–90.

49. Mayrav Saav, *OCR,* 18 February 2001; Carol Masciola et al., *OCR,* 21 May 1995.

50. Gianpiero Palermo, Hubert Joris, Paul Devroey, and Andre C. Steirteghey, "Pregnancies after Intracytoplasmic Injection of Single Spermatoon into an Oocyte," *Lancet,* 340 (1992):17–18.

51. Alastair E. Sutcliff, "Intracytoplasmic Sperm Injection and Other Aspects of New Reproductive Technologies," *Archives of Disease in Childhood,* 82 (2000):98–101.

52. Jennifer Kurinczuk and Carol Bowers, "Birth Defects in Infants Conceived by Intracytoplasmic Sperm Injection: An Alternative Interpretation," *British Medical Journal,* 315 (15 November 1997):1260–1265.

53. Andrew A. Toledo, Graham Wright, Amy E. Jones, Scott S. Smith, Jill Johnson-Ward, Wendy W. Brockman, Florence Ng, and David J. Wininger, "Blastocyst Transfer: A Useful Tool for Reduction of High-Order Multiple Gestations in a Human Assisted Reproduction Program," *American Journal of Obstetrics and Gynecology,* 183 (2000):377–379; see also Mary Ann Davis Moriarity, "Addressing In Vitro Fertilization and the Problem of Multiple Gestations," *St. Louis University Law Review,* 18 (1999):503–518.

54. Gina Kolata, *NYT,* 1 January 2002.

55. Thomas H. Murray, "Money-Back Guarantees for IVF: An Ethical Critique," *Journal of Law, Medicine, & Ethics,* 25 (1997):292–294. For an opposing viewpoint see John Robertson and Theodore Schnoyer, "Professional Self-Regulation and the Shared-Risk Programs for In Vitro Fertilization," *Journal of Law, Medicine & Ethics,* 25 (1997):284–290.

56. Debra Gordon, *OCR,* 26 March 1998; Ann Wozencraft, *NYT,* 25 August 1996.

57. Diane Vaughan, "The Macro-Micro Connection in White-Collar Crime Theory," pp. 124–145 in *White-Collar Crime Reconsidered,* ed. Kip Schlegel and David Weisburd (Boston: Northeastern University Press, 1992), p. 132.

58. Samuel McCulloch, *Instant University: The History of the University of California, Irvine, 1957–1993* (San Diego: Continental Graphics, 1996), p. 96.

59. Paul Starr, *The Social Transformation of American Medicine* (New York: Basic Books, 1982).

60. Clinical Panel Report, 17 March 1995, pp. 15–16.

Acknowledgments

Our work was dependent on the goodwill and forthcomingness of a large number of people who held often divergent views about aspects of the fertility clinic scandal. We are grateful to those who shared with us facts and interpretations of what had gone on. Human subject restrictions prevent us from listing numerous people who were gracious with their time and thoughts; others have requested anonymity. Surprisingly few of the persons we sought to interview felt unable to cooperate.

We want to express our deep appreciation to the following (in alphabetical order): Ricardo Asch, José Balmaceda, Byron Beam, Ed Benoe, Michelle Berner, Thomas Bienert, Arnie Binder, Warren Bostick, Valerie Cass, Debbie and John Challender, Robert Chatwin, Susan Coutin, John Crab, Alan DeCherney, Joe Dimento, Scott Dorfman, Gary Ellis, Warren Ernest, James Fallon, Ryan Fischer, Concepcion Franco, Richard Friedenberg, Colleen Gately, Ellen Dagny Geis, Rosemary Gido, Larry Graham, Michael Grinfeld, Wayne Gross, Breckenridge and Mary Lynn Grover, Josephine Hardin, Dana and Steve Harmes, Joseph Hartley, Ted Houston, Christine Hrountas, Paul Jesilow, Bruce Johnson, Julie Johnston, Susan Kelleher, W. Noel Keyes, Walter Koontz, Debra Krahel, Stuart Krassner, Beth McClain, Samuel McCulloch, Anna Miriam McKee, Stephen L. Meagher, Alan Mobley, Deborah Neese, Yossi Neev, Martha Newkirk, Corina Oliver, Jean Oliver, Judy Omiya, Mary Piccione, Henry Pontell, Fred Rainquet, Anne Ready, Oscar Reyer, Steve Reynard, John Robertson, Greg Sarkisian, Dale Sechrest, David Shichor, Tammy Shuminsky, Allen C. Snyder, Herb Spiwak, Abby Stahl, Philip Stanford, Sergio Stone, Rania Sweis, Karen L. Taillon, Gary Taylor, Dennis Temko, Janet Temko, William Thompson, Kathleen Tuttle, Marilyn Wahlert, Joseph Wells, Ted Wentworth, Jerry Williams, Richard Wright, Carol Wyatt, Kathy Wycoff. We would also like to thank Kerry P. Callahan and Darrin Pratt at the University of Colorado Press, as well as the Faculty Grant Award program at the University of Colorado, Denver, for its generous support.

The people at Northeastern University Press have been gracious and expert in moving our manuscript into book form. We particularly want to express our appreciation to Bill Frohlich, Director, and Sarah Rowley, his assistant, as well as Ann Twombly and Jill Bahcall, the press's production and marketing directors, and also to Judy Loeven for helpful proofreading and Greg Jewett for an excellent index.

Any shortcomings that exist in this book are of our own creation, despite the wisdom and guidance of those who provided information.

Index

227